teach®
yourself

french grammar

teach®
yourself

french grammar
robin adamson
and
brigitte edelston

The **teach yourself** series does
exactly what it says, and it works.
For over 60 years, more than
40 million people have learnt over
750 subjects the **teach yourself**
way, with impressive results.

be where you want to be
with **teach yourself**

For UK order queries: please contact Bookpoint Ltd, 130 Milton Park, Abingdon, Oxon OX14 4SB. Telephone: +44 (0) 1235 827720, Fax: +44 (0) 1235 400454. Lines are open 9.00–18.00, Monday to Saturday, with a 24-hour message answering service. You can also order through our website www.madaboutbooks.com.

For USA order queries: please contact McGraw-Hill Customer Services, PO Box 545, Blacklick, OH 43004-0545, USA. Telephone: 1-800-722-4726. Fax: 1-614-755-5645.

For Canada order queries: please contact McGraw-Hill Ryerson Ltd, 300 Water St, Whitby, Ontario L1N 9B6, Canada. Telephone: 905 430 5000. Fax: 905 430 5020.

Long renowned as the authoritative source for self-guided learning – with more than 30 million copies sold worldwide – the *Teach Yourself* series includes over 300 titles in the fields of languages, crafts, hobbies, business, computing and education.

British Library Cataloguing in Publication Data: A catalogue entry for this title is available from The British Library.

Library of Congress Catalog Card Number: on file

First published in UK 1998 by Hodder Headline Ltd, 338 Euston Road, London, NW1 3BH.

First published in US 1998 by Contemporary Books, a Division of the McGraw Hill Companies, 4255 West Touhy Avenue, Lincolnwood (Chicago), Illinois 60646 – 1975 USA.

This edition published 2003.

The 'Teach Yourself' name and logo are registered trade marks of Hodder & Stoughton Ltd.

Typeset by Transet Limited, Coventry, England.
Printed in Great Britain for Hodder & Stoughton Educational, a division of Hodder Headline Ltd, 338 Euston Road, London NW1 3BH by Cox & Wyman Ltd, Reading, Berkshire.

Impression number   10 9 8 7 6 5 4 3 2 1
Year   2008 2007 2006 2005 2004 2003

contents

18   **imagining what could happen**   **226**
saying what would have to take place before
something else could happen; imagining how
you would react in certain circumstances;
saying what you thought would happen.

abbreviations

masc./m.	masculine
fem./f.	feminine
sing.	singular
plu./pl.	plural
infinit.	infinitive
past.part/pp	past participle
pt.p	present participle
Q	question
A	answer

introduction

Congratulations! You've decided to get to grips with the grammar of French. We're here to help you and this book is clear and easy to use, whether you're in a class or studying by yourself. You don't need to know a lot about grammar before you start. Everything is explained simply and we've given you lots of examples. There's also an on-going storyline to put the grammar in context.

The authors

Learning languages works best if you have two teachers: one who speaks your language and one who speaks the language you're learning. Robin Adamson (a native speaker of English) and Brigitte Edelston (a native speaker of French) have a wide variety of qualifications and experience.

We have enjoyed working together over many years with all kinds of learners – university students, primary school pupils, teachers, people in business, holiday makers. We wanted to write a book that would be fun to use but that would also be based on ways of learning that worked. **Teach Yourself French Grammar** is the result of our collaboration and it is based on the ways of learning that our different kinds of students have enjoyed and found most successful: we've based a story to put all the French into a context and we've underpinned and encouraged the learning process by the close relationships between the sections in each unit. Feedback from the first edition tells us that the book has helped people who wanted – for all sorts of reasons – to learn French grammar. We hope you'll find it helpful too.

How to use this book

Teach Yourself French Grammar is divided into 18 units and each one will help you to use French for specific things like talking about yourself, asking about people, describing people and so on. You'll see in the **Contents** (page v) that each unit is based on a theme connected with the story of the Lemaires and the Dicksons, ranging from the family to banking. All the examples come from the story and all are in modern French. You won't find obscure or old-world examples in this book. Every time you read an example, you'll know it fits into the story so it will be easier and quicker for you to understand and you'll be able to concentrate on the grammar.

We know you're all at different stages, so, although the book starts with the basics and goes on to the more complex grammar, we've organized it so that you can begin wherever you like. If there's a particular point you need, you can use the **Index** (page 270) and the **Contents** and go straight to it. If terminology is a problem, the **Glossary** (page 263) is there to take the strain. Just need to work on those irregular verbs? The **Verb tables** (page 250) have all the details.

The book will work for you because it's a partnership between you and us. You decide what you need – and we help you to decide. Then we show you how to get to where you want to be.

All the units follow the same pattern. They start by showing you the theme of the unit and what you will learn in it. Then there are six carefully inter-related sections. Each unit begins with **Getting started**. This lets you check if you're ready for that unit. Then we show you how the grammar works in real life (**Say it in French**) so that you're already prepared for what you find in the grammar section (**The main points**). **The story** will show you how much you've learned. Different sorts of language activities (in **A quick check**) make sure you've learned the grammar – and there's a **Key** at the back of the book (page 244). If you're hooked and want to know more, go on to **The next stage**. You'll never feel lost because we've given you cross-references to other units wherever we think they'll help.

You'll soon get more confident and then it's a good idea to cover up the English on the right hand side of the page, and just look at the French.

Your notebook is an essential tool. Use it where we suggest it and make it your own, unique record of learning French grammar.

Storyline

The storyline runs through the whole book, with a new chapter in each unit. You'll meet the same people and follow some of their activities in a momentous year. All the examples in the book fit into the context of this important year in the lives of the Lemaires and the Dicksons. You'll get to know the characters and see how their lives change – and we hope that learning French grammar may also change yours!

The Lemaire family live in Saint-Amand-les-Eaux in the north of France, and the Scottish family, the Dicksons, live in Dundee in Scotland. Georges and Isabelle Lemaire have two children, Stéphanie, aged 20, and Nicolas, 17. Stéphanie is on a six-month work experience placement with an oil company in Aberdeen as part of the last year of her commerce degree (*le D.U.T.*). Nicolas is in his 7th year of secondary school, studying sciences. Stéphanie met Mark Dickson, a research engineer in the same oil company, at the beginning of her stay in Aberdeen. They are planning to become engaged at the end of the summer.

Mark has one sister Sandy, 20, who is in her second year of university, studying English and French. Their younger brother, Andrew, is in his final year at school. Stéphanie and Mark go to St Amand at the beginning of May and the Lemaires meet Mark for the first time. Mark's parents – Alison and Patrick Dickson – are hoping to spend a few days with Stéphanie's parents in July and have enrolled to learn French at evening classes in preparation for the big event.

How are Alison Dickson, a history and geography teacher, and Patrick, manager of a supermarket, going to communicate with the Lemaires? Georges Lemaire, a highly-skilled plumber and Isabelle, a busy housewife actively involved in voluntary work with the Catholic church, speak no English. Will the date of the engagement be decided during the Dicksons' stay? Read on!

We hope you enjoy discovering French grammar while getting to know the Lemaire and the Dickson families. You can contact us through Hodder Headline if you'd like to let us know how you get on.

01

greetings and introductions

In this unit you will learn
- to introduce yourself / someone else
- numbers to 100
- to greet people
- to talk about yourself / someone else
- to ask questions about someone (age, address, nationality, occupation, family circumstances)

Topic
- meeting people

Grammar

- Subject pronouns: **je** (*I*), **tu** (*you*), **il** (*he*), **elle** (*she*), **on** (*one/we/they*), **nous** (*we*), **vous** (*you*), **ils/elles** (*they*)
- Verbs: present tense of **avoir** (*to have*), **être** (*to be*)
- -**er** verbs: regular **habiter** (*to live*); irregular **aller** (*to go*)
- A reflexive verb: **s'appeler** (*to be called*)
- Using **tu** or **vous**?
- Asking questions
- The negative form: **ne...pas / n'...pas** (*not*)
- Stressed pronouns: **moi, toi, lui/elle, nous, vous, eux/elles**
- Gender

The next stage

- Expressions with **avoir** and **être**
- Changes in spelling of -**er** verbs
- Questions: inversion of verb and subject pronoun
- Gender rules and exceptions

Getting started

So that you can say a little about yourself in French, it is important to learn some key verbs, such as **avoir** *to have*, **être** *to be*, **habiter** *to live*, **s'appeler** *to be called* and the subject pronouns (i.e. **je** *I*, **tu** *you*, **il** *he* etc.). With a few numbers and a little vocabulary you are well on your way.

Say it in French

1 Introducing yourself / someone else

Bonjour, **je m'appelle** Georges Lemaire.
Hello, my name is Georges Lemaire.

J'ai 46 ans.
I'm 46 years old.

J'habite St Amand-les-Eaux.
I live in St Amand-les-Eaux.

Je suis Georges.
I'm Georges.

Je vous **présente** ma famille.
This is my family.

2 Numbers to 100

Here is a list of numbers to 100. Learn them at your own pace and refer to the list frequently.

Note that after 60, the French count in 20s. 70 is **soixante-dix**, 80 is **quatre-vingts** and 90 is **quatre-vingt-dix**.

0	zéro	10	dix	20	vingt
1	un	11	onze	21	vingt et un
2	deux	12	douze	22	vingt-deux
3	trois	13	treize	23	vingt-trois
4	quatre	14	quatorze	24	vingt-quatre
5	cinq	15	quinze	25	vingt-cinq
6	six	16	seize	26	vingt-six
7	sept	17	dix-sept	27	vingt-sept
8	huit	18	dix-huit	28	vingt-huit
9	neuf	19	dix-neuf	29	vingt-neuf

30	trente	40	quarante	50	cinquante	60	soixante
31	trente et un	41	quarante et un	51	cinquante et un	61	soixante et un
32	trente-deux	42	quarante-deux	52	cinquante-deux	62	soixante-deux

70	soixante-dix	80	quatre-vingts	90	quatre-vingt-dix
71	soixante et onze	81	quatre-vingt-un	91	quatre-vingt-onze
72	soixante-douze	82	quatre-vingt-deux	92	quatre-vingt-douze
73	soixante-treize	83	quatre-vingt-trois	93	quatre-vingt-treize
74	soixante-quatorze				
75	soixante-quinze			100	cent
76	soixante-seize				
77	soixante-dix-sept				
78	soixante-dix-huit				
79	soixante-dix-neuf				

3 Greeting people

Stéphanie présente son petit ami Mark à la famille Lemaire. (*Stéphanie introduces her boyfriend Mark to the Lemaire family.*)

Stéphanie	Mark, **je** te **présente** mon père et ma mère.	*Mark, this is my father and my mother.*
Mark	Enchanté.	*Pleased to meet you.*
Stéphanie	**Je** vous **présente** Mark, mon copain.	*This is my friend Mark.*

Isabelle ⎫ Georges ⎭	Ravis de faire votre connaissance.	*Delighted to make your acquaintance.*
Georges	Comment **allez-vous**?	*How do you do?*
Mark	Bien, merci.	*I'm well, thank you.*
Stéphanie	Voici mon frère, Nicolas.	*This is my brother Nicolas.*
Mark	Salut, ça va?	*Hi, how are you?*
Nicolas	Ça **va** bien, merci. Et toi?	*Fine, thank you. What about you?*
	Comment **tu vas**?	*How's it going?*

4 Talking about yourself / someone else

Voici ma femme Isabelle:
Elle a 43 (quarante-trois) ans.
Moi, **j'ai** 46 (quarante-six) ans.

This is my wife Isabelle:
She's 43.
(Myself) As for me, I'm 46 years old.

Nous avons deux enfants.
Ils s'appellent Stéphanie et
et Nicolas.
Stéphanie **a** 20 (vingt) ans et
Nicolas **a** 17 (dix-sept) ans.

We have two children.
They're called Stéphanie and Nicolas.
Stéphanie is 20 and Nicolas is 17.

5 Asking questions about someone

Georges	**Vous habitez** Aberdeen aussi?	*Do you live in Aberdeen too?*
Mark	Oui, **je suis** ingénieur dans une compagnie pétrolière.	*Yes, I'm an engineer in an oil company.*
Isabelle	Est-ce que vos parents **habitent** Aberdeen?	*Do your parents live in Aberdeen?*
Mark	Non, **ils** n'**habitent** pas Aberdeen. **Ils habitent** Dundee.	*No, they don't live in Aberdeen. They live in Dundee.*
Isabelle	**Êtes-vous** né en Écosse?	*Were you born in Scotland?*
Mark	Oui, à Dundee.	*Yes, in Dundee.*
Georges	**Vous aimez** Aberdeen?	*Do you like Aberdeen?*
Mark	Oui, beaucoup.	*Yes, very much.*

The main points

1 Subject pronouns

The subject pronouns and matching verbs are shown in bold type in **Say it in French** above. Here they are in full:

1st person singular	**je (j'** in front of vowel / vowel sound)	*I*
2nd	**tu**	*you*
3rd	**il/elle/on**	*he/she/one*
1st person plural	**nous**	*we*
2nd	**vous**	*you*
3rd	**ils/elles**	*they*

2 Verbs *avoir* and *être*

Look for the different forms of **être** and **avoir** and the matching nouns or subject pronouns in the examples in **Say it in French 1** and **4**.

avoir to have
j'**ai**
tu **as**
il/elle/on **a**
nous **avons**
vous **avez**
ils/elles **ont**

être to be
je **suis**
tu **es**
il/elle/on **est**
nous **sommes**
vous **êtes**
ils/elles **sont**

M. Lemaire (=il) **est** plombier.

Mr Lemaire (=he) is a plumber.

Mme Lemaire (=elle) **est** femme au foyer.

Mrs Lemaire (=she) is a housewife.

Elle **a** 43 ans.

She is 43.

Ils **ont** deux enfants.

They have two children.

Remember that in French you use the verb **avoir** to say your age.

Nicolas **a** dix-sept ans.

Nicolas is 17.

J'**ai** 46 ans.

I am 46.

3 Verbs ending in *-er*

80% of French verbs end in -**er** and most of them are regular.

Regular verbs such as *habiter* to live

To use -**er** verbs you just: take the -**er** off the infinitive, this gives you the *stem*; add the endings.

For example:

habiter: take the -**er** off to get the stem (**habit-**); add the endings (table below); match them to the subjects. Because the **h** at the beginning of **habiter** is not pronounced, the first sound is **a** and so the **e** on **je** is dropped.

Pronoun	**Stem**	**Ending**
j'	habit-	**E**
tu	habit-	**ES**
il/elle/on	habit-	**E**
nous	habit-	**ONS**
vous	habit-	**EZ**
ils/elles	habit-	**ENT**

habiter

j'habit**E** Londres	*I live in London*
tu habit**ES** Paris	*you live in Paris*
il/elle habit**E** Marseille	*he/she lives in Marseilles*
nous habit**ONS** Édimbourg	*we live in Edinburgh*
vous habit**EZ** Cardiff	*you live in Cardiff*
ils/elles habit**ENT** Lille	*they live in Lille*

Les Lemaire habit**ent**	*The Lemaires live in*
St Amand-les-Eaux	*St Amand-les-Eaux*
dans le nord de la France.	*in the north of France.*

Useful verbs such as **aimer** *to like*, **détester** *to hate*, **donner** *to give*, **quitter** *to leave*, follow the same pattern. Here are some more regular -**er** verbs. Compile your own list now in your notebook and keep adding to it as you learn.

List of regular -*er* verbs

aider	*to help*	**fermer**	*to close*
aimer	*to like*	**fumer**	*to smoke*
chercher	*to look for*	**gagner**	*to win*
commander	*to order*	**jouer**	*to play*
danser	*to dance*	**laisser**	*to leave*
déjeuner	*to have breakfast*	**louer**	*to rent/hire*
		marcher	*to walk*
demander	*to ask*	**monter**	*to go up*
désirer	*to wish*	**oublier**	*to forget*
détester	*to hate*	**parler**	*to talk*
discuter	*to discuss*	**porter**	*to carry*
écouter	*to listen to*	**raconter**	*to tell*
emprunter	*to borrow*	**remercier**	*to thank*
expliquer	*to explain*		

• The stems of some -**er** verbs change their spelling with some subjects:

appeler	*to call*
préférer	*to prefer*

These verbs are given in full on page 262.

aller

There is one key verb in **Say it in French 3** that is irregular. **Aller**, *to go* does not follow the pattern given above for **habiter**. It is used in expressions such as:

| Ça va? | *How is it going?* |
| Comment **allez**-vous? | *How do you do?/How are you?* |

je **vais** très bien	*I'm very well*
tu **vas** à Dundee	*you are going to Dundee*
il/elle/on **va** au travail	*he/she/one (we go) goes to work*
nous **allons** à l'arrêt de bus	*we're going to the bus stop*
vous **allez** à St Amand	*you're going to St Amand*
ils/elles **vont** en France	*they're going to France*

4 A reflexive verb

s'appeler	je **m**'appelle Stéphanie	*I'm called Stéphanie*
	tu **t**'appelles Mark?	*you're called Mark?*
	il/elle/on **s**'appelle Dickson	*he/she is / we're called Dickson*
	nous **nous** appelons Lemaire	*we're called Lemaire*
	vous **vous** appelez Alison?	*you're called Alison?*
	ils/elles **s**'appellent Dupont	*they're called Dupont*

In French you say *I call myself, we call ourselves, …* This type of verb is called **reflexive**. You will find out more about reflexive verbs in Unit 3.

The main points 2, 3.

Stéphanie a un frère.	*Stéphanie has a brother.*
Il **s'appelle** Nicolas.	*He is called Nicolas.*
Ils **s'appellent** Lemaire.	*They're called Lemaire.*

5 Using *tu* or *vous*

Did you notice, in **Say it in French 3**, that Nicolas says:

Comment tu vas? when talking to Mark. He uses **tu**, the informal, friendly form, as opposed to: **Comment allez-vous?** which is a formal way of speaking to *one* person. Georges says: **Comment allez-vous?** He addresses Mark more formally because they do not know one another.

Here are some guidelines on when to use the formal **vous** and the informal **tu:**

TU for	**VOUS** for
• friends	• adults meeting someone for the first time
• family	• someone you don't know well

- children
- students
- teenagers
- animals

- someone with whom you do not have a friendly/personal relationship; i.e. unless your doctor or a shop assistant was a personal friend of yours you would always say **vous**.
- people you want to show respect to: a superior / somebody in authority, an employee, in-laws etc.

6 Asking questions

As you can see from **Asking questions about someone** on page 5, there are three ways of asking questions:

- You can make a statement and let your voice rise

  Ça va? (↑)
  Vous habitez Aberdeen? (↑)

- You can add **est-ce-que** at the beginning of your sentence

  Est-ce que vos parents habitent Aberdeen?

- You can change the order of the verb and the subject pronoun

  Êtes-vous né en Écosse?

When you do this with an **-er** verb and the pronoun **il/elle/on**, if the verb ends in a vowel, you insert **-t-**:

Aime-**t**-il Dundee?	*Does he like Dundee?*
Joue-**t**-elle au football?	*Does she play football?*

These three ways of asking questions can also be used with question words, *when? how?* etc. See Unit 2 **The main points 8**.

7 The negative forms: *ne … pas / n'… pas*

Compare these two sentences:

J'habite Aberdeen.	*I live in Aberdeen.*
Je **n'**habite **pas** Dundee.	*I do not live in Dundee.*

To say that you 'do *not* do something / are *not*' you use **ne … pas**. Ne comes after the subject. **Pas** comes after the verb.

Les Lemaire **ne** sont **pas** écossais. *The Lemaires are not Scottish.*

Ne, like **je**, drops the **e** and becomes **n'** in front of a vowel or vowel sound:

Stéphanie **n'**habite **pas** Lille.	*Stéphanie does not live in Lille.*
Mark **n'**aime **pas** Londres.	*Mark doesn't like London.*

8 Stressed pronouns: *moi, toi, lui/elle*

Stressed pronouns are useful if you want to find out something about someone.

- If you are speaking to one person, you say:

    et *toi*? (informal register), or et *vous*? (formal register)

J'aime ma famille. **Et toi?**	*I love my family. What about you?*
Je n'aime pas le football. **Et vous?**	*I don't like football. Do you?*

- If you are speaking to several people, you say:

    et vous?

Nous aimons beaucoup l'Angleterre. **Et vous?**	*We like England very much. Do you?*

- If you want to know what other people think, you say:

    et elle? (feminine singular); **et lui?** (masculine singular)
    et elles? (feminine plural); **et eux?** (masculine plural)

Sandy va bien maintenant. **Et lui?**	*Sandy is fine now. What about him?*
Tous les garçons sont ici. **Et elle?**	*All the boys are here. What about her?*
Nous allons en France. **Et eux?**	*We're going to France. How about them?*

Here is a complete list of stressed pronouns and the subjects they correspond to:

moi	*me*	corresponds to	**je**
toi	*you*	→	**tu**
lui	*him*	→	**il**
elle	*her*	→	**elle**
soi	*oneself*	→	**on**
nous	*us*	→	**nous**
vous	*you*	→	**vous**
eux	*them*	→	**ils**
elles	*them*	→	**elles**

These pronouns can also be used to add emphasis to the subject:

Moi, je m'appelle Georges.	*(Myself / As for me), I'm called Georges.*

They can be used after **et** (*and*) and after prepositions such as **après** (*after*), **avant** (*before*) etc. See Unit 6 **The main points 3**.

Moi, je vais bien. **Et toi?**   *I am well. What about you?*
Après **vous**./Après **toi**.   *After you.*

9 Gender

Subjects:

* to say *she* in French you use **elle**
* to talk about several girls or women (*they*), you use **elles**
* to say *he* you use **il**
* to talk about more than one man or a mixed group (*they*) you use **ils**

Stressed pronouns:

* to say *and her* you use **elle**: et *elle*
* to say *and them* (feminine group) you use **elles**: et *elles*
* to say *and him* you use **lui**: et *lui*
* to say *and them* (masculine or mixed group) you use **eux**: et *eux*

However, not only people have gender in French. All nouns, objects, ideas, fruit and vegetables – *everything* has gender. For example **une table** (*a table*) is feminine → **elle**. **Une voiture** (*a car*) is also feminine. As you progress through the book you will discover that gender is extremely important in French because it affects verb and adjective endings, pronouns etc.

In your notebook, keep separate lists of masculine and feminine nouns, and add to them as you learn more nouns.

Here is a list to help you separate French nouns into the two groups:

Masculine
* days of the week
* male members of the family
* vegetables and countries not ending in **-e**
* nouns ending in **-isme, -asme, -age, -ège, -ème, -ède**

Feminine
* most words ending in **-e**
* female members of the family
* vegetables and countries ending in **-e**
* words ending with a double consonant + **-e** (**une allumette** *a match*)
* nouns ending in **-tion/-sion**

The story

In this passage look for **verbs**, **subject pronouns** and **verb endings**.

Nicolas	Moi, j'ai 17 ans. Et toi?	*(Me/myself) I'm 17. And you?*
	Quel âge as-tu?	*How old are you?*
Mark	J'ai 24 ans. Tu es lycéen?	*I'm 24. Are you a student?*
Nicolas	Oui, je suis en première, section S. Et toi, tu travailles?	*Yes, I'm in 6th year science stream. And how about you, do you work?*
Mark	Oui, je suis ingénieur dans une compagnie pétrolière à Aberdeen. Est-ce que tu aimes l'école?	*Yes, I'm an engineer with an oil company in Aberdeen. Do you like school?*
Nicolas	Non, pas du tout. Je n'aime pas les profs, surtout mon prof d'anglais … Toi et moi, nous partageons la même chambre. On monte? Je t'aide à porter tes valises. D'accord?	*No, not at all. I don't like the teachers, especially my English teacher … You and I are sharing the same room. Shall we go up? I'll help you carry your suitcases. All right?*
Mark	Oui, merci.	*Yes, thank you.*
Nicolas	Comment s'appellent tes parents?	*What are your parents called?*
Mark	Ils s'appellent Patrick et Alison.	*They're called Patrick and Alison.*
Nicolas	Tu as des frères et des soeurs?	*Do you have brothers and sisters?*
Mark	Oui, j'ai un frère et une soeur. Mon frère s'appelle Andrew et ma soeur s'appelle Sandy.	*Yes, I have a brother and a sister. My brother called Andrew and my sister's called Sandy.*
Nicolas	Est-ce que tes parents travaillent?	*Do your parents work?*
Mark	Ma mère est professeur d'histoire-géographie. Mon père est directeur de supermarché.	*My mother is a history and geography teacher. My father is the manager of a supermarket.*

A quick check

Voici la famille Dickson

ALISON

48 ans
prof
d'histoire-
géographie

PATRICK

54 ans
directeur de
supermarché

MARK

24 ans
ingénieur –
industrie du
pétrole

SANDY

20 ans
2e année de
sciences
humaines
(+ français)

ANDREW

17 ans
lycéen

1 Introduce the Dickson family in French by filling in the gaps:
   a Je vous _____ Alison. Elle _____ 48 ans.
   b Elle _____ professeur d'histoire-géographie.
   c Voici Patrick. _____. _____ 54 ans.
   d Il _____ _____.
   e Ils _____ trois enfants: Mark, Sandy, Andrew.
   f Andrew _____ travaille ___. Il _____ à l'école.

2 Complete the following questions:
   a Comment _____ les parents de Mark?
   b Quel âge _____ Sandy?
   c _____ Sandy travaille?
   d Les Dickson _____ -ils (à) Aberdeen?
   e Et Stéphanie? _____ – ___ – ___ (à) Dundee?

3 Answer in French the questions you have just completed in 2 above.

The next stage

1 Expressions with *avoir* and *être*

Avoir is sometimes used in French where **être** (*to be*) is used in English:

J'**ai** 20 ans.	*I am 20 years old.*
J'**ai** faim.	*I am hungry.*
J'**ai** froid.	*I am cold.*
J'**ai** chaud.	*I am hot.*

Avoir and **être** are also used as auxiliary verbs in some past tenses: the perfect (see Unit 13, **The main points 2, 3**), the pluperfect (see Unit 15 **The main points 1**) and the perfect subjunctive (see Unit 17 **The main points 5**).

2 Changes in spelling *-er* verbs

Some **-er** verbs have a change in spelling in some tenses. See Verb tables page 262.

a Verbs ending in *-yer*

envoyer *to send*	
j'**envoie**	nous **envoyons**
tu **envoies**	vous **envoyez**
il/elle/on **envoie**	ils/elles **envoient**

b Verbs ending in *-ger*

Verbs such as **manger** *to eat*, **nager** *to swim*, **plonger** *to dive* add an -e in the first person plural (**nous** form) to retain the same pronunciation (a soft **g**) as in the infinitive:

nous mangeons, nous nageons, nous plongeons,...

c Verbs ending in *-cer*

Verbs such as **commencer** (*to begin*) have a cedilla on the **c** in the first person plural (**nous** form) to retain the soft **c** sound of the infinitive:

nous commençons

d Verbs ending in *-ter/-ler*

Verbs such as **jeter** or **appeler** double the **t** or **l** except for the **nous** and **vous** forms:

jeter *to throw*	
je **jette**	nous **jetons**
tu **jettes**	vous **jetez**
il/elle/on **jette**	ils/elles **jettent**

épeler *to spell*	
j'**épelle**	nous **épelons**
tu **épelles**	vous **épelez**
il/elle/on **épelle**	ils/elles **épellent**

or add a grave accent:

acheter *to buy*	
j'**achète**	nous **achetons**
tu **achètes**	vous **achetez**
il/elle/on **achète**	ils/elles **achètent**

3 Questions: Inversion of verb and subject pronoun

As-tu faim? *Are you hungry?*
Ont-ils des frères et des soeurs? *Do they have brothers and sisters?*

It is only possible to invert a verb and a pronoun. If a noun such as **Mark** or **la soeur de Mark** is used, you use a matching pronoun after the verb while retaining the noun:

Mark, a-t-il faim? *Is Mark hungry?*
La soeur de Mark (Sandy) *Does Mark's sister (Sandy)*
aime-t-elle Dundee? *like Dundee?*
Alison, joue-t-elle au tennis? *Does Alison play tennis?*

4 Gender rules and exceptions

The guidelines given in **The main points 9** are useful suggestions which you should bear in mind, but do not be surprised if you encounter words which break the rules:

• Most words ending in -**age**, for example, are masculine except: **la cage** (*the cage*), **la nage** (*swimming*), **l'image** (*image, picture*), **la page** (*page*), **la plage** (*the beach*), **la rage** (*rabies*).

• Most words ending in -**tion** are feminine, but there are exceptions such as **le bastion** (*stronghold*).

• Although most animals, like humans, have both a masculine and a feminine form, there are some animals which are always feminine in gender: **la girafe** (*giraffe*), **l'autruche** (*ostrich*), **la perruche** (*budgie*).

• Some professions remain masculine and do not have a feminine form:

le professeur (*teacher*) Il est professeur. Elle est professeur.
l'auteur (*author*) Il est auteur. Elle est auteur.
le juge (*judge*) Il est juge. Elle est juge.
le chauffeur (*driver*) Il est chauffeur. Elle est chauffeur.

• Some words have a different meaning depending on whether they are masculine or feminine:

le livre (*book*) **la livre** (*pound*)
le mort (*dead man*) **la mort** (*death*)
le physique (*physique*) **la physique** (*physics*)
le poste (*post/job*) **la poste** (*post office*)

02

likes and dislikes

In this unit you will learn
- to express preferences
- to ask about likes, dislikes and hobbies
- question words
- days and dates

Topics
- hobbies
- sport

Grammar

- Definite articles **le, la, l', les** (*the*) and indefinite articles **un, une, des** (*a, an*)
- Articles with nouns in the plural
- Contracted articles: definite articles after *at/with/to*: **au, aux** and after *of/from*: **du, des**
- Partitive articles: **du, de la, de l', des** (*some/any*)
- Demonstrative adjectives: **ce/cet, cette, ces** (*this, that, these, those*)
- Possessive adjectives: **mon/ma/mes** (*my*)
- The verb **faire** (*to do*) in the present tense
- Question words: **comment?, qui?, quand?** (*how?, who?, when?*)

The next stage

- Partitive articles after negatives
- Irregular plurals
- More about demonstratives
- More about possessive adjectives
- When to use **faire** and **jouer**

Getting started

As you saw in Unit 1 **The main points 2**, the article in French is omitted after **être** before a profession. You say:

Il est professeur.   *He is a teacher.*

This is an exception to the ground rule, as articles are usually used in French:

Mark aime **le** football.   *Mark likes football.*
Nicolas a **des** amis sur   *Nicolas has friends on the*
l'internet.   *Internet.*

1   In this unit you will learn when to use the definite articles **le, la, les** and when to use the indefinite articles **un, une, des**:

Georges regarde **un** match de   *Georges is watching a football*
football à **la** télévision.   *match on the television.*
Il adore **le** football.   *He loves football.*

2   You will find out more about the plural of nouns and the use of definite and indefinite articles in French with plural nouns.

In some cases you will see they are used in French when they would not be used in English:

Nicolas aime **les** ordinateurs. *Nicolas likes computers.*
Nicolas rencontre **des** amis *Nicolas is meeting friends this*
ce soir. *evening.*

3 You will learn to say *any/some* in French:

Avez-vous **des** passe-temps? *Do you have any hobbies?*
J'ai **des** amis français. *I have some French friends.*

4 You will also learn how definite articles contract with the prepositions **à** (*at/with/to*) and **de** (*of/from*):

Nicolas va **au** cinéma. *Nicolas goes to the cinema.*
Nicolas joue **du** piano. *Nicolas plays the piano.*

5 An article can be replaced by a demonstrative adjective (**ce/cet, cette, ces**) if you want to refer specifically to one or more things. In the following examples the demonstrative adjective singles out a particular video, a specific picture or specific ideas:

Nicolas préfère **cette** vidéo. *Nicolas prefers this video.*
Stéphanie adore **ce** tableau *Stéphanie likes this painting by*
de Monet. *Monet very much.*
Aimez-vous **ces** idées d'avant- *Do you like these avant-garde*
garde? *ideas?*

6 A noun can also be preceded by a possessive adjective (**mon/ma/mes**,...) which indicates possession or refers to family members etc.:

Leur père, Georges, a des *Their father, Georges,*
trophées de chasse. *has hunting trophies.*
Stéphanie admire **sa** mère car *Stéphanie admires her mother*
elle fait du travail bénévole. *because she does voluntary*
work.

7 The verb **faire** is very useful when you are talking about your hobbies/activities. In this unit you will learn to use it in the present tense:

Mark **fait** du football et du *Mark plays football*
rugby. *and rugby.*

8 You have already met (Unit 1 **The story**) the question words

quel? (*what*) in **Quel âge as-tu?** (*How old are you?*) and
comment? (*how*) in **Comment allez-vous?** (*How are you?*). In
this unit you will meet more question words **où?** (*where?*),
quand? (*when?*) etc.:

Quand est-ce que Mark joue au rugby?	*When does Mark play rugby?*
Où joue-t-il au rugby?	*Where does he play rugby?*

Look carefully at all the structures in the following examples
before moving on to the **The main points**.

Say it in French

1 Discussing hobbies, likes and dislikes

Georges adore **le** football.	*Georges adores football.*
Moi, je préfère **la** broderie et **le** canevas.	*Myself, I prefer embroidery and cross-stitch.*
Nicolas déteste **le** sport. Il préfère **les** ordinateurs.	*Nicolas hates sport. He prefers computers.*
Mark joue **au** squash. Il fait **du**	*Mark plays squash. He skis*

ski et **de la** plongée sous-marine.	*and dives.*
Nicolas adore **la** cuisine d'Isabelle, surtout **sa** purée Parmentier.	*Nicolas loves Isabelle's cooking especially her Parmentier purée.*

2 Asking about hobbies, likes and dislikes, places

Qu'est-ce que tu fais comme loisirs?	*What do you do in your spare time?*
Qu'est-ce que tu aimes?	*What do you like?*
Quel plat préfères-tu?	*What is your favourite dish?*
Que détestes-tu?	*What do you hate?*
Quand jouez-vous au squash?	*When do you play squash?*
Qui joue avec vous?	*Who plays with you?*
Où se trouve Aberdeen?	*Where is Aberdeen?*
Comment allez-vous au travail?	*How do you go to work?*

3 Days and dates

Mark joue au squash **le lundi** et **le mardi**.	*Mark plays squash on Mondays and Tuesdays.*
Il joue au rugby **le samedi** ou **le dimanche après-midi**.	*He plays rugby on Saturday or Sunday afternoons.*
Est-ce que tu joues au rugby **samedi**?	*Are you playing rugby this Saturday?*
Georges est né **le 26 novembre** 1958.	*Georges was born on November 26th, 1958.*
Stéphanie est née **le 1er janvier**.	*Stéphanie was born on January 1st.*
Mark est né **le 3 septembre**.	*Mark was born on September 3rd.*

The main points

1 Definite and indefinite articles

Articles are different in French according to the **gender** of the noun (Unit 1 **The main points 9**) and to the **number** of the noun (singular or plural).

	definite article: *the*	indefinite article: *a, an, -*
masc. sing.	**le, l'** (in front of a vowel)	**un**
fem. sing.	**la, l'** (in front of a vowel)	**une**
masc. fem. plural	**les**	**des**

Definite article

The definite article is used in French even when you are talking about something in general terms. In English you talk and write about *football/swimming* etc., French uses the definite article **le/la** in front of the noun (depending on its gender): **le football** (*football*), **la natation** (*swimming*). See **Say it in French 1**.

Aimez-vous **le** football?	*Do you like football?*
Stéphanie aime **le** chant.	*Stéphanie likes singing.*
Georges regarde **le** football sur *Canal +*.	*Georges watches football on Canal plus.*
Georges regarde **le** match Paris-Nice.	*Georges is watching the Paris-Nice match.* (a specific match)

Indefinite article

The indefinite article also changes according to the gender of the noun. You use **un** in front of a masculine noun and **une** in front of a feminine noun:

Mark habite **un** appartement à Aberdeen.	*Mark lives in a flat in Aberdeen.*
Nicolas va à la vidéothèque et emprunte **une** vidéo.	*Nicolas goes to the video library and borrows a video.*
Georges regarde **un** match de football à la télévision.	*Georges is watching a football match on the television.* (not specific)

2 Articles with nouns in the plural

French normally adds an -s to nouns to show that they are plural. Plural articles also have the ending -s. The plural of **le/la** (*the*) is **les**, and the plural of **un/une** (*a/an*) is **des**.

In English, plural nouns are most often used *without* an article, while in French an article *is* used.

Il y a souvent **des** matches de football sur *Canal +*.	*There are often football games on Canal +.*
Nicolas adore **les** plats comme **les** frites et **les** pizzas.	*Nicolas adores dishes such as chips and pizzas.*

3 Contracted articles

The definite articles **le**, **les** contract with **de** (*of/from*) and **à** (*at/with/to*) to become **du/des** and **au/aux**.

You will need to keep referring to this section. Contracted articles are used often and can be surprising as there are no equivalents in English.

Here is a pattern to help you:

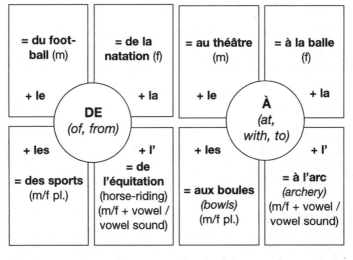

Mark joue **au** squash.   *Mark plays squash.*
Georges fait **du** ball-trap.   *Georges does clay pigeon*
                                    shooting.
Nicolas va souvent **au** cinéma.   *Nicolas often goes to the*
                                    cinema.
Il aime jouer **aux** échecs.   *He likes to play chess.*
Isabelle reste **à la** maison   *Isabelle stays at home or goes*
ou va **au** centre d'accueil   *to the drop-in centre at the*
du presbytère.   *presbytery.*
Alison joue **du** piano.   *Alison plays the piano.*

Aimer can be followed directly by an infinitive (e.g. **jouer**).

4 Partitive articles: some, any

If you want to talk about a quantity or use *some* or *any* you use **de** with the definite article. This is called the **partitive article**. As you saw in **3** above, there is a contraction with **le** and **les** and you say:

J'ai **du** temps libre. (**de** combines with **le** to become **du**)
J'ai **des** problèmes. (**de** combines with **les** to become **des**)

More about these in Unit 4 **The main points 2**.

5 Demonstrative adjectives: this, that, these, those

These also change according to the gender and number of nouns. Look at the following grid and examples and refer to it when you find demonstratives in other situations.

masc. sing.	fem. sing.	masc. fem. plural
ce	**cette**	**ces**
cet + vowel / vowel sound		
this/that	*this/that*	*these/those*

Ce match est formidable.	*This match is wonderful.*
Cet ordinateur est bien.	*This computer is good.*
Cette émission est intéressante.	*This TV programme is interesting.*
J'aime bien ces tableaux.	*I really like these paintings.*

6 Possessive adjectives: *mon, ma, mes*

In French it is important to remember that possessive adjectives agree in number and gender with *what is possessed* and not with the person who owns it (More about this in Unit 7 **The main points 1**). The gender of the person who owns something is totally irrelevant in French and does not affect the choice of possessive adjective.

Nicolas taquine **sa** soeur (fem.) et Stéphanie n'aime pas toujours **son** frère (masc.)	*Nicolas teases his sister and Stéphanie doesn't always like her brother.*

Here is a complete grid:

masc. sing.	fem. sing.	masc. fem. plural	
mon	**ma**	**mes**	*my*
	mon + vowel		
ton	**ta**	**tes**	*your*
	ton + vowel		
son	**sa**	**ses**	*his/her/its*
	son + vowel		
notre	**notre**	**nos**	*our*
votre	**votre**	**vos**	*your*
leur	**leur**	**leurs**	*their*

See **Getting started 6**.

7 The verb *faire*

Faire is very useful for talking about your leisure activities. See **Say it in French 1** and **The main points 3**. It is an irregular verb:

faire		
	je **fais** le ménage	*I do the housework*
	tu **fais** du sport	*you play sport*
	il/elle/on **fait** du football	*he/she plays football*
	nous **faisons** des promenades	*we go for a walk*
	vous **faites** du travail bénévole	*you do voluntary work*
	ils/elles **font** du ski	*they go skiing*

Mark **fait** du football, du ski et de la plongée sous-marine.	*Mark plays football and goes skiing and diving.*

The present tense in French is also used where in English you would use the form *is + ing*: Mark **fait** du football. (*Mark is playing football.*) The present tense can also be used in speech to talk about future actions, which are indicated by time expressions e.g. **demain** (*tomorrow*), **l'année prochaine** (*next year*). See the future tense in Unit 11 **Getting started 1, 2** and **The main points 1, 2**.

Demain, il **fait** de la plongée. *He is diving tomorrow.*

8 Question words

The three ways of asking questions that were given in Unit 1 **The main points 6**, can also be used with question words:

Quel âge tu as?	*How old are you?*
Quel âge est-ce que tu as?	*How old are you?*
Quel âge as-tu?	*What age are you?*
J'ai 24 ans.	*I'm 24.*

Quel? is an adjective and it changes to match the gender and number of the noun it accompanies:

Quels sports (masc. plural) tu fais?	*What sports do you play?*
Quelle est votre date (fem. sing.) de naissance?	*What is your date of birth?*
Quelles activités (fem. plural) est-ce que tu fais?	*Which activities do you do?*

Other question words:

Comment?	Comment s'appellent-ils?	*(How) What are they called?*
Qui?	Qui joue avec moi?	*Who is playing with me?*
Que?, qu'?	Qu'est-ce que tu fais?	*What are you doing?*
Où?	Où habitez-vous?	*Where do you live?*
Pourquoi?	Pourquoi dites-vous ça?	*Why do you say that?*
Quand?	Quand faites-vous du sport?	*When do you play sport?*
	Quand allez-vous en vacances?	*When do you go on holiday?*
Combien / combien de?	Combien de temps est-ce que Mark reste en France?	*How long is Mark staying in France?*

In spoken French the question word can be placed at the end of the sentence:

Vous faites du sport **quand**?
Vous habitez **où**?

9 More days and dates

Here are the names of other days and months so that you can say what the date is and answer some of the questions above:

| Aujourd'hui, c'est **le lundi** 2 (deux) février. | *Today is Monday, February 2nd.* |

le ...

lundi (*Monday*)	1er janvier (*January*)	5 mai	9 septembre
mardi (*Tuesday*)	2 février (*February*)	6 juin	10 octobre
mercredi (*Wednesday*)	3 mars (*March*)	7 juillet	11 novembre
jeudi (*Thursday*)	4 avril (*April*) etc.	8 août	12 décembre
vendredi (*Friday*)			
samedi (*Saturday*)			
dimanche (*Sunday*)			

In French, days and months do not have a capital letter.

You only use an ordinal number – **le premier** (*the first*) – for the first of the month. After that, say **le deux, le trois, le quatre** etc. when you say the date.

Note the difference between:

| Qu'est-ce que tu fais **lundi**? | *What are you doing on Monday?* |
| Qu'est-ce que tu fais **ce lundi**? | *What are you doing this Monday?* |

and

Qu'est-ce que tu fais **le lundi**? *What do you do on Mondays?*
(every Monday).

You also use **le** when talking about a specific day followed by a date:

Qu'est-ce que tu fais **le**   *What will you be doing*
lundi 20 mars?   *on Monday, March 20th?*

The story

Look for the different **articles** and **question forms** in the dialogue below.

Stéphanie	Mark, Nicolas! Le dîner est prêt.	*Mark, Nicolas! Dinner is ready.*
Nicolas	Nous arrivons.	*We're coming.*
Isabelle	Georges, on mange. Qu'est-ce que tu fais?	*Georges we are eating. What are you doing?*
Georges	Je regarde un match de foot.	*I'm watching a football match.*

(Isabelle to Mark)

Isabelle   Georges adore le football. Moi, je préfère la cuisine et la couture. Est-ce que vous jouez au football?

Georges adores football. Myself, I prefer cooking and sewing. Do you play play football?

Mark	Oui, je joue au football et aussi au rugby.	*Yes I play football and rugby too.*
Stéphanie	Il joue aussi au squash, au golf et il fait de la plongée sous-marine.	*He also plays squash, golf and goes diving.*
Nicolas	Maman, qu'est-ce qu'on mange?	*Mum, what are we having?*
Isabelle	Nicolas n'aime pas le sport. Il préfère son ordinateur et son estomac.	*Nicolas doesn't like sport. He prefers his computer and his stomach.*

	N'est-ce pas, Nicolas?	*Isn't that right, Nicolas?*
Stéphanie	Qu'est-ce que tu fais ce soir?	*What are you doing this evening?*
Nicolas	Je vais au cinéma puis à la pizzéria.	*I am going to the cinéma and then to the pizzeria.*
Isabelle	Quand rentres-tu? Pas trop tard, j'espère.	*When are you coming home? Not too late, I hope.*

A quick check

Mark montre des photos de sa famille. Georges et Isabelle posent des questions.

Mark is showing pictures of his family. Georges and Isabelle are asking questions. As they don't know one another well, they are using **vous**.

1 Complete the following questions and answers, using question words, articles and possessive adjectives. (One word per gap)

   a _____'est-ce que _____ maman fait comme passe-temps?

   b Elle aime ___ randonnées en montagne, ___ photographie et faire ___ ski.

   c Et _____ père? _____ sports fait-il?

   d Il joue ___ golf.

   e ___ est-ce qu'il joue au golf? (where)

   f ___ est sur ___ photo?

   g C'est ___ frère Andrew et ici c'est ___ soeur Sandy.

   h ___ 'est-ce qu'elle fait dans ___ vie?

   i Elle est étudiante. Elle fait ___ études de sciences humaines et de français.

2 One way of asking questions with interrogative words is suggested in the following sentences. Write out the other two ways.

   Comment est-ce que tu t'appelles?
   Où habites-tu?
   Tu joues au rugby quand?

3 Give your date of birth and the date today.

The next stage

1 Partitive articles after negatives

After negatives or after expressions of quantity (Unit 4 **The main points** 3) the partitive article – **du, de la, de l', des** – becomes simply **de** or **d'**:

Nicolas n'a **pas d**'argent.   *Nicolas doesn't have any money.*
                                Nicolas has no money.
Il a **beaucoup de** temps libre.   *He's got a lot of free time.*

2 Irregular plurals

Most plurals are indicated by -**s**. However, there are nouns which have irregular plurals. Here are some that form the plural with -**x**:

- Most nouns in -**eau/-eu**:

le bateau	les bateaux	*boats*
le gâteau	les gâteaux	*cakes*
le cheveu	les cheveux	*hair*
le jeu	les jeux	*games*

- Some nouns in -**al**:

le cheval	les chevaux	*horses*
le journal	les journaux	*newspapers*

- Nouns in -**ou** add an -**s** except: **hibou** (*owl*), **joujou** (*toy*), **caillou** (*stone*), **chou** (*cabbage*), **genou** (*knee*), **pou** (*louse*) which add -**x**:

le hibou	les hiboux
le pou	les poux

3 More about demonstratives

To be more specific in pinpointing something, you can use a demonstrative adjective and add -**ci** or -**là** (*here* or *there*) after the noun. A hyphen is used between the noun and -**ci** and -**là**:

Cette raquette-**ci**   *This particular racket*
Ce ballon-**là**   *That ball there*

4 More about possessive adjectives

The possessive adjectives **mon, ton, son** are used before a vowel, even if the noun is feminine. This can seem surprising, but it is to make the pronunciation easier:

Mon/ton/son amie	*My/your/his/her girl friend.*
Mon/ton/son ordinateur	*My/your/his/her/its computer.*

5 When to use *faire* and *jouer*

(See **Say it in French 1, The main points 3**). With **jouer** (*to play*) you use **à** for sports et **de** with musical instruments:

Il **joue au** rugby.	*He plays rugby.*
Vous **jouez du** piano.	*You play the piano.*

Jouer à can be replaced by **faire de**:

Il **fait du** rugby.	*He plays rugby.*

Faire can also be used for activities other than sports:

Nicolas **fait du** dessin assisté par ordinateur.	*Nicolas does computer-aided design.*
Isabelle **fait de la** couture.	*Isabelle sews.*
J'aime **faire des** promenades.	*I like to go for walks.*

03 describing people, things and routines

In this unit you will learn
- to describe people: their age, their size, their appearance, their clothes
- to describe things
- to talk about regular activities
- to tell the time

Topic
- routines

Grammar

- Adjectives
- Reflexive verbs
- Questions with reflexive verbs
- More numbers (from 100 onwards, saying *1st*, *2nd*, *3rd* ...,
  saying you are in your *twenties* etc. ...)

The next stage

- More about adjectives – position of adjectives
- Adjectives with adverbs
- Present participles: the *-ing* form of verbs

Getting started

As you saw in Unit 2 **The main points 1–6**, the gender and
number of nouns affect other words in the sentence, such as
articles, interrogative adjectives **quel?**, **quels?**, **quelle?**, **quelles?**
and demonstrative adjectives **ce/cet**, **cette**, **ces**.

1 In this Unit you will see that adjectives also agree in gender
and number with the nouns they relate to. This means that
their endings change, unlike in English where they remain the
same:

Mark est **grand**.	*Mark is tall.*
Sandy est **grande**.	*Sandy is tall.*

In English most adjectives come before the noun. In French,
they usually come after the noun:

Mark a les cheveux **noirs**.   *Mark has black hair.*

– except for a few short adjectives, which you will also meet
in this unit:

Andrew et son copain ont   *Andrew and his mate have*
de **belles** bicyclettes.   *great bicycles.*

You will see that some adjectives can have different meanings
according to whether they come before or after the noun:

Patrick aime avoir une voiture   *Patrick likes to have a **clean***
propre et bien entretenue.   *and well-maintained car.*

Andrew voudrait sa **propre**   *Andrew would like his **own** car.*
voiture.

2 You have already met the reflexive verb **s'appeler** in Unit 1 **The main points** 4. Reflexive verbs use the extra pronoun **se** which changes according to the subject (**je, tu, il** ...):

Quand **vous** réveillez-vous? *When do you wake up?*
À quelle heure **te** couches-tu? *(At) what time do you go to bed?*

The extra pronoun (reflexive pronoun) can mean *myself, yourself, yourselves* etc.:

Je **me** lave. *I wash (myself).*

– but it can also mean *one another, each other*:

Nous **nous** parlons souvent. *We often talk to each other.*
Stéphanie et Nicolas **se** *Stéphanie and Nicolas often*
disputent souvent. *argue (with one another).*

3 In this unit you will also meet numbers from 100 onwards and learn to say the approximate age of someone (e.g. *in his late twenties/thirties*).

Say it in French

Read the following examples, identify all the **adjectives** and look carefully at their **position** and their **agreement** with the nouns they refer to.

1 Describing people

Mark est un **beau** garçon
bronzé.
Il mesure 1,82m.

Mark is a good-looking boy
with a tan.
He is 1.82m tall.

Il a les yeux **bleus** et les cheveux **noirs**.	*He has blue eyes and black hair.*
Il est **musclé** car il est très **sportif**.	*He has good muscles because he is very keen on sport.*
Son père a les cheveux **gris** et les yeux **bleus**.	*His father has grey hair and blue eyes.*
Sa mère Alison a les cheveux **brun clair** et elle a les yeux **gris-vert**.	*His mum Alison has light brown hair and greyish green eyes.*
Elle mesure 1,57m. Elle est **mince** et très **élégante**. Elle a la quarantaine.	*She is 1.57m tall. She is slim and very smart. She is in her a forties.*
Sandy est **brune**. Elle est très **jolie**.	*Sandy is dark. She is very pretty.*
Elle travaille comme modèle pour un magazine de mode.	*She works as a model for a fashion magazine.*
Andrew a les cheveux **noirs bouclés**.	*Andrew has curly black hair.*
Il a l'air très **coquin**.	*He looks very cheeky.*
Il mesure 1,70m et il est **bronzé**.	*He is 1.70m tall and is suntanned.*

2 Describing people's clothing

Alison porte une **jolie** jupe **bleue**, un **beau** chemisier **blanc** et des chaussures **assorties**.	*Alison is wearing a pretty blue skirt, a nice white blouse and matching shoes.*
C'est une jupe **longue, classique**, taille 40.	*It is a long skirt, in a classical style, size 12.*
Patrick porte un **vieux** survêtement, car il fait du jardinage.	*Patrick is wearing an old tracksuit, because he is gardening.*

3 Talking about daily activities

Andrew est souvent à l'extérieur.	*Andrew is often outdoors.*
Il **se lève** très tôt pour distribuer les journaux en vélo.	*He gets up very early to deliver newspapers on his bike.*
Il **se douche** en vitesse.	*He has a quick shower.*
Il **s'habille** rapidement et il déjeune.	*He gets dressed quickly and has breakfast.*

Il **se dépêche** de distribuer les journaux car il **se rend** à l'école à 8h30.
Le soir, il **s'amuse** avec ses amis.

He delivers the papers quickly because he goes to school at 8.30.
In the evenings he enjoys himself with his friends.

4 Describing things/places

Il **se déplace** en vélo.
Son vélo est un V.T.T. **bleu** et **blanc** avec 22 vitesses.
Il travaille pour un **petit** magasin **populaire,** qui vend des journaux près de chez lui.
Il n'a pas le temps de ranger sa chambre. Elle est mal **rangée.**
Alison porte de **jolies** boucles d'oreille **rondes.**
Ce sont des boucles d'oreille en or, très **chic.**

He goes around on his bike.
His bike is a blue and white mountain bike with 22 gears.
He works for a small popular shop selling newspapers near his house.
He doesn't have time to tidy up his bedroom. It is untidy.
Alison is wearing pretty round earrings.
They are very smart gold earrings.

5 Telling the time

Je me réveille **à 7 heures** du matin et je me couche **à 11 heures** du soir.
Andrew se lève **à 6 heures et demie** pour distribuer les journaux.
Ses cours commencent à **8h45** et finissent à **15h55.**
Il sort avec des amis et rentre à **23h15.**

I get up at seven in the morning and go to bed at eleven in the evening.
Andrew gets up at half past 6 to deliver papers.

His lessons start at a quarter to nine and finish at five to four.
He goes out with friends and comes home at a quarter past eleven.

The main points

1 Adjectives

être + adjective

To describe a person or a thing, the verb **être** can be used to link the noun and the adjective that relates to it:

Mark est très **sportif**.	*Mark is very keen on sport.*
La chambre d'Andrew est mal **rangée**.	*Andrew's bedroom is untidy.*

If there is more than one adjective after **être**, they are separated by **et** (*and*), **ou** (*or*), **mais** (*but*) or by a comma:

Patrick est **grand** et **fort**.	*Patrick is big and strong.*
Le vélo est **bleu, blanc** et **rouge**.	*The bike is blue, white and red.*

Most adjectives end: in any letter if they are masculine singular
in **-s** if they are masculine plural
in **-e** if they are feminine singular
in **-es** if they are feminine plural

Mark est intelligen**t**.	*Mark is intelligent.*
Patrick, Mark et Andrew sont sportif**s**.	*Patrick, Mark and Andrew are keen on sport.*
Alison est élégant**e** et bien habillé**e**.	*Alison is elegant and well dressed.*
Sa bicyclette est bleu**e** et blanch**e**.	*His bike is blue and white.*
Ses chaussures sont assorti**es** à sa robe.	*Her shoes match her dress.*

As you can see from these examples and **Say it in French 1**, after the verb **être** adjectives agree in gender and number with the subject.

Noun + adjective

Most adjectives follow the noun:

Mark a les yeux **bleus**.	*Mark has blue eyes.*
Il a les cheveux **noirs**.	*He has black hair.*

These adjectives also agree in number and gender with the noun they qualify:

Patrick porte un survêtement **usagé** (masc. sing.).

Patrick wears a worn tracksuit.

Alison porte une jupe **bleue** (fem. sing.), une veste **bleue** (fem. sing.) et des chaussures **assorties** (fem. pl.).

Alison is wearing a blue skirt, a blue jacket and matching shoes.

Andrew a les cheveux **bouclés** (masc. pl.).

Andrew has curly hair.

Change of spelling

Some adjectives change their endings when they qualify a feminine noun.

- Adjectives ending in -**eau**

masc. sing.	fem. sing.	masc. plural	fem. plural	
beau	**belle**	**beaux**	**belles**	*beautiful*
un **beau** garçon	une **belle** fille	de **beaux** garçons	de **belles** filles	
nouveau	**nouvelle**	**nouveaux**	**nouvelles**	*new/recent*
un **nouveau** film	une **nouvelle** amie	de **nouveaux** amis	de **nouvelles** amies	

See **The main points, noun + adjective** for the position of **beau** and **nouveau**.

- Adjectives ending in -**euf**:

masc. sing.	fem. sing.	masc. plural	fem. plural	
neuf	**neuve**	**neufs**	**neuves**	*new, not old*
un vélo **neuf**	une robe **neuve**	des vêtements **neufs**	des robes **neuves**	
veuf	**veuve**	**veufs**	**veuves**	*widowed*
un homme **veuf**	un femme **veuve**	des hommes **veufs**	des femmes **veuves**	

• Adjectives ending in **-eur**

masc. sing.	fem. sing.	masc. plural	fem. plural	
menteur	**menteuse**	**menteurs**	**menteuses**	*lying*
il est	elle est	ils sont	elles sont	
menteur	**menteuse**	**menteurs**	**menteuses**	
rieur	**rieuse**	**rieurs**	**rieuses**	*cheerful*
il est	elle est	ils sont	elles sont	
rieur	**rieuse**	**rieurs**	**rieuses**	

Many adjectives ending in **-teur** have **-trice** in the feminine:

masc. sing.	fem. sing.	masc. plural	fem. plural	
innovateur	**innovatrice**	**innovateurs**	**innovatrices**	*innovative*
un projet	une idée	ils sont	elles sont	
innovateur	**innovatrice**	**innovateurs**	**innovatrices**	

• Adjectives ending in **-l, -n, -s** double the consonant and add **-e**:

masc. sing.	fem. sing.	masc. plural	fem. plural	
bas	**basse**	**bas**	**basses**	*low*
cruel	**cruelle**	**cruels**	**cruelles**	*cruel*
gentil	**gentille**	**gentils**	**gentilles**	*nice, kind*
gros	**grosse**	**gros**	**grosses**	*fat*
mignon	**mignonne**	**mignons**	**mignonnes**	*cute*
pareil	**pareille**	**pareils**	**pareilles**	*same*

Nicolas a une **grosse** chatte.   *Nicolas has a big (female) cat.*
Elle est **gentille,** plutôt   *She is nice, rather cute, but cruel*
mignonne, mais **cruelle** avec   *with birds.*
les oiseaux.
Ces deux jupes sont **pareilles.**   *These two skirts are alike.*

• Adjectives ending in **-t** either double the **-t**:

masc. sing.	fem. sing.	masc. plural	fem. plural	
coquet	**coquette**	**coquets**	**coquettes**	*smart*

Alison est très **coquette**. *Alison is very particular about her appearance.*

or add a grave accent è and an e (→ **ète**):

masc. sing.	fem. sing.	masc. plural	fem. plural	
complet	**complète**	**complets**	**complètes**	*complete/full*

Cette auberge de jeunesse
est **complète**. *This youth hostel is full.*

• Adjectives ending in **-er** also add a grave accent and an **-e** in the feminine:

masc. sing.	fem. sing.	masc. plural	fem. plural	
cher	**chère**	**chers**	**chères**	*dear, expensive*
dernier	**dernière**	**derniers**	**dernières**	*last*

Chères amies… *Dear (female) friends…*
L'année **dernière** je… *Last year I…*

• Adjectives ending in **-ic** become **-ique**:

masc. sing.	fem. sing.	masc. plural	fem. plural	
public	**publique**	**publics**	**publiques**	*public*

• Some adjectives are highly irregular:

masc. sing.	fem. sing.	masc. plural	fem. plural	
blanc	**blanche**	**blancs**	**blanches**	*white*
favori	**favorite**	**favoris**	**favorites**	*favourite*
frais	**fraîche**	**frais**	**fraîches**	*fresh*
franc	**franche**	**francs**	**franches**	*frank, straight*
vieux	**vieille**	**vieux**	**vieilles**	*old*
vieil + vowel				

Nicolas regarde son émission
favorite. *Nicolas is watching his favourite programme.*

Adjective + noun

Some adjectives come before the noun. See Say it in French 2. These are usually short common adjectives, such as **beau, bon, grand** etc.

Here is a list of adjectives that usually come *before the noun*:

autre	*other*	**long**	*long*
***beau (bel)**	*handsome*	**mauvais**	*bad*
bon	*good*	***nouveau (nouvel)**	*new*
chaque	*each*	**petit**	*small*
grand	*big/tall*	**tel**	*such*
gros	*big/fat*	**vaste**	*vast*
haut	*high*	***vieux (vieil)**	*old*
jeune	*young*	**vilain**	*naughty*
joli	*pretty*		

*When the masculine adjectives **beau, nouveau, vieux** come before a singular noun beginning with a vowel or a vowel sound, they change their endings to become **bel, nouvel** and **vieil**:

Patrick est un très **bel** homme.	*Patrick is a very handsome man.*
Andrew va acheter un **nouvel** album.	*Andrew's going to buy a new album.*
Ce n'est pas un **vieil** homme.	*He is not an old man.*

Most of the adjectives in the box above are one-syllable adjectives. They agree in number and gender with the noun they relate to:

Patrick porte aussi de **vieilles** baskets.	*Patrick is also wearing old trainers.*
Patrick porte un **vieux** survêtement.	*Patrick is wearing an old tracksuit.*
Andrew a la grippe. Il a **mauvaise** mine.	*Andrew's got the flu. He looks poorly*

Colour adjectives, although short, come after the noun:

Alison porte une jupe **bleue**.	*Alison is wearing a blue skirt.*
Patrick porte un survêtement **gris**.	*Patrick is wearing a grey tracksuit.*

Exceptions to the rules on agreement of adjectives

Some adjectives remain unchanged:

• Adjectives derived from fruit and nuts:

Nouns	Adjectives	Examples
un marron / des marrons (wild chestnut)	**marron**	des yeux **marron**
une noisette / des noisettes (hazelnut)	**noisette**	des yeux **noisette**
une orange / des oranges (orange)	**orange**	des boules **orange**

• **chic** – des boucles d'oreille très **chic**
• hyphenated adjectives with two colours do not change their spelling:

Elle a les yeux **gris-vert**.	*She has greyish-green eyes.*

• When there are two adjectives, a colour and an adjective that refers to it, neither of them agrees:

Il a les yeux **bleu clair**.	*He has light-blue eyes.*
Les nuages sont **gris foncé**.	*The clouds are dark grey.*

Look at the difference between the spelling of the adjectives in the following examples:

Elle a les cheveux **bruns** et **foncés**.	*She has dark-brown hair.*
Elle a les yeux **brun foncé**.	*She has dark-brown eyes.*

2 Reflexive verbs

Reflexive verbs (where the subject and the object are the same person) are easily noticeable in French as they have an extra pronoun: **se** in front of the infinitive, which changes form to match the subject of the verb (See Unit 1 **The main points 4**).

They mean that:

• the subject is doing something to himself/herself (*myself, yourself, himself/herself/oneself* etc.):

Andrew **se lève** tôt, il **se douche**, il **s'habille** et **se dépêche**.	*Andrew gets up early, has a shower (showers), gets dressed and hurries up.*

As you can see from these examples and **The main points** 3, the object of a reflexive verb is not always expressed in English. The formula *to get dressed* is more usual in English than *to dress oneself*.

In French the subject performs the action on him/herself, i.e. *Andrew gets **himself** up, showers himself* etc.

• the subject and another person or other persons (also subject of the verb) are doing something to one another:

Stéphanie et Nicolas **se disputent** souvent, mais ils **s'aiment** quand même.	*Stéphanie and Nicolas often quarrel, but they like each other all the same.*

The idea of interaction (each other/one another) is not always explicit in English:

Mark et Stéphanie **se rencontrent** toujours après le travail.	*Mark and Stéphanie always meet after work.*

3 Questions with reflexive verbs

When asking questions with reflexive verbs using inversion, remember that the reflexive (object) pronoun does not move. It always remains before the verb:

Comment **t'**appelles-tu? / Comment est-ce que tu **t'**appelles? / Comment **vous** appelez-vous?	*What are you called? / What's your name?*
Vous promenez-vous à la campagne?	*Do you walk in the country?*
Vous entendez-vous bien?	*Do you get on well?*

4 More numbers

Asking/telling the time

Quelle heure est-il?	*What time is it?*

For the 12-hour clock system you simply add the expression in bold below to indicate *a quarter past, half past, a quarter to…*:

Il est une heure.	*It's one o'clock.*
Il est une heure **et quart**.	*It's a quarter past one.*
Il est une heure **et demie**.	*It's half past one.*
Il est deux heures **moins le quart**.	*It's a quarter to two.*
Il est midi.	*It's noon.*
Il est minuit.	*It's midnight.*

This 12-hour system does not show whether it is in the morning or in the afternoon. If it is not obvious from the context, you add the time of day, just as in English:

Il est une heure **du matin.**	*It's one o'clock in the morning.*
Il est une heure **de l'après-midi.**	*It's one o'clock in the afternoon.*
Il est onze heures **du soir.**	*It's eleven o'clock at night / in the evening.*

The 24-hour system is used more formally in business timetables, schedules etc. In this system, you do not use **et quart, et demie, moins le quart,** but simply the number of minutes: **quinze, trente, quarante-cinq:**

Il est 23h00 (vingt-trois heures).	*It's 23.00.*
Il est 23h15 (vingt-trois heures quinze).	*It's 23.15.*
Il est 23h30 (vingt-trois heures trente).	*It's 23.30.*
Il est 23h45 (vingt-trois heures quarante-cinq).	*It's 23.45.*

The word **heures** cannot be omitted.

Ordinal numbers

• To speak about *first, the first,* you say:

le premier / la première, les premiers, les premières.

le deuxième	**le neuvième**
le troisième	**le dixième**
le quatrième	**le vingtième**
le cinquième	**le vingt et unième**
le sixième	**le vingt-deuxième**
le septième	**le vingt-troisième...**
le huitième	

These numbers agree with the person or noun referred to:

Mark se lève le premier.	*Mark gets up first.*
Stéphanie quitte le travail **la première.**	*Stéphanie leaves work first.*

• To say *second, third, fourth...,* again put the definite article **le/la/les** first, and then add **-ième/s** to the number:

Nicolas est le **deuxième** de sa classe en maths.	*Nicolas is second in his class in maths.*
Georges regarde souvent la **cinquième.**	*Georges often watches Channel 5.*

• **le second / la seconde** can replace **le deuxième / la deuxième** when talking about ranks/classes:

C'est **la seconde** fois qu'il gagne.   *It's the second time that he has won.*

Il voyage en **seconde** classe.   *He travels second class.*
En **second** lieu …   *Secondly...*

To say that someone is in their twenties, thirties etc.

You remove the -e from the number and add **-aine**. These numbers are always **feminine**:

Isabelle a **la quarantaine**.   *Isabelle is in her forties.*
Alison a aussi **la quarantaine**,   *Alison is also in her forties,*
mais Patrick a une petite   *but Patrick is in his early*
cinquantaine.   *fifties.*

To count after 100

100	cent, cent un, cent deux, cent trois...
200	deux cents , deux cent un, deux cent deux, deux cent trois...
300	trois cents, trois cent un, trois cent deux...
370	trois cent soixante-dix, trois cent soixante et onze …
1 000	mille, mille un, mille deux...
2 000	deux mille, deux mille un, deux mille deux...
10 000	dix mille …
10 280	dix mille deux cent quatre-vingts...
10 372	dix mille trois cent soixante-douze...
1 000 000	**un** million...
2 000 000	deux millions, deux millions un...
2 120 000	deux millions cent vingt mille...
1 000 000 000	**un** milliard...
1000 000 115	**un** milliard cent quinze...

Vingt and **cent** are spelt with an -s when they are not followed by other numbers:

quatre-vingts but **quatre-vingt-deux**
deux cents but **deux cent deux**
mille never adds an -s

With numbers after 1,000, a full stop or a space is used in French, whereas a comma is used in English:

1.000 or 1 000 mille   1,000   *a thousand*
2.331 or 2 331 deux mille   2,331   *two thousand three*
trois cent trente et un   *hundred and thirty-one*

The words **million** and **milliard** take **de** when they are followed by a noun:

Il y a plus de 56.000.000 **de** gens   *There are over 56,000,000*
en France.   *people in France.*

(cinquante-six millions)

The story

When reading this dialogue look for **expressions of time**, **reflexive verbs** and **adjectives**.

Mark et Stéphanie parlent d'Aberdeen et de leur appartement.
Mark and Stéphanie are talking about Aberdeen and their flat.

Mark	Je me lève vers 7 heures. Je me douche et je m'habille. Stéphanie se réveille un plus tard. Nous quittons peu l'appartement vers 8 heures.	*I get up about 7 o'clock. I have a shower and get dressed. Stéphanie wakes up a little later. We leave the flat about 8 o'clock.*
Stéphanie	Nous partageons l'appartement mais Mark est souvent absent. Il se rend sur la plate-forme pétrolière pour plusieurs semaines. Je m'occupe donc de l'appartement.	*We share the flat but Mark is often away. He goes to the oil platform for several weeks. So I look after the flat.*
Isabelle	Il est joli?	*Is it pretty?*

Stéphanie	Oui, c'est un petit apparte-ment situé dans le centre-ville.	*Yes it is a small flat situated in the town centre.*
	Il est bien décoré, clair, bien chauffé et très confortable. Les voisins sont très sympathiques.	*It is well decorated, well lit, well heated and very comfortable. The neighbours are very friendly.*
Mark	Stéphanie et moi, nous nous rencontrons souvent pour le déjeuner. Nous rentrons ensemble le soir.	*We often meet for lunch, Stéphanie and I. We go home together in the evening.*

A quick check

La famille Lemaire

1 a Complete the sentences given below, using the information provided on Georges and Isabelle and the adjectives in brackets.

Georges (blond) (grand) (long) **visage** **yeux** (bleu) **cheveux** (bouclé) **1.92m** **46 ans**	**Isabelle** **cheveux** (brun), (mi-long) (mince), (joli) **yeux** (marron) **43 ans**	**Stéphanie** (joli) **yeux** (bleu) (blond) **cheveux** (blond) (bouclé) (mince)

George est un homme _____.
Il mesure _____.
Il est _____. Il ___ les cheveux _____ et les yeux _____.
Isabelle a les _____ _____, _____.
Elle est _____ et _____.
Elle a les _____ _____.
Ils ont la _____ (*in their forties*).

Nicolas **cheveux** (blond) **yeux** (noisette) (grand) (mince) **1.90m**

b Write a few sentences to describe Stéphanie and Nicolas.

2 Say and write the following figures/times in French (in words).

231 456
245 985

3 500 765
6.15, 3.45, 3.05 (using the 12-hour system)
13.55, 22.35, 23.45 (using the 24-hour system)

The next stage

1 More about adjectives

Adjectives following a verb

As you saw in **The main points 1**, adjectives can follow the verb
être, and they agree with the subject:

Il est **fatigué**. *He is tired.*

They can also follow other verbs and qualify the subject:

- verbs of state, such as **sembler** (*to look*), **paraître/apparaître** (*to appear*):

Il semble **épuisé**. He seems exhausted.
Elle paraît **charmante**. She looks charming.

- verbs of action, such as **rentrer** (*to come back*), **sortir** (*to go out*):

Ils rentrent **fatigués** le soir. *They get home tired in the evening.*

When a noun is qualified by two adjectives, they can be placed
after the noun and are linked by **et** (and), **mais** (*but*) or **ou** (*or*):

Cette voiture paraît ancienne *This car looks old but/and*
mais / **et** bien entretenue. *well kept.*

Position of adjectives

- Some adjectives can have a different meaning according to
  their position *before* or *after* the noun:

Georges est un homme **grand**. *George is a tall man.*
Le Général de Gaulle est un **grand** *General de Gaulle is a great*
homme de l'histoire française. *man in French history.*

Ce n'est pas la **même** idée. *It is not the same idea.*
L'idée **même** m'amuse. *The very idea amuses me.*

Isabelle rencontre souvent des *Isabelle often meets poor*
gens **pauvres**. *people.*

L'entreprise caritative fait *The charity does a lot for*
beaucoup pour ces **pauvres** gens. *these unfortunate people.*

Here is a list of adjectives which have a different meaning depending on their position:

ancien + noun = former	une **ancienne** élève	*a former pupil (female)*
noun + **ancien** = old	un village **ancien**	*an old village*
certain + noun = certain	un **certain** 'je ne sais quoi'	*a certain 'je ne sais quoi'*
noun + **certain** = sure	un fait **certain**	*a sure fact*
cher + noun = dear	**chers** amis	*dear friends*
noun + **cher** = expensive	une voiture **chère**	*an expensive car*
même + noun = same	C'est la **même** chose.	*It's the same thing.*
noun + **même** = itself	C'est cette personne **même**.	*It's the very same person.*
propre + noun = own	Son **propre** ordinateur.	*His own computer.*
noun + **propre** = clean	Il a un appartement **propre**.	*He has a clean flat.*

• If several adjectives which usually go before the noun are used, such as **joli, nouveau,** only *one* adjective goes before the noun and the other adjectives go after the noun:

Alison porte une **jolie** jupe nouvelle.
Alison is wearing a pretty new skirt.

Other adjectives may follow the second adjective, provided a comma or a link word such as **et** (*and*), **mais** (*but*), **ou** (*or*) is used:

Andrew a un **beau** VTT **propre et neuf.**
Andrew has a nice clean new mountain bike.

Patrick porte un **vieux** survêtement **foncé**, légèrement **usé**.
Patrick is wearing an old dark tracksuit, slightly worn.

• A few adjectives can be joined to other adjectives: **demi-/mi-/semi-** (*half*) (+ hyphen). They do not agree when they are joined to another adjective.

The main adjective agrees with the noun it relates to:

Isabelle a les cheveux **mi**-longs.
Isabelle has longish hair.

Elle aime le lait **demi**-écrémé.
She likes semi-skimmed milk.

C'est une région **semi**-autonome.
It's a semi-autonomous region.

• Some noun + adjective combinations are so common that they act as a single noun. In this case, the adjective agrees with the noun:

Les **grands**-parents	*Grand-parents*
Il faut faire attention aux **ronds**-points.	*One must be careful at roundabouts.*

Tel/telle/tels/telles (such)

These adjectives can be used with or without an indefinite article. In each case, the meaning is slightly different:

Une **telle** personne	*Such a person*
Telle personne	*A certain person*

Adjectives ending in '-ic' in English

These adjectives often end in **-ique** (fem./masc.) in French:

Noun	**Adjective**
l'ecclésiastique	ecclésiastique(s)
l'économie	économique(s)
l'élastique	élastique(s)

public is an exception:

le public	public/publique/publics/publiques

2 Adjectives with adverbs

Adjectives can have an adverb before them (Unit 6 **The main points. Position of adverbs**), such as **très** (*very*), **trop** (*too much*), **complètement** (*completely*) etc. if they come after the verb **être** or another verb:

Ils sont **trop fatigués**.	*They are too tired.*
Ils rentrent **complètement épuisés**.	*They come back completely exhausted.*

Adjectives which go before the noun can also be preceded by **trop** (*too*), **très** (*very*):

Isabelle est une **très petite** femme.	*Isabelle is a very small woman.*

If an adjective which usually goes before the noun is modified by an adverb – except **très** (*very*) and occasionally, **trop** (*too*) – it comes after the noun:

Isabelle est une femme **vraiment petite**.	*Isabelle is a really small woman.*

3 Present participles: the '-ing' form

(See **Verb tables** page 250.) For most verbs you just take off the -**ons** from the second person plural (**nous** form) of the present tense and add -**ant**, for example:

descendre *to go down*	nous descendons	descend-	+ ant **descendant**
partir *to leave*	nous partons	part-	+ ant **partant**
précéder *to precede*	nous précédons	précéd-	+ ant **précédant**

There are three exceptions to this ground rule:

avoir	nous avons	ayant
être	nous sommes	étant
savoir	nous savons	sachant

Present participles are **verbs**, always ending in -**ant**. They do not agree in number or gender with the subject:

Le magasin **vendant** des journaux... See **Say it in French** 4.

Andrew et Mark **étant** jeunes, beaux et forts, ils sont très populaires avec les filles.	*Being young, handsome and strong Andrew and Mark are very popular with girls.*
L'horloge s'**étant** arrêtée, je ne connais pas l'heure exacte.	*The clock having stopped, I do not know the exact time.*

Many **adjectives** in French also end in -**ant** but they agree in gender and number with the noun they relate to:

Cette émission est intéress**ante**.	*This programme is interesting.*
Les acteurs sont très amus**ants**.	*The actors are very funny.*

If you are using a French word ending in -**ant,** it is important to check to see if it is an adjective or a verb.

04 making requests

In this unit you will learn
- to say what you want or need
- ask what / where / how much something is
- to ask what / which one someone would like
- quantities and sizes

Topic
- shopping

Grammar

- Verbs and expressions to say what you want or need: **je voudrais** (*I'd like*), **avoir besoin de** (*to need*)
- Partitive articles **du, de la, de l', des** (*some, any*)
- Expressions of quantity and size
- Question adjectives and pronouns: *what/which, which one*(s)
- More negatives: **ne ... plus** (*no longer / no more*), **ne ... jamais** (*never*)

The next stage

- More about articles
- More expressions of quantity
- More about using articles after negatives
- **ne ... personne, personne ne,** (*nobody*), **rien ne, ne ... rien** (*nothing*)
- **Avoir besoin de** (*to need*) in the negative
- **La plupart de** (*most of*)

Getting started

Look back at Unit 1 **The main points 3** for verbs which can express what you want / desire, such as **aimer, désirer** + noun or + infinitive:

Nous **aimons** la France.	*We like France.*
Nicolas **désire** sortir.	*Nicolas wants to go out.*

1 In this unit, you will meet other verbs and expressions to express needs, likes and dislikes:

Nicolas **voudrait** acheter un cédérom.	*Nicolas would like to buy a CD-ROM.*
Nicolas **a besoin de** nouvelles disquettes.	*Nicolas needs some new disks.*

2 You will also learn to use more partitive articles **du, de la, de l', des** (*some, any*). See Unit 2 **The main points 4**.

Mark voudrait acheter **des** cadeaux pour sa famille.	*Mark would like to buy some presents for his family.*

3 You will meet expressions of quantity:

Mark voudrait acheter **deux boîtes de** chocolats pour des amis et **une bouteille de** bon vin pour son père.

Mark would like to buy two boxes of chocolates for some friends and a bottle of good wine for his father.

4 To ask what sort of thing someone wants or does, you can use interrogative adjectives **quel(s)**, **quelle(s)** (*which/what*), which agree with the noun they accompany. See Unit 2 **The main points 8**. Also look back at Unit 1 **The main points 6**, if you have problems with asking questions.

Quelle sorte voulez-vous?
Qu'est-ce que vous désirez?

What type do you want?
What do you want?
(*What would you like?*)

In this unit you will meet interrogative pronouns **lequel?**, **laquelle?** (*which one(s)*)?, which replace the noun they refer to and help you to ask more specific questions:

Lequel (masc. sing.) voulez-vous? *Which one do you want?*
Lequel préférez-vous? *Which one do you prefer?*

5 You have already used the negative **ne ... pas** (*not*). See Unit 1 **The main points 7**. In this unit you will meet other useful negatives such as **ne ... plus** (*no longer, no more*):

Mark **n'**aime **pas** faire les courses. *Mark does not like shopping.*
Mark **n'**a **plus** beaucoup de temps pour faire ses achats. *Mark doesn't have a lot of time to do his shopping any more.*

Say it in French

1 Saying what you need or want

Stéphanie, je **voudrais** acheter des cadeaux pour mon père, ma mère, Andrew et Sandy. | *Stéphanie, I would like to buy presents for my father, my mother, Andrew and Sandy.*

Je **voudrais** une bonne bouteille de vin pour mon père. | *I'd like a good bottle of wine for my father.*

Je **désire** acheter un St Émilion ou un Bourgogne. | *I want to buy a St Émilion or a wine from Burgundy.*

Je **voudrais** acheter un CD ou un T-shirt pour Andrew. | *I'd like to buy a CD or a T-shirt for Andrew.*

Pour maman, j'**aimerais** acheter du parfum à l'aéroport. | *For mum I'd like to buy some perfume at the airport.*

J'**ai** aussi **besoin de** lames à rasoir pour moi. | *I also need some razor blades for myself.*

2 Asking what/which one someone would like

Quel parfum voudrais-tu acheter? | *Which perfume would you like to buy?*

Lequel préfères-tu? | *Which one do you prefer?*

Une eau de toilette est aussi très bien. | *An eau de toilette is also quite good.*

Laquelle préfères-tu? | *Which one do you prefer?*

Il y a de jolis T-shirts. | *There are some nice T-shirts.*

Lesquels préfères-tu? | *Which ones do you prefer?*

3 Finding out where to get things and prices

Qu'est-ce que vous avez **comme** vins? | *What wines do you have?*

Où est-ce qu'il y a un marchand de vins? | *Where is there a wine store?*

Combien coûte ce vin? | *How much does this wine cost?*

Ça fait combien en tout? | *How much is it all together?*

C'est combien? | *How much is it?*

4 Quantities and sizes

Je désire **une bouteille de** vin.
Je voudrais **deux boîtes de** chocolats.
Pour sa mère, Stéphanie a **une liste de** courses. Elle voudrait:
1 kilo de pommes de terre,
une demi-livre de beurre,
500 g de pâté, **deux litres de** vin rouge, **deux briques de** lait,
un paquet de sucre.

Je voudrais un T-shirt **demi-patron** ou **patron**.
Je ne veux **plus rien,** merci.

I want a bottle of wine.
I'd like two boxes of chocolates.
Stéphanie has a shopping list for her mother. She would like:
1 kg of potatoes, half a pound of butter, 500 g of pâté, two litres of red wine, two cartons of milk, a packet of sugar.
I'd like a medium size or large size T-shirt.
I don't need anything else, thank you.

The main points

1 Verbs and expressions to say what you want or need

Désirer **and** *vouloir*

The verb **désirer** can be followed by a noun:

Je **désire du jambon** fumé.   *I want / I'd like some smoked ham.*

It can also be followed by an infinitive:

Je **désire faire** des achats.   *I want / I'd like to do some shopping.*

The verb **désirer** is used in French to say *what you want* and also to ask *what someone wants*: **Que désirez-vous?** However, it is not the most commonly used expression to say *what you would like*. The most polite way is to use the conditional of **vouloir** (*to want*). See Unit 8 **The main points 1, Vouloir** and Unit 18 **The main points 3.**

The conditional of vouloir:

je **voudrais**	nous **voudrions**
tu **voudrais**	vous **voudriez**
il/elle/on **voudrait**	ils/elles **voudraient**

Using **vouloir** in the present tense to say what you want: **Je veux** un café au lait (*I want a white coffee.*) could be too abrupt. See Unit 8 **The main points 1, Vouloir.**

Je **voudrais** un café et deux croissants.

I'd like a coffee and two croissants.

Mark **voudrait** acheter un St. Émilion pour son père.
Nous **voudrions** regarder les T-shirts.

Mark would like to buy a St. Émilion for his father.
We'd like to look at the T-shirts.

avoir besoin de to need

Mark **a besoin de** beaucoup d'argent pour acheter ses cadeaux.

Mark needs a lot of money to buy his presents.

2 Partitive articles: some, any

See grid, Unit 2 **The main points 3.**

Partitive articles follow the same contraction rule as **de** + definite article:

> **le** combines with **de** to make **du**
> **les** combines with **de** to make **des**

Here is a complete list of partitive articles:

masc. sing.	fem. sing.	masc. plural	fem. plural
du	**de la**	**des**	**des**
de l' + vowel	**de l'** + vowel		
du fromage	**de la margarine**	**des croissants**	**des baguettes**
(some cheese)	*(some margarine)*	*(some croissants)*	*(some baguettes)*
de l'ail	**de l'aspirine**		
(some garlic)	*(some aspirin)*		

Mark voudrait **du** vin rouge.

Mark would like some red wine.

Il voudrait aussi acheter **des** fleurs pour Isabelle.
Stéphanie achète **du** beurre, **du** pâté, **de l'**ail, **de la** limonade, **de l'**huile, des pommes de terre … pour sa mère.

He would also like to buy some flowers for Isabelle.
Stéphanie buys some butter, paté, garlic, lemonade, oil, potatoes … for her mother.

As you can see from these examples, articles in a list are repeated in French, even if they have the same gender and number.

3 Expressions of quantity and size

The partitive article becomes **de**, not only after a negative (Unit 2 **The next stage 1**), but also after expressions of quantity.

Je voudrais **un peu de** fromage. Nous voudrions **un morceau de** brie, **un paquet de** café moulu et **une boîte de** choucroute garnie.	*I would like a little cheese. We would like a piece of brie, a packet of ground coffee and a tin of sauerkraut with meat.*

Non-specific quantities and sizes

assez de	*enough of*		
beaucoup de	*a lot of*	**un paquet de**	*a packet of*
moins de	*less*	**une plaque de**	*a bar of*
plus de	*more*	**une plaquette de**	*a bar of*
une boîte de	*a box/tin of*	**un pichet de**	*a pichet*
un bouquet de	*a bunch of*		*(jugful/*
une brique de	*a carton of*		*carafe) of*
	(milk, juice)		
une carafe de	*a carafe of*	**une pincée de**	*a pinch of*
une cuillerée de	*a spoonful of*	**une portion de**	*a portion*
un morceau de	*a piece of*		*/helping of*
un pack de...	*several*	**une tasse de**	*a cup of*
	cartons/	**une tranche de**	*a slice of*
	bottles of...	**un verre de**	*a glass of*

Pour faire une mousse au chocolat, Isabelle a besoin de **500g de** chocolat, de six oeufs et de **200 cl de** crème fraîche.	*To make a chocolate mousse Isabelle needs 500g of chocolate, six eggs and 200 cl of fresh cream.*

Precise quantities

un litre de	*(100cl) a litre of*
une bouteille de	*(75cl) a bottle of*
100 grammes de	*100 g of*
1 kg de	*one kilo of*
une livre de	*one pound of*
une demi-livre de	*half a pound of*

4 Question adjectives and pronouns

Interrogative adjectives

Interrogative **adjectives**, Unit 2 **The main ponts 8**, are shown in the grid below. As you can see, they are followed by a noun, and they agree with it in number and gender:

masc. sing.	fem. sing.	masc. plural	fem. plural
quel	**quelle**	**quels**	**quelles**
quel parfum?	**quelle** crème?	**quels** T-shirts?	**quelles** pommes?
(Which perfume?)	*(Which cream?)*	*(Which T-shirts?)*	*(Which apples?)*

Interrogative pronouns

Interrogative **pronouns** replace the noun. They are formed with the definite article **le/la/les + quel/le/s**. They agree with the noun they replace in gender and number: *le*quel, *la*quelle etc.:

masc. sing.	fem. sing.	masc. plural	fem. plural
lequel	**laquelle**	**lesquels**	**lesquelles**
Lequel	**Laquelle**	**Lesquels**	**Lesquelles**
voulez-vous?	désirez-vous?	prenez-vous?	désirez-vous?
(Which one do you want?)	*(Which one do you want?)*	*(Which ones are you taking?)*	*(Which ones do you want?)*

More examples with interrogative pronouns:

Je voudrais un T-shirt.	*I'd like a T-shirt.*
Lequel désirez-vous?	*Which one would you like?*
Il y a deux sortes de crèmes hydratantes.	*There are two types of moisturising lotion.*
Laquelle préfères-tu?	*Which one do you prefer?*
Ta mère aime les parfums français?	*Does your mum like French perfumes?*
Lesquels préfère-t-elle?	*Which ones does she prefer?*
Ces fleurs sont toutes très jolies.	*These flowers are all very pretty.*
Lesquelles préférez-vous?	*Which ones do you prefer?*

5 More negatives

As you will remember, when you use the negative **ne ... pas,** the ne comes after the subject and the **pas** comes after the verb (See Unit 1 **The main points** 7). The same applies to other negatives.

Useful negatives:

ne ... plus	*no longer, not any of, no more of*
ne ... jamais	*no longer, never*
ne ... guère	*hardly*
ne ... point	*emphatic 'no'*
ne ... rien	*nothing*
ne ... que	*only*
ne ... personne	*nobody*
ne ... aucun(e)	*no, none*
ne ... ni ... ni	*neither ... nor*

Je n'ai **rien** à faire.	*I have nothing to do.*
Je suis au régime. Je **ne** mange **ni** gâteaux **ni** bonbons.	*I am on a diet. I eat neither cakes nor sweets.*
Je **ne** veux **qu'**un verre d'eau.	*I only want a glass of water.*
Je n'ai **aucune** idée au sujet d'un cadeau pour Sandy.	*I have no ideas about a present for Sandy.*
Il **n'**y a **personne** à la caisse.	*There is nobody on the till.*
Des ennuis, je **n'**en veux **point.**	*I do not want **any** worries.*

When negatives are used as expressions of quantity meaning *not/never... any of,* they are followed by **de** without an article (See Unit 2 **The next stage** 1 and **The main points** 3 above).

Stéphanie ne boit **jamais de** whisky.	*Stéphanie never drinks whisky.*
Mark ne veut **plus de** fromage.	*Mark does not want any more cheese.*
Il n'achète **jamais de** roquefort.	*He never buys roquefort.*
Je n'ai **pas de** monnaie.	*I haven't got any change.*
Je ne bois **plus de** vin rouge.	*I don't drink red wine any more.*

The story

Make a list of the **interrogative adjectives** and **interrogative pronouns** used in the dialogue. Identify the **nouns** which the interrogative pronouns replace.

Au supermarché *At the supermarket*

Stéphanie	On va au rayon de vêtements.	*Let's go to the clothes department.*
	Il y a beaucoup de vêtements en solde.	*There are lots of clothes in the sale.*
Mark	D'accord.	*All right.*
Stéphanie	Ces T-shirts sont jolis.	*These T-shirts are pretty.*
	Lequel préfères-tu?	*Which one do you prefer?*
Mark	Je préfère le bleu avec la vue de la Tour Eiffel.	*I prefer the blue one with the picture of the Eiffel Tower.*
Stéphanie	De quelle taille as-tu besoin?	*What size do you need?*
Mark	Je ne sais pas quelle taille. 'Patron'? Qu'est-ce que ça veut dire?	*I do not know what size. 'Patron'? What does that mean?*
Stéphanie	Ça veut dire *large*. Grand patron c'est *extra large*.	*It means large. 'Grand patron' is extra large.*
Mark	Je voudrais taille patron. Mon frère est grand pour son âge.	*I'd like the large size. My brother is big for his age.*
Stéphanie	Qu'est-ce que tu achètes pour Sandy?	*What are you buying for for Sandy?*
Mark	Je n'ai aucune idée.	*I have no idea.*

Stéphanie	Peut-être des magazines français ou un roman?	*Perhaps French magazines or a novel?*
Mark	Lesquels à ton avis?	*Which ones, do you think?*
Stéphanie	*Marie-Claire, le Point, l'Express.*	Marie-Claire, le Point, l'Express.
Mark	Quel roman suggères-tu?	*Which novel do you suggest?*
Stéphanie	On va à la librairie. Ils ont plus de choix.	*We'll go to the bookshop. They have more choice.*
Mark	Laquelle? La librairie sur la place?	*Which one, the bookshop on the market-place?*
Stéphanie	Oui, mais d'abord il faut passer à la caisse.	*Yes, but first of all we'll have to go to the till.*

A quick check

1 Rewrite the sentences below by putting the words in the right order. Add capital letters and hyphens wherever necessary.

a je un rouges kilo belles voudrais de pommes.
b taille vous acheter quelle désirez ?
c je plus ne de veux viande merci
d nous ma acheter mère du voudrions parfum pour
e vous laquelle ces voudriez de robes ?

2 a Add the appropriate articles in the following sentence:

Isabelle voudrait ___ pâté, ___ beurre, ___ fromage, ___ pommes de terre, ___ limonade, ___ croissants.

b Add an appropriate expression of quantity to the phrases below:

Stéphanie would like to cook for her mother. She needs ...

Stéphanie a besoin de/d':

    ___ bouteille de bordeaux.
    ___ gros poulet.
  un ___ ___ oignons.
  500 _____ ___ champignons.
  une _____ ___ beurre.
  5 _____ ___ pommes de terre.

3 Your friend would like to buy the following items. Ask him/her which one s/he prefers.

Je voudrais:

une chemise
un pantalon
des bonbons
des cerises
du whisky

Laquelle préfères-tu?
_____ préfères-tu?
_____ préfères-tu?
_____ préfères-tu?
_____ préfères-tu?

The next stage

1 More about articles

All articles normally have to be repeated in a list in French. See Unit 2 **Say it in French 1, 3** and Unit 4 **The main points 2**.

Voici les activités offertes: **les** randonnées, **le** golf, **la** natation…	*Here are the available activities: walks in the forest, golf, swimming…*

However, they are sometimes omitted in advertisements or in brochures:

Voici les nombreuses activités offertes par St Amand: randonnées en forêt, golf, natation, ball-trap, canoë-kayac…	*Here are the numerous activities available at St Amand: walks, golf, swimming, clay-pigeon, shooting, canoeing…*

As gender is crucial in French, get into the good habit of always using the correct article with every noun. Don't forget to keep adding to the lists of masculine and feminine nouns in your notebook.

2 More expressions of quantity

The adjective **demi/e-**: (**une demi-livre** *half a pound*) can be used with many nouns to mean *half*. See Unit 3 **The main points 1**.

un **demi**-fromage	*half a cheese*
un **demi**-camembert	*half a camembert*
une **demi**-heure	*half an hour*

When it comes **before** the noun, **demi-** is joined to it by a hyphen and it is invariable, whatever the gender of the noun. If **demi** follows the noun, it agrees with it in gender:

| une heure et **demie** | *an hour and a half* |
| deux portions et **demie** | *two and a half portions* |

3 Using articles after negatives

Articles are not used after the negatives: **ne ... pas**, **ne ... guère**, **ne ... point**, **ne ... jamais**, **ne ... plus** when talking about quantities, or when *any/some* are used. See **The main points 5**.

In these cases you say: **pas** *de*, **guère** *de*, **point** *de*, **jamais** *de*, **plus** *de*:

Elle **n'**a **pas** d'excuses.	*She doesn't have any excuses.*
Vous **n'**avez **guère de** patience.	*You have hardly any patience.*
Il **ne** mange **jamais de** poisson.	*He never eats fish (any fish).*
Je **n'**ai **plus** d'argent.	*I don't have any more money.*

However, if you want to refer to something specific, the definite article (examples 1 and 2, below) can be used and you can say:

| Ils n'ont pas **le** chocolat, indiqué dans la recette, pour faire une bonne mousse au chocolat. | *They haven't got **the** chocolate mentioned in the recipe to make a good chocolate mousse.* |
| Je n'ai **plus le** vin que vous aimez tant. | *I haven't got any more of **the** wine you like so much.* |

The indefinite article can also be used after a negative and you can say:

| Il n'a **plus un** sou. | *He is penniless (doesn't have a penny).* |
| Il n'a **pas une** seule excuse. | *He doesn't have **a** single excuse.* |

4 *ne ... personne, personne ne* (nobody); *ne ... rien, rien ne* (nothing)

Personne can be the subject of the sentence. In that case, it comes before the **ne/n'**:

Personne ne sait pourquoi.   *Nobody knows why.*

When **rien** is the subject of the sentence, it also comes before the **ne/n'**:

Rien ne l'intéresse.   *Nothing interests him/her.*

5 *avoir besoin de...* (to need) in the negative

Note that the preposition **de** always follows **besoin** when it is used with a negative:

Je n'ai pas **besoin de** sel.   *I do not need any salt.*
Je n'ai **besoin de** rien.   *I don't need anything / need nothing.*
Il n'a **besoin de** personne.   *He doesn't need anybody.*

6 *la plupart de* (most of)

After most expressions of quantity followed by **de**, e.g. **beaucoup de, un peu de** (The main points 3), the partitive article becomes **de**. After the expression **la plupart de** (*most of*), the partitive article is **du/de l'/de la/des**:

La plupart **des** gens   *Most of the people*
La plupart **du** temps   *Most of the time*

05 saying what you prefer

In this unit you will learn
- to ask and say what someone prefers
- to compare things, places, people

Topic
- shopping

Grammar

- Verbs in -**ir**, such as **choisir** (*to choose*) and verbs in -**re**, such as **vendre** (*to sell*)
- Demonstrative pronouns (*this/that/these/those*)
- More personal pronouns: direct object pronouns **me** (*me*), **te** (*you*), **le/la/les** (*him/her/them*) and the pronoun **en** (*some of it/of that*)
- Comparatives (*less / more*)

The next stage

- The irregular verb **prendre** (*to take*), and **re**- before verbs (meaning *again*)
- **C'est** or **il est / elle est**?
- **Plus de** (*more than*)
- The difference between **bon** (*good*) and **bien** (*well*), **meilleur** and **mieux** (*better*)

Getting started

1 You have already met regular and irregular verbs ending in -**er**. See Unit 1 **The main points** 3. In this Unit you will meet regular verbs ending in -**ir** such as **choisir** and in -**re** such as **vendre**:

Je **choisis** ce livre-ci.   *I choose this book.*
Le supermarché **vend** des   *The supermarket sells all*
vins de toutes qualités.   *qualities of wine.*

2 Demonstrative adjectives **ce**, **cet**, **cette** (*that, this*), **ces** (*these, those*) were explained in Unit 2 **The main points** 5. To pinpoint something without repeating the noun, you need to use demonstrative pronouns:

Quel vin désirez-vous?   *Which wine would you like?*
Je voudrais **celui**-ci.   *I'd like this one.*
Celui-là coûte combien?   *How much does that one cost?*
Ceci est important.   *This is important.*

3 You already know how to say that you like or want something.

Je **voudrais** un nouveau logiciel.   *I'd like a new computer programme.*

Je voudrais un café. Je **le**   *I'd like a coffee. I take it*
prends noir et sans sucre.   *black and without sugar.*

To avoid repeating the noun, you use direct object pronouns, which, just as in English, are different from subject pronouns: *I* (subject), *me* (object), *he* (subject), *him* (object) etc.:

Il **la** voit tous les jours.	*He sees her every day.*
Je vais **l'**acheter demain.	*I am going to buy it tomorrow.*
(le cadeau de mon père)	*(the present for my dad).*
Je **le** choisis car il est bien.	*I choose it because it's good.*
J'**en** voudrais un peu.	*I'd like a little (of it).*

4 In this unit you will learn how to compare things and to express an opinion.

Je préfère un vin **plus** doux.	*I prefer a sweeter wine.*
Je préfère les fruits **moins** amers.	*I prefer less bitter fruit.*

Say it in French

1 Which one do you prefer?

Quel tableau préfères-tu?	*Which painting do you prefer?*
Celui-ci ou **celui-là?**	*This one or that one?*
Quelle carte choisis-tu?	*Which postcard do you choose?*
Je choisis **celle-ci.**	*I choose this one.*
Vous voulez **ceux-ci** (ces chocolats)?	*Do you want these (these chocolates?)*
Oui, je **les** prends.	*Yes, I'll have them.*
Lesquels voulez-vous?	*Which ones do you want?*
Je prends **ceux-ci.**	*I'll take these/those.*

2 Comparing things, places and people

Je préfère les endroits **moins** fréquentés.	*I prefer places which are less crowded.*
Cet ordinateur est **plus** puissant **que celui-là**.	*This computer is more powerful that that one.*
Les livres sont **plus** chers à la librairie **qu'**au supermarché.	*Books are more expensive at the bookshop than at the supermarket.*
Mais, le choix est **plus** grand à la librairie.	*But there is a wider choice at the bookshop.*

The main points

1 Verbs in -ir/-re

-ir verbs

For regular -**ir** verbs you follow the same principle as for -**er** verbs. Take the -**ir** off the infinitive and add the endings given below.

Pronoun	Stem	Ending
je	chois-	**IS**
tu	chois-	**IS**
il/elle/on	chois-	**IT**
nous	chois-	**ISSONS**
vous	chois-	**ISSEZ**
ils/elles	chois-	**ISSENT**

choisir

je choisis un livre	*I choose a book*
tu choisis un disque compact	*you choose a compact disc*
il/elle/on choisit un nouvel ordinateur	*he/she(we are) is choosing a new computer*
nous choisissons du bon vin	*we choose good wine*
vous choisissez vos amis?	*do you choose your friends?*
ils/elles choisissent de nouveaux vêtements	*they are choosing new clothes*

Some regular -ir verbs

accomplir	*to accomplish*	**punir**	*to punish*
atterrir	*to land (of a plane)*	**rafraîchir**	*to refresh*
		ralentir	*to slow down*
choisir	*to choose*	**réfléchir**	*to think of*
envahir	*to invade*	**réussir**	*to succeed*
finir	*to finish*	**rougir**	*to redden, blush*
fournir	*to provide*	**salir**	*to dirty*
grandir	*to grow up*	**vieillir**	*to grow old*
mûrir	*to ripen*		

Mark **réfléchit** et **choisit** un joli vase pour les fleurs d'Isabelle.	*Mark thinks and chooses a pretty vase for Isabelle's flowers.*

Mark et Stéphanie **réussissent** à trouver la plupart des cadeaux.	*Mark and Stéphanie manage to find most of the presents.*
Mark adore manger des cerises, mais elles ne **mûrissent** et ne **rougissent** qu'en juin.	*Mark loves to eat cherries but they only ripen and turn red in June.*

-re **verbs**

For regular -**re** verbs, take the -**re** off the infinitive to get the stem and add the endings given below:

Pronoun	Stem	Ending
je	vend-	**S**
tu	vend-	**S**
il/elle/on	vend-	**-**
nous	vend-	**ONS**
vous	vend-	**EZ**
ils/elles	vend-	**ENT**

vendre

je vends mes vieux livres	*I sell my old books*
tu vends les tiens?	*do you sell yours?*
il/elle/on vend beaucoup de choses	*he/she/we sell a lot of things*
nous vendons des produits verts	*we sell 'green' products*
vous vendez quelque chose?	*do you sell anything?*
ils/elles vendent des vêtements	*they sell clothes*

Some regular -re **verbs**

correspondre	*to correspond*	**perdre**	*to lose*
défendre	*to defend*	**pondre**	*to lay (eggs)*
dépendre de	*to depend on*	**rendre**	*to give back*
descendre	*to go down*	**répondre**	*to answer*
entendre	*to hear*	**tondre**	*to mow*

St Amand est célèbre pour les carillonneurs. Tu **entends** les cloches de St Amand?	*St Amand is famous for its bellringers. Can you hear the bells of St Amand?*
Le vendredi beaucoup de St Amandinois **se rendent** au marché pour acheter leurs fruits et légumes.	*On Fridays many people in St Amand go to the market to buy their fruit and vegetables.*

Les boulangeries **vendent** du bon pain.
The bakers sell good bread.

Stéphanie et Mark montent
les 370 marches de l'Abbaye
et **redescendent**.

*Stéphanie and Mark go up the
370 steps of the Abbey and
come down again.*

2 Demonstrative pronouns

ce + être + adjective

To say *it is, this is,* **ce** is used with **être** + adjective when you
mention something you have already been speaking or writing
about:

Ce n'est pas important.	*This is not important.*
(… un problème)	*(… a problem)*
C'est plutôt cher. (… le prix)	*It is rather expensive. (… the price)*

It can also be used with **être** and a following noun:

C'est un magasin bien achalandé.	*It is a well-stocked shop.*

ci (here), là (there)

If you are referring to something specific you add **ci** (*here*) and
là (*there*) to **ce**:

ceci (*this*); cela (*that*)

Ceci est à moi.	*This is mine.*
Cela est à lui.	*That's his.*

ça – cela

ça (*this/that*) is an abbreviation of **cela**:

Je ne comprends pas **ça**.	*I don't understand that.*
Ça n'a pas d'importance.	*That doesn't matter.*

ceci/cela

Ceci and **cela** refer to one object, one situation or something
general.

celui-ci, celui-là

If you are choosing between different objects, ideas or situations, you use the following demonstrative pronouns.

They replace a noun and agree with it in gender and number:

masc. sing.	fem. sing.	masc. pl.	fem. pl.
celui-ci	**celle-ci**	**ceux-ci**	**celles-ci**
(this one)	*(this one)*	*(these ones)*	*(these ones)*
celui-là	**celle-là**	**ceux-là**	**celles-là**
(that one)	*(that one)*	*(those ones)*	*(those ones)*

See **Say it in French 1.**

J'ai besoin de piles pour mon baladeur.	*I need some batteries for my personal stereo.*
Lesquelles choisissez-vous?	*Which ones will you choose?*
Celles-ci.	*These (ones).*
Celles-là ne sont pas de longue durée.	*Those (ones) are not long life.*
Ces fleurs-ci sont jolies mais je prends **celles-là.**	*Those flowers are pretty but I'll take those.*

celui de, celui qui / que

The following demonstrative pronouns:

> **celui** (masc. sing.)/**celle** (fem. sing.) (*this, that*)
> **ceux** (masc. plural)/**celles** (fem pl) (*these, those*)

are used with:

> **de** to indicate possession. See Unit 7 **The main points 3.**

> **que/qui** (*that*). See Unit 11 **The main points 5.**

Ce vélo, c'est **celui de** Nicolas.	*That bike is Nicolas'.*
Celui que je voudrais	*The one (that) I'd like*

3 More personal pronouns

Remember that, although these pronouns usually refer to *people* (personal), they can also refer to things: **il/le/la** (*it*); **ils/les** (*they*).

Direct object pronouns

Subject pronouns		Direct object pronouns	
je	*I*	**me**	*me*
tu	*you*	**te**	*you*
il/elle/on	*he/she/one*	**le/la**	*him/her/it*
nous	*we*	**nous**	*us*
vous	*you*	**vous**	*you*
ils/elles	*they*	**les**	*them*

Direct object pronouns come before the verb but after the subject in a statement:

Alors, tu **les** prends? (les fleurs) — *Well are you taking them? (the flowers)*

Mark adore Stéphanie. Il **la** regarde avec passion. — *Mark adores Stéphanie. He looks at her passionately.*

Mark donne une pâquerette à Stéphanie. Elle tire les pétales un à un et dit: 'Je **t'**aime un peu, beaucoup, passionnément, à la folie, pas du tout.' — *Mark gives a daisy to Stéphanie. She pulls the petals one by one and says: 'I love you a little, a lot, passionately, madly, not at all.'*

Et toi, est-ce que tu **m'**aimes? — *And you, do you love me?*

Stéphanie laisse tomber sa liste de courses. Mark **la** ramasse. — *Stéphanie drops her shopping list. Mark picks it up.*

Patrick aime sa voiture. Il **la** lave tous les week-ends. — *Patrick likes his car. He washes it every week-end.*

Patrick s'occupe du gazon. Il **le** tond tous les week-ends. — *Patrick looks after the lawn. He mows it every weekend.*

en (some of it, of that) as a personal pronoun

When you want to replace a noun by a pronoun, it is not always possible to use the direct object **le**, **la** when referring to things. For example, if you are talking about **quantities** – **du** poisson (*some fish*), **de** l'argent (*some money*) – you will need to use the pronoun **en** which means *some* (*of it / of that*).

Je **le** veux. (something specific, precise) *I want it.*

but

J'**en** veux. — *I want some (of it).*

| Combien **en** voulez-vous? | *How much (of it) / How many (of them) would you like?* |
| J'**en** voudrais deux, s'il vous plaît. | *I'd like two (of them) please.* |

4 Comparatives

There are three ways of comparing things or objects.

aussi ... que

To say that something or someone is *as ... as* something else you use **aussi ... que**:

| Mark est **aussi** intéressé par le sport **que** son frère. | *Mark is as interested in sport as his brother.* |

moins ... que

To say that something or someone is *less ... than* you use **moins ... que**:

Nicolas est beaucoup **moins** athlétique **qu'**Andrew.	*Nicolas is much less athletic than Andrew.*
Les parents de Stéphanie parlent **moins** vite **que** les gens dans la rue.	*Stéphanie's parents talk less quickly than people in the street.*
Le vin coûte **moins** cher en France **qu'**en Grande-Bretagne.	*Wine costs less in France than in Great Britain.*

plus ... que

To say that something or someone is *more ... than* you use **plus ... que**:

| Le vin de qualité supérieure coûte **plus** cher **que** le vin de table. | *Top quality wine costs more than table wine.* |

Just as in English, the comparison doesn't have to be specific. You can just say **aussi, plus, moins**, without saying **que** (*than*) (something else):

| Il coûte **plus** cher. | *It costs more.* |
| C'est **aussi** intéressant. | *It is just as interesting.* |

Two useful comparative adjectives

bon → becomes **meilleur/e/s** (*better*)
mauvais → becomes **pire/s** (*worse*)

| Est-ce que le boudin blanc est **meilleur que** le haggis? | *Is boudin blanc better than haggis?* |

Stéphanie pense que c'est **meilleur,** mais que les andouillettes sont **pires.**	*Stéphanie thinks that it is nicer, but that chitterlings are worse.*

There is one adverb which changes its form when it is used as a comparative:

bien becomes **mieux** (*better*)

Je vais **mieux.**	*I feel better.*

The story

When reading this dialogue look particularly for **demonstrative pronouns, direct object pronouns** and **-ir** and **-re** verb endings.

Mark achète des cadeaux à la librairie.

Mark is buying presents at the bookshop.

Stéphanie	Voici le rayon des magazines. Lesquels choisis-tu?	*Here is the magazine section. Which ones are you choosing?*
Mark	Celui-ci a l'air intéressant.	*This one looks interesting.*
Stéphanie	Si tu préfères un magazine plus littéraire, il y a *l'Express, le Point, le Nouvel Observateur.*	*If you'd rather have a more literary magazine, there are* l'Express, le Point, le Nouvel Observateur.
Mark	Je prends *le Point.* Je voudrais aussi des journaux régionaux, mais j'attends la fin de la semaine.	*I'll take* le Point. *I'd also like some regional papers, but I'll wait till the end of the week.*

Stéphanie	Voici le rayon des livres de poche. Voici deux romans populaires. Celui-ci est plus passionnant que celui-là. C'est l'histoire d'un ménage à trois à Paris.	*Here is the paperback section. Here are two popular novels. This one is more exciting than that one. It's the story of a love triangle in Paris.*
Mark	Ce genre d'histoire te passionne. Moi, je préfère les livres de science fiction. C'est plus stimulant que les histoires d'amour.	*This type of story really appeals to you. As for me, I prefer science fiction. It is more stimulating than love stories.*
Stéphanie	Merci beaucoup Mark!	*Thanks a lot Mark!*
Mark	Sandy est aussi sentimentale que toi. Alors je prends celui-ci.	*Sandy is as sentimental as you. So I'll take this one.*
La vendeuse	Et avec ceci, Monsieur?	*Something else, sir?*
Mark	C'est tout, merci madame.	*That's all, thank you.*
Stéphanie	Il y a un marchand de cadeaux juste à côté. Ils vendent de jolies assiettes en porcelaine. Celle-ci montre la place et la station thermale. Celle-là montre l'Abbaye.	*There is a gift shop just next door. They sell gorgeous china plates. This one shows the square and the spa centre. That one shows the Abbey.*
Mark	Je préfère celle-ci. Elle est beaucoup plus fine que l'autre. Et elle coûte aussi moins cher. D'accord, je la prends pour ma voisine.	*I prefer this one. It's a lot finer than the other one. And it also costs less. OK I'll take it for my neighbour.*
La vendeuse	Monsieur, vous désirez un emballage-cadeau?	*Would you like it gift-wrapped, sir?*
Mark	Oui, merci, madame.	*Yes, thank you.*
La vendeuse	Je l'emballe aussi dans du polystyrène pour la protéger.	*I'll also wrap it in some polystyrene to protect it.*
Mark	Je vous en remercie.	*Many thanks.*

A quick check

1   Write six pairs of sentences using a pronoun from the left-hand column and the word opposite it in the right-hand column. Use the verb **choisir** and the structure given in the example.

(Je) choisis (une assiette en porcelaine). Je prends (celle-ci).

a   je   une fleur
b   tu   un pot de confiture
c   il/elle/on un stylo-plume
d   nous   un livre
e   vous   des brochures
f   ils/elles   des biscuits

2   a   Add the appropriate endings to the verbs used in the following sentences:

A St Amand nous entend____ **les cloches de l'Abbaye** sonner tous les jours.

Ils entend____ **leurs voisins** partir très tôt.

Quand Mark joue au rugby, il sal____**son maillot.**

Mark réfléch____ et chois____ **l'assiette en porcelaine** pour sa voisine.

   b   Replace the expressions in bold above with the corresponding **object pronoun**.

3   Using the outlines in the box below, write two sentences, each one using a comparative.

Example: Il fait chaud – l'Afrique – le Pôle Nord
           Il fait **plus** chaud en Afrique **qu**'au Pôle Nord.
           Il fait **moins** chaud au Pôle Nord **qu**'en Afrique.

Un hôtel quatre étoiles – luxueux – un hôtel deux étoiles
La Tour Eiffel – haut – la Tour de Blackpool.
Mark – âgé – Stéphanie.

The next stage

1 An irregular verb in -re: prendre

• **Je, tu, il/elle/on** are regular, but the stem changes in the plural.

For other irregular **-re** and **-ir** verbs see Unit 6 **The main points 2**.

prendre *to take*	
je **prends**	nous **prenons**
tu **prends**	vous **prenez**
il/elle/on **prend**	ils/elles **prennent**

• -re in verbs like **reprendre** (*to take back, to retake*)

You can add **re-** before many French verbs to mean that you do the action again:

recommencer *to restart,*
refaire *to do again,*
repartir *to go again,*
reprendre *to take again,*
reconnaître *to recognize.*

2 *C'est* or *il est*?

Sometimes you have to choose between **c'est** (see **The main points 2**) and **il est**.

Il est / elle est + **adjective**

• **Il est / elle est** is used when you are referring to a specific person:

Il / elle est **riche.**	*He/she is wealthy.*
(ton père / ma femme)	(your father / my wife)

or to a specific thing:

Elle est très **importante.**	It is very important.
(cette tâche)	(this task)

• **Il est / elle est** + noun (without an article) is used when you are saying what someone's job or profession is. (See Unit 1 **The main points 2**):

Il est commerçant.	*He is a shopkeeper.*
Elle est professeur.	*She is a teacher.*

Il est meaning 'it is'

• **Il est** + adjective

There are many impersonal expressions in French based on **il est** meaning *it is*:

Il est important, il est probable, il est possible... See Unit 10 **The next stage, Impersonal expressions** and Unit 17 **The main points, Probability and possibility.**

• **Il est** + adjective + **de** + infinitive (*it is* + adjective + *to*) is used to refer *forward* to something later in the sentence:

Il est important d'acheter des cadeaux avant de partir.	*It is important to buy presents before leaving.*
Il est difficile de comprendre cette liste.	*It is difficult to understand this list.*

C'est (it is) + adjective

See **The main points 3**. This refers *back* to an idea or situation but not to a person.

C'est vraiment très intéressant.	*It is really very interesting.*
C'est vrai, tu sais.	*It is true, you know.*

The structure **c'est** + noun + adjective can be used to refer to a person:

C'est un homme intelligent.	*He is an intelligent man.*
C'est une femme intelligente.	*She is an intelligent woman.*

3 *Plus de* (more than)

The expression *more than* is not always expressed by **plus que** when you are using figures. **Plus *de*** is used instead of **plus *que*** when figures are used:

Il fait **plus de** 30 degrés.	*It is more than (over) 30 degrees.*
Il y a **plus de** 100 élèves.	*There are more than (over) 100 pupils.*

4 *Bon/bien* (good/well), *meilleur/mieux* (better)

The adverb **bien** (*well*) is sometimes used in French where in English you would use the adjective *good*:

Ce travail est **bien**.	*This is good work.*

Because there is sometimes a problem for English speakers in choosing between **bon** and **bien**, it might also be difficult to know when to use the comparatives **meilleur** and **mieux**. The **adjective meilleur/e/s** (*better*) is the comparative of **bon/bonne/s** (*good*). It agrees with the appropriate noun in gender and number and goes before the noun it relates to:

Cette confiture est **meilleure** (lit. *more good*) que celle-là.	*This jam is better than that.*
Mark a **meilleur** caractère qu'Andrew.	*Mark has a better temper than Andrew.*

The **adverb mieux** (*better*) is the comparative of **bien** (*well/fine*) and remains invariable (does not agree):

Ces nouvelles baskets sont mieux.	*These new trainers are better.*

Mieux, being an adverb, follows the verb:

Ça va **mieux.**	*I am better. / Things are going better.*
Ça va **mieux?**	*Are you better? Are things any better?*

06

saying what you are going to do

In this unit you will learn
- to talk about where you are going
- to talk about what you are going to do
- to ask about people, places and things
- to locate people, places and things

Topic
- travel

Grammar

- The immediate future: **aller** + infinitive (*going to* + infinitive)
- Irregular -**ir** and -**re** verbs
- Prepositions *in*, *at*, *to*, *with*
- Adverbs
- Superlatives *the least / the most*

The next stage

- -**ir** / -**re** reflexive verbs
- Verbs followed by prepositions
- More about adverbs in set expressions

Getting started

1 To say where you are going and what you are going to do, you can use the present tense in conversational French.

Je **vais** à Paris la semaine   *I am going to Paris next week.*
prochaine.

J'**ai** une réunion dans deux   *I have a meeting in two weeks.*
semaines.

The future action is indicated by the time expression: *next week / next year...* In writing, or to emphasize the fact that the action will take place in the future, you will need to use the future tense (see Unit 11). However, just as in English, there is a way of saying that an action will take place in the immediate future (*going to* + infinitive): *I'm going to go abroad soon.*

In French you use the verb **aller** + the infinitive of the verb indicating the action:

Je **vais aller** à Paris la semaine   *I am going to go to Paris next*
prochaine.   *week.*

You have already learned the present tense of **aller**, which is an irregular verb. If you are unsure refer back to Unit 1 **The main points 3**.

2 In this unit you will also meet more irregular verbs ending in -**ir** and -**re** such as **prendre** (*to take*), **partir** (*to leave*):

Les Français **prennent** souvent   *French people often take a*
un mois de vacances en juillet   *month off in July or August.*
ou en août.

Ils **partent** à la mer ou à
la montagne.

*They go to the seaside or to
the mountains.*

3 To say where you are going to, or to locate people, things or
places, you need to use a preposition, for example: *to, in,
with*,...

St Amand-les-Eaux se trouve
dans le nord **près de** la
frontière belge.

*St Amand-les-Eaux is situated
in the north near the
Belgian border.*

4 To say **when, where, how, how often** you do something you
use adverbs. In this unit you will find out about common
adverbs such as **souvent** (*often*). You will also find out how
most other adverbs in French are formed, for example:
rarement (*rarely*).

Isabelle va **souvent** à Paris.
Elle va à Paris **principalement**
pour les expositions dans les
musées.

*Isabelle often goes to Paris.
She goes to Paris mainly for
exhibitions in museums.*

5 You have used adjectives for comparisons in Unit 5 **The main
points 4** and **Say it in French 2**. In this Unit you will learn how
to use the superlative form, how to say *the most, the least* and
so on:

Paris est **la plus** belle capitale
du monde.

*Paris is the most beautiful capital
in the world.*

Say it in French

Look more closely at **verb structures, prepositions** and **adverbs**
in the following examples.

1 Where you are and where you are going

Mark **est** en vacances à St
Amand-les-Eaux. St Amand
offre de nombreuses attractions
touristiques.

*Mark is on holiday in St
Amand-les-Eaux. St Amand
has many tourist attractions.*

Mark visite la station thermale.
Elle **se trouve près de** la source
du clos **de** l'Abbaye.

*Mark visits the spa centre. It is
situated near the spring at
the clos de l'Abbaye.*

Mark et Stéphanie se
promènent **dans** la forêt de
St Amand.

*Mark and Stéphanie are walking
in the forest of St Amand.*

La forêt de St Amand **est au centre du** Parc naturel régional.

St Amand forest is in the centre of the regional country park.

Mark et Stéphanie **vont visiter** l'Abbaye et **écouter** le carillon **de** 48 cloches.

Mark and Stéphanie are going to visit the Abbey and listen to the peal of 48 bells.

Ils **vont** aussi **faire** des courses et **prendre** un verre à la terrasse d'un café.

They are also going to go shopping and have a drink at a pavement café.

2 What you are going to do

Demain je **vais aller** à la pharmacie **pour** acheter des aspirines.

Tomorrow I am going to go to the chemist to buy some aspirins.

Les parents de Mark **vont venir en** France **afin de** rencontrer les parents **de** Stéphanie.

Mark's parents are going to come to France to meet Stéphanie's parents.

Les Dickson **vont suivre** des cours **du** soir en français.

The Dicksons are going to take evening classes in French.

Ils **vont venir en** France **en** juillet.

They are going to come to France in July.

Sandy **va** bientôt **passer** ses examens en français.

Sandy is going to take her French exams soon.

Elle **va** beaucoup **réviser** pendant plusieurs semaines.

She is going to revise a lot for several weeks.

3 Asking about people, places and things

Qu'est-ce qu'il y a à voir dans la région?

What is there to see in the area?

Pourquoi la ville porte-t-elle ce nom?

Why does the town have this name?

Où est-elle située?

Where is it situated?

Pourquoi est-elle célèbre?

Why is it famous?

Quelles sont les spécialités de St Amand?

What are the specialities of St Amand?

Qui est le maire de St Amand?

Who is the mayor of St Amand?

Comment est-ce que ça s'appelle?

What's that called?

4 Locating people, places and things

Stéphanie et Mark **sont** au café
près de la gare.
La ville **est située dans** le nord de
la France, **à** 30 km de Lille.

Le musée **se trouve sur** la place
du marché.

*Stéphanie and Mark are at
the café near the station.*
*The town is situated in the
north of France, 30 kms
from Lille.*
*The museum is situated in
the market place.*

The main points

1 The immediate future

aller (to go) + infinitive

The immediate future tells you what is going to happen in the not
too distant future and replaces the future tense in conversational
French, when no specific point about the future is being made.
See **Say it in French 2**.

Les Dickson **vont mettre** leur
français en pratique durant
leurs vacances.
Ils **vont faire** la connaissance
de la famille de Stéphanie.
Où **allez**-vous **passer** vos
vacances?
Nous n'**allons** pas **passer** les
vacances en Italie.
Allez-vous **visiter** Marseille?

*The Dicksons are going to put
their French to use during
their holidays.*
*They are going to meet
Stéphanie's family.*
*Where are you going to spend
your holidays?*
*We aren't going to spend the
holidays in Italy.*
*Are you going to visit
Marseilles?*

2 Irregular -ir and -re verbs

Verbs in *-ir*

A small group of irregular verbs ending in **-ir** add the following
endings to the stem:

-e, -es, -e, -ons, -ez, -ent.

The stem of these verbs does not change in the plural:

cueillir *to pick*	cueille, cueilles, cueille,	cueillons, cueillez, cueillent
offrir *to offer*	offre, offres, offre,	offrons, offrez, offrent

ouvrir *to open*	ouvre, ouvres, ouvre,	ouvrons, ouvrez, ouvrent
souffrir *to suffer*	souffre, souffres, souffre, souffrons, souffrez, souffrent	

Mark **cueille** un brin de muguet pour Stéphanie.

Mark picks a sprig of lily of the valley for Stéphanie.

A group of irregular verbs ending in two consonants before -**ir** have the -**ir** and also one preceding consonant removed to form the stem for the first three persons in the singular. The following endings are added:

-s, -s, -t, -ons, -ez, -ent.

The stem does not change in the plural:

dormir *to sleep*	dors, dors, dort,	dormons, dormez, dorment
mentir *to lie*	mens, mens, ment,	mentons, mentez, mentent
partir *to leave*	pars, pars, part,	partons, partez, partent
sortir *to go out*	sors, sors, sort,	sortons, sortez, sortent

courir *(to run)* has the same endings:		
	cours, cours, court,	courons, courez, courent

Le vendredi soir Mark et Stéphanie **sortent** à Aberdeen.

On Friday nights Mark and Stéphanie go out in Aberdeen.

Two -**ir** verbs are highly irregular:

tenir *to hold*	tiens, tiens, tient,	tenons, tenez, tiennent
venir *to come*	viens, viens, vient,	venons, venez, viennent

Verbs with similar spelling such as **devenir** (*to become*), **revenir** (*to come back*), **retenir** (*to hold back*) etc. follow the same pattern:

Isabelle **tient** les cordons de la bourse.

Isabelle holds the purse-strings.

Les parents de Mark **viennent** de Dundee.

Mark's parents come from Dundee.

Verbs in -*re*

The stem of irregular -**re** verbs changes in the present tense with plural subjects.

For **prendre** the stem becomes **pren**- so that the plural forms of the present tense are:

nous prenons, vous prenez, ils prennent

The endings of the present tense of the other irregular -re verbs are: -s, -s, -t, -ons, -ez, -ent.

Here is a more complete list of irregular verbs in -re.

Look at the way the stem changes in the plural:

boire *to drink*	bois, bois, boit,	buvons, buvez, boivent
croire *to believe*	crois, crois, croit,	croyons, croyez, croient
conduire *to drive*	conduis, conduis, conduit,	conduisons, conduisez, conduisent
connaître *to know*	connais, connais, connaît,	connaissons, connaissez, connaissent
dire *to say*	dis, dis, dit,	disons, dites, disent
écrire *to write*	écris, écris, écrit	écrivons, écrivez, écrivent
lire *to read*	lis, lis, lit,	lisons, lisez, lisent
prendre *to take*	prends, prends, prend,	prenons, prenez, prennent
suivre *to follow*	suis, suis, suit,	suivons, suivez, suivent
vivre *to live*	vis, vis, vit	vivons, vivez, vivent

Cette année Mark et Stéphanie **prennent** une semaine de vacances en mai.	*This year Mark and Stéphanie are taking a week's holiday in May.*
Les Dickson ne **connaissent** pas encore les Lemaire.	*The Dicksons do not know the Lemaires yet.*
Mark **écrit** quelques cartes.	*Mark writes some postcards.*
Stéphanie les **lit** et ajoute un petit mot.	*Stéphanie reads them and adds a few words.*

For more information on irregular verbs, see the **Verb tables**, page 250.

3 Prepositions 'in, at, to, with'

Prepositions can go with verbs, for example: **sortir de** (*to go out of / to come from*) but they mainly introduce adverbial phrases which explain *where*, *when*, *how*, *why* things happen. See **The main points 4** below.

Here is a list of prepositions (both single words and groups of words) you have already met in examples in this book:

Prepositions and prepositional groups for place (where)

à	to/in/at	contre	against
à côté de	beside / next to	dans	in
à l'intérieur de	inside	de	of/from/by
après	after	derrière	behind
au bord de	on / at the edge of	devant	in front of
au coin de	on / at the corner of	en	to/in/of
		en face de	opposite
au-dessous de	below/ underneath	entre	between
		loin de	far from
au-dessus de	above	parmi	among
autour de	around	près de	near
avant	before	sous	under
chez	at / at the home of (someone)	sur	on
		vers	towards

L'Abbaye se trouve **sur** la place **en face de** l'hôtel de ville.

The Abbey is situated in the market place opposite the town hall.

L'agence de voyages se trouve **au coin de** la rue, **à côté du** marchand de légumes **près de** l'Abbaye.

The travel agency is situated on the corner of the street, next to the greengrocer's near the Abbey.

À St Amand il y a un marché **sur** la place tous les vendredis **de** 9 heures **à** 13 heures.

In St Amand there is a market in the square every Friday from 9.00 to 13.00.

Prepositions for time (when)

à	at	jusque	until
avant	before	pendant	during
après	after	pour	for
depuis	since/for		

Stéphanie habite à Aberdeen **depuis** six mois.
Avant ça elle était à l'université de Lille **pendant** 2 ans.

Stéphanie has been living in Aberdeen for six months. Before that she was at the University of Lille for two years.

Elle va travailler à Aberdeen **jusqu'**à la fin de son stage, puis elle espère y trouver un autre emploi.

She is going to work in Aberdeen until the end of her work placement and then she is hoping to find another job there.

Other prepositions and prepositional groups showing how or why:

afin de	*in order to*	**par**	*by / through*
à cause de	*because*	**pour**	*in order to*
au lieu de	*instead of*	**presque**	*almost*
avec	*with*	**sans**	*without*
comme	*like, such as*	**sauf**	*except*
d'après	*according to*	**selon**	*according to*
de façon à	*in order to*	**suite à**	*following*

Stéphanie travaille **comme** stagiaire pour une compagnie pétrolière à Aberdeen.	*Stéphanie works as a trainee for an oil company in Aberdeen.*
Elle travaille **avec** Mark. **Selon lui,** elle est très douée et elle se débrouille très bien dans son emploi. Mark a tous les cadeaux **sauf** un pour son meilleur ami.	*She works with Mark. In his opinion she is very gifted and is doing very well in her job. Mark has all his presents except one for his best friend.*

As mentioned in Unit 1 **The main points 8** and **Say it in French 3**, when prepositions are followed by personal pronouns, stressed pronouns are used: **moi, toi, lui/elle/soi, nous, vous, eux/elles.** See also Unit 7 **The main points 6**.

Tu viens **avec moi?**	*Are you coming with me?*
Elle va à la librairie **avec lui.**	*She is going to the bookshop with him.*
Selon toi, Mark, est-ce que Stéphanie va obtenir un emploi à temps complet à la fin de son stage?	*Mark, in your opinion, is Stéphanie going to get a full-time job at the end of her work placement?*
Tu y vas **sans moi?**	*Are you going without me?*

4 Adverbs

Adverbs describe *where, when, how,* or *why* something happens. They work with words such as verbs, adjectives or other adverbs to change or explain the basic meaning. There are two main groups of adverbs:

Short, frequently used adverbs

assez	*fairly/enough*	**toujours**	*very*
bien	*well*	**très**	*always*
moins	*less*	**trop**	*too*
plus	*more*	**vite**	*fast*
souvent	*often*	**vraiment**	*really/truly*

Adverbs formed from adjectives

For these adverbs you simply add **-ment**, usually to the feminine form of the adjective:

actif (m)	**active** (f)	active**ment**
heureux (m)	**heureuse** (f)	heureuse**ment**
mondial (m)	**mondiale** (f)	mondiale**ment**
passif (m)	**passive** (f)	passive**ment**
principal (m)	**principale** (f)	principale**ment**
régulier (m)	**régulière** (f)	régulière**ment**

For adjectives which already end in **-e**, add **-ment** without any change:

simple (m, f)	simple**ment**
véritable (m, f)	véritable**ment**

The position of adverbs

Adverbs can accompany/modify **verbs**, **adjectives** or **other adverbs**.

• When adverbs modify **verbs**, they usually come after the verb (or after the first part of the verb: **être** or **avoir** in the perfect tense, see Unit 13 **The main points 3**):

Mark travaille **souvent** sur la plate-forme pétrolière.	*Mark often works on the oil platform.*
Il téléphone **régulièrement** à Stéphanie.	*He phones Stéphanie regularly.*
Il a **déjà** acheté un téléphone portable.	*He has already bought a mobile phone.*

• When adverbs modify **adjectives**, they come directly before the adjective:

Mark trouve les parents de Stéphanie **vraiment** sympathiques.	*Mark finds Stéphanie's parents really friendly.*

Il est **très** heureux d'être en France.

He is very happy to be in France.

• Short adverbs such as **trop**, **plus**, **très** can also modify **other adverbs** and are placed before them:

Certains Français roulent **trop** vite.

Some French people drive too fast.

Les Britanniques roulent **plus** prudemment.

The British drive more cautiously.

5 Adverbial phrases

There are some frequently used adverbial phrases which are formed from a preposition + a **noun**:

avec plaisir	*with pleasure*
en ce moment	*at the moment*
en retard	*late*

Georges et Isabelle accueillent Mark **avec plaisir**.

Georges and Isabelle welcome Mark with pleasure.

6 Time phrases

To say when something happened, there are some time phrases which do not start with a preposition in French, although they do in English:

le samedi soir	*on Saturday nights*
le dimanche matin	*on Sunday mornings*
le matin	*in the morning*
lundi	*on Monday*
le lundi	*on Mondays*

7 *en* + the present participle

See Unit 3 **The next stage 3**.

In English you form the present participle from the infinitive of the verb by adding *-ing*:

to drive → *driving; to go* → *going*

In French you find the stem of the verb and add -**ant**:

rouler → roul- → roul**ant** (*driving*); **aller** → all- → all**ant** (*going*)

Se couch**ant** tard à cause de ses examens, Sandy est très fatiguée.

Going to bed late because of her exams, Sandy is very tired.

To show that one thing causes another (*by/in ...ing*), in French you add the preposition **en** before the present participle (the **-ant** form of the verb):

En pren**ant** des cours du soir, les parents de Mark espèrent apprendre assez de français pour communiquer avec les Lemaire.	*By taking evening classes Mark's parents hope to learn enough French to communicate with the Lemaires.*

8 Superlatives: the least, the most

The most ...

To say that something or someone is *the most...*, or for adjectives that end in *-est* in English (great*est*, old*est*, new*est*), you use: **le/la/les plus** + adjective. The adjective agrees in number and gender with the noun, and its position does not change.

Most adjectives go *after* the noun:

Nicolas est le cinéphile **le plus** passionné de toute la famille.	*Nicolas is the keenest cinema enthusiast of the whole family.*
St Amand est une des villes **les plus** connues du nord, ayant participé plusieurs fois aux jeux d'Interville.	*St Amand is one of the most famous cities in the north, having taken part in the Interville Games several times.*
L' eau de St Amand est une des eaux **les plus** riches en minéraux et en magnésium et c'est **la plus** consommée dans le nord.	*St Amand water is among the richest in minerals and magnesium and is the one most people drink in the north.*

Here are some examples of adjectives which go *before* the noun. See Unit 3 **The main points 1**.

Nicolas est **le plus grand** garçon de sa classe.	*Nicolas is the tallest boy in his class.*
A la maison, il a **la plus petite** chambre.	*At home, he has the smallest bedroom.*

The least...

To say that something or someone is *the least* you use: **le/la/les moins** + adjective. The adjective agrees in number and gender with the noun:

Nicolas est **le moins** sportif de toute la famille.	*Nicolas is the least sporty of the whole family.*

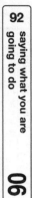

L'eau de St Amand est aussi une des eaux minérales **les moins** chères.	*St Amand water is also one of the least expensive mineral waters.*

The story

In the following conversation, look for **expressions of time** and of **place**, and for verbs **expressing an immediate future**:

Isabelle parle de Paris à Mark.
Isabelle is talking to Mark about Paris.

Isabelle	Mark, connaissez-vous Paris?	*Mark, do you know Paris?*
Mark	Non, mais j'aimerais beaucoup y aller un jour avec Stéphanie. Est-ce que vous allez souvent à Paris?	*No, but I would very much like to go there one day with Stéphanie. Do you go to Paris often?*
Isabelle	Environ une fois par an. J'ai des cousins qui vivent là-bas. Exceptionnellement, je vais y aller la semaine prochaine, afin de rendre visite à ma cousine Jacqueline. Elle est à l'hôpital suite à un accident de la route. Je pars mercredi matin.	*About once a year. I have some cousins who live there. Exceptionally, I'm going to go there next week, to visit my cousin Jacqueline. She is in hospital as the result of a road accident. I'm leaving on Wednesday morning.*
Mark	Est-ce que c'est très grave?	*Is it very serious?*
Isabelle	Assez grave. D'après les docteurs elle a vraiment de la chance d'être en vie. Sa voiture est complèment inutilisable. Elle a les deux jambes cassées et quelques blessures aux bras et au visage. Elle dort très mal et elle se sent plutôt déprimée. Je vais donc aller la voir.	*Fairly serious. According to the doctors she is very lucky to be alive. Her car is a complete write-off. Both her legs are broken and she has a few cuts to her arms and face. She is sleeping very badly and feels rather depressed. So I'm going to go and see her.*
Mark	Combien de temps allez-vous rester à Paris?	*How long are you going to stay in Paris?*

| Isabelle | Trois ou quatre jours seulement. Je vais en profiter pour faire quelques courses pendant mon séjour là. Je voudrais aller à la Samaritaine, près du Pont-Neuf. C'est le magasin le mieux situé et le plus populaire de Paris. C'est au coeur de Paris, près du musée du Louvre et pas très loin de Notre-Dame de Paris. Il est extrêmement populaire avec les touristes. On a la plus belle vue de Paris de la terrasse de la Samaritaine. | *Only three or four days. I'm going to take the opportunity to do some shopping during my stay there. I'd like to go to the Samaritaine near the Pont-Neuf. It is the most convenient and the most popular shop in Paris. It is in the centre of Paris near the Louvre, not too far from Notre-Dame. It is extremely popular with tourists. You have the best view of Paris from the roof-top of Samaritaine.* |

A quick check

1 Put the words in the following sentences in the correct order, adding capitals and punctuation as necessary:

a vais St Amand je visiter de l'Abbaye
b est-ce des vas cartes que postales tu acheter
c le j' aller les sangliers aimerais bois dans voir les de St Amand

2 Make the verbs in brackets agree with their subject and add the correct prepositions in the following sentences:

a Mark (écrire) des cartes postales ___ St Amand et les (envoyer) ___ sa famille ___ Dundee et ___ ses amis.
b Les parents ___ Mark (vivre) ___ un quartier résidentiel ___ Dundee.
c Mr. Dickson (prendre) le bus ___ se rendre au travail le matin.
d Il est directeur ___ un supermarché ___ quelques kilomètres ___ centre ville ___ de la rivière Tay.
e Il (partir) ___ 8 heures le matin et (revenir) ___ 18 heures, ___ le jeudi soir car il travaille ___ 21 heures.

3 Select adverbs from the lists on pages 87–90 above, and add them to the following sentences:

Dundee occupe une position _____ privilégiée sur la côte est de l'Écosse. Les deux collines, Balgay et Law, offrent une vue _____ superbe de la Tay et de la campagne. Dundee est une ville _____ connue pour le bateau *Discovery*, et l'observatoire de Balgay avec ses vues féériques. Dundee est une ville _____ accueillante pas très loin de St Andrews _____ célèbre pour le golf.

The next stage

1 *-ir/-re* **reflexive verbs**

Most reflexive verbs are **-er** verbs. See Unit 3 **The main points 3**. Some **-ir/-re** verbs can also be used as reflexives. The extra pronoun **se** which comes in front of the verb changes form according to the subject of the verb.

Here are a few examples of **-ir** and **-re** reflexive verbs:

s'asseoir	*to sit down*	Tu t'assieds.
se comprendre	*to understand one another*	Nous nous comprenons.
se conduire	*to behave (oneself)*	Ils se conduisent bien.
se connaître	*to know oneself / know each other*	Vous vous connaissez?
se dire	*to tell oneself*	Je me dis...
s'écrire	*to write to each other*	Nous nous écrivons.
se tenir	*to stand/behave/hold*	Ils se tiennent bien.

Mark et Stéphanie **se tiennent** la main.	*Mark and Stéphanie hold hands.*
Les Dickson et les Lemaires ne **se connaissent** pas encore.	*The Dicksons and the Lemaires don't know each other yet.*

2 Verbs followed by prepositions

Prepositions are often used differently in English and French. This is most noticeable in **verb groups** (**s'habituer à, penser à, se contenter de**). For example the preposition **à** can be translated by *at/in* and it also means *to*:

| Mark s'habitue **à** la vie française. | *Mark is getting used to French life.* |

à can also mean *of/about* in expressions such as:

penser **à** (*to think of/about*)

de can also mean *with* in expressions such as:

se contenter **de** (*to be satisfied with*)

par can mean with *in* expressions such as:

commencer **par** (*to begin with*),
remplacer **par** (*to replace with*)

| Mark pense **à** écrire **à** ses amis. | *Mark is thinking of writing to his friends.* |

| Mark et Stéphanie se contentent **de** sortir le week-end. | *Mark and Stéphanie are satisfied with going out at weekends.* |

Many French verbs are almost always followed by a preposition, forming a **verb group**.

It is important to remember the verb *with its preposition* and to look up the verb in a good dictionary whenever you are unsure.

Here is a list of French verbs followed by the preposition **à**:

aboutir à	*to lead to*
***aider quelqu'un à**	*to help someone to*
s'amuser à (+ inf)	*to amuse oneself* (+ verb + *ing*)
appartenir à	*to belong to*
***chercher à**	*to try to*
***commencer à**	*to begin to*
consentir à	*to consent to*
***continuer à**	*to continue to*
s'habituer à	*to become used to*
***inviter quelqu'un à**	*to invite someone to*
***penser à**	*to think of*
***réussir à**	*to succeed in*

| Stéphanie s'habitue **à** vivre **à** Aberdeen. | *Stéphanie is getting used to living in Aberdeen.* |
| Elle cherche **à** rester en Écosse. | *She is trying to stay in Scotland.* |

The verbs marked with * above and overleaf are not always followed by a preposition, either in English or in French. Some can also be followed by a direct object:

| Il commence **son travail** à 8h 30. | *He starts work at 8.30.* |

Here is a list of French verbs followed by the preposition **de**. As you can see, this preposition can be translated in many ways: *to, from, of, for, with*. Note that the equivalent English verb may not be followed by a preposition.

s'arrêter de (+ inf)	*to stop (doing something)*
avoir l'air de	*to look like*
avoir besoin de	*to need*
avoir envie de	*to be afraid of*
se contenter de	*to be satisfied with*
se dépêcher de	*to hurry to*
douter de	*to doubt*
***éviter de**	*to avoid (doing something)*
s'excuser de	*to apologize for*
***finir de**	*to finish*
***offrir de**	*to offer to*
***ordonner à quelqu'un de**	*to order someone to*
parler de	*to talk about*
se passer de	*to do without*
penser de	*to have an opinion about*
se souvenir de	*to remember*

The reflexive verbs (**s'arrêter, se contenter, se dépêcher** …) are followed by a preposition when they have an infinitive. You would say:

Je me dépêche.	*I hurry up*
but	
Je me dépêche **de faire** quelque chose.	*I hurry to do something.*
Mark se dépêche **de téléphoner** à Stéphanie.	*Mark rushes to phone Stéphanie.*

There are some verbs which are followed by a preposition in English, but not in French:

chercher	*to look **for***
écouter	*to listen **to***
entrer	*to come **in***
regarder	*to look **at***

Nous cherchons St Amand-les-Eaux.	*We're looking **for** St Amand-les-Eaux.*
Nicolas écoute la radio.	*Nicolas is listening **to** the radio.*

Only a few prepositions can be followed by a verb – usually the infinitive:

- à, de
- compound prepositions containing de such as: loin de, avant de, au lieu de
- pour, sans, par
- après can be followed by avoir or être (See Unit 15 The next stage 3):

Après avoir acheté ses cadeaux, il ne lui reste plus beaucoup d'argent.	*After buying his presents he doesn't have a lot more money left.*

3 More about adverbs

Cher

The adjective cher can become an adverb. It is invariable when it is used in the set expression coûter cher:

Cette robe coûte cher.	*This dress costs a lot.*
Ces logiciels coûtent cher.	*These software packages are expensive.*

Vite

Vite is an adverb and not an adjective.

You say:

Ces trains sont rapides.   *These trains are fast.*
(adjective qualifying the noun trains masc. plural)

But if you use vite, it is invariable:

Stéphanie roule vite.   *Stéphanie drives fast.*
(adverb modifying the verb roule).

Mal

Mal is also an adverb, not an adjective, so it does not show agreement:

Cela fait mal.	*It hurts.*
La cousine d'Isabelle se sent plutôt mal.	*Isabelle's cousin feels rather unwell.*

Beaucoup trop

You can say beaucoup trop (*far too much*).

Mark aime beaucoup trop les sucreries.	*Mark likes sweet things (far) too much.*

07

saying who owns what

In this unit you will learn
- to speak about personal ownership
- to say and ask who owns something

Topic
- homes and possessions

Grammar
- More about possessive adjectives *my*, *your*, *her/his/its*
- Possessive pronouns *mine*, *his*, *hers*
- The preposition **de** to show possession
- The preposition **à** to show belonging
- Useful verbs for possession and ownership: **être** (*to be*); **avoir** (*to have*), **appartenir** (*to belong to*) in the present tense
- Stressed pronouns after **à** and **de**

The next stage
- More about possessive adjectives and pronouns
- More about possession

Getting started

You have already met possessive adjectives which show ownership. See Unit 2 **The main points 6.**

Voilà l'appartement de **mes** amis.	*That is my friends' flat.*
Leur appartement est situé près des magasins.	*Their flat is situated near the shops.*

As you can see from the above examples, possessive adjectives always come before the noun and agree in gender and number with the noun they precede and **not with the owner.**

Stéphanie cherche **son** livre.	*Stéphanie is looking for her book.*
«Où est **mon** livre?» demande-t-elle à Nicolas.	*"Where is my book?" she asks Nicolas.*

1 You use possessive pronouns to avoid repeating a noun:

Leur appartement is replaced by **le leur.**
Mon livre is replaced by **le mien.**

Cet appartement est **le leur.**	*This flat is theirs.*
Ce livre est **le mien.**	*This book is mine.*

2 In English, possession can also be expressed by the use of '*s* or *s*'. In French the preposition **de** is used to show ownership:

Les amis **de** mes parents ont une propriété sur la Côte d'Azur.	*My parents' friends have a property on the Côte d'Azur.*

3 In this unit you will also meet the preposition **à** to show ownership, useful verbs to show ownership and possession – **être** (*to be*), **avoir** (*to have*), **appartenir** (*to belong to*) – and will learn to ask questions about ownership and possession: *Whose is it/this?*, *Who do they/these belong to?*

C'est à Nicolas? Non, c'est
à Stéphanie.

*Is it Nicolas'? No, it
is Stéphanie's.*

4 As mentioned in Unit 6 **The main points 3**, if a preposition is followed by a personal pronoun, the stressed pronoun is used: **moi, toi, lui/elle/soi, nous, vous, eux/elles.**

The other grammatical structures you will find useful to express possession are:

- Demonstrative adjectives (Unit 2 **The main points 5**)
- Demonstrative pronouns (Unit 5 **The main points 2**)

Ce livre est à moi. Est-ce que
celui-ci est à toi?

*This book is mine. Is this
one yours?*

Say it in French

The following examples show the different structures used in French to express possession. Look at them and check with the English translation if necessary before going on to the **The main points**.

1 Showing personal ownership

Voici la maison **de** la famille Lemaire.	*This is the Lemaires' house.*
Leur maison est individuelle.	*Their house is detached.*
La chambre **de** Stéphanie est la plus grande.	*Stéphanie's room is the biggest.*
Voici la chambre **de son** frère.	*This is her brother's bedroom.*
Sa chambre est toujours en désordre.	*His bedroom is always untidy.*
Isabelle et George ont la chambre la plus spacieuse.	*Isabelle and George have the most spacious room. Theirs*
La leur a un balcon et une salle de bains complète.	*has a balcony and an en suite bathroom.*
Nicolas trouve **la sienne** trop petite.	*Nicolas thinks his is too small.*
Comment est **la tienne**?	*What is yours like?*

2 Asking who owns something

A qui est cette chambre?	*Whose is this bedroom?*
A qui appartient la plus grande chambre?	*Who does the biggest bedroom belong to?*
Tu **as** la plus grande chambre?	*Do you have the biggest bedroom?*
C'**est** l'ordinateur **de qui**?	*Whose computer is it?*
À qui sont ces logiciels?	*Who do these computer programmes belong to?*
Est-ce que ces logiciels **appartiennent** à Nicolas?	*Do these computer programmes belong to Nicolas?*

The main points

1 More about possessive adjectives

Possessive adjectives must agree in both gender and number with the noun they accompany, so there are more variations in French than in English:

mon, ma, mes	*my*
ton, ta, tes	*your*
son, sa, ses	*his/her/its*
notre, nos	*our*
votre, vos (plural and formal)	*your*
leur, leurs	*their*

Nicolas, est-ce que c'est ta chambre ou celle de **ta** soeur?
Nicolas, is this your bedroom or your sister's?

Stéphanie ne trouve pas **son** album de photos.
Stéphanie can't find her photo album.

Nos livres sont dans le bureau en bas.
Our books are in the office downstairs.

Leurs voisins se plaignent souvent du bruit.
Their neighbours often complain about the noise.

2 Possessive pronouns (mine, his, hers, ours,...)

As you can see from the possessive pronouns in bold in the examples below (**la mienne, la sienne** etc.), they also agree in number and gender with the noun they replace. They *agree* in both number and gender *with whatever is owned* – not with the owner as in English. They are like nouns because they are accompanied by the definite articles **le/la/les**, which also vary according to the gender and number of the thing owned.

Forms of the possessive pronoun				
masc. sing.	fem. sing.	masc. plural	fem. plural	
le mien	la mienne	les miens	les miennes	*mine*
le tien	la tienne	les tiens	les tiennes	*yours (informal)*
le sien	la sienne	les siens	les siennes	*his/her/its*
le nôtre	la nôtre	les nôtres	les nôtres	*ours*
le vôtre	la vôtre	les vôtres	les vôtres	*yours (plural, formal)*
le leur	la leur	les leurs	les leurs	*theirs*

A qui est cette radio?
Whose radio is this?

C'est **la mienne**.
It's mine.

Nicolas emmène **la sienne** au lycée.
Nicolas takes his to the secondary school.

Ce disque n'est pas **le tien**. *This record is not yours.*
Nos voisins se plaignent *Our neighbours often complain.*
souvent. Comment sont **les** *What are yours like?*
vôtres (plural)?

3 The preposition *de* to show possession or ownership

Very often in French **de** is used, particularly with a person's name, to show that someone owns something. There is no equivalent structure to the English *'s, s'*.

La chambre **de** Stéphanie est *Stéphanie's room is always*
toujours très bien rangée. *very tidy.*
Celle **de** Nicolas est toujours *Nicolas' is always untidy.*
en désordre. *(i.e. the one of ...)*
La chambre **de** leurs parents *Their parents' room has a*
offre une jolie vue sur la *lovely view over the*
campagne. *countryside.*

4 The preposition *à* to show belonging

In French, the preposition **à** is used in questions to ask *Whose is...?* or *Whose are...?* **À qui est...?, À qui sont...?** as shown in these examples. It is also used to say to whom something belongs.

À qui sont ces magazines? *Whose are these magazines?*
À qui est cette vidéo-ci? *Whose is this video?*
Ces logiciels ne sont pas **à toi.** *These computer programmes*
Ils sont à ton ami. *are not yours. They belong to your*
friend.

À qui est la nouvelle voiture *Whose is the new car parked*
garée devant la maison de nos *in front of our neighbours'*
voisins? *house?*

5 Useful verbs for possession and ownership

• **Avoir**: as with the English verb *to have*, **avoir** can be used to show ownership or possession:

Nicolas **a** deux disques de *Nicolas has two Westlife*
Westlife. *albums.*
Mark **a** aussi leur dernier disque. *Mark also has their latest*
album.

- **Être + à**: can be used to show possession. See **The main points 4**.

C'est à qui?	*Whose is it?*
C'est à Nicolas.	*It's Nicolas'.*

- **Appartenir + à** + noun: this can be used in similar situations to être à:

La voiture garée juste en face de la maison **appartient aux*** parents de Stéphanie.	*The car parked right in front of the house belongs to Stéphanie's parents.*

*As usual, **à** + **les** contract to make **aux**.

6 Stressed pronouns after *à*

If you want to indicate possession using **à** + a pronoun, you use the stressed form of the pronoun: **toi, moi, lui/elle** etc. See Unit 1 **The main points 8**; Unit 6 **The main points 3**.

Cette voiture est **à eux**.	*This car belongs to them.*
Est-ce que ce disque est **à toi**?	*Does this record belong to you?*
Non, c'est **à lui**.	*No, it belongs to him.*
Stéphanie a sa voiture bien **à elle**, mais elle n'est pas assurée en ce moment.	*Stéphanie has her very own car but it is not insured at present.*

The story

Look for **possessive adjectives** and **possessive pronouns** in the following conversation between Stéphanie and Nicolas.

Stéphanie cherche son album de photos pour le montrer à Mark.
Stéphanie is looking for her photo album to show it to Mark.

Stéphanie	Où est mon album de photos? Il n'est pas à sa place habituelle. Je me demande si Nicolas l'a. Nicolas, as-tu mon album de photos?	*Where is my photo album? It isn't in its usual place I wonder if Nicolas has it. Nicolas, have you got my photo album?*
Nicolas	J'ai un album mais c'est le mien.	*I've got an album but it is mine.*
Stéphanie	Mais non, ce n'est pas le tien, c'est le mien.	*No, it isn't yours, it's mine.*

	Le tien est sûrement enfoui sous un tas de vêtements. Tu es si désordonné! Et ça? Ce n'est pas à toi non plus. C'est mon logiciel.	*Yours is probably buried under a pile of clothes. You are so untidy! And this? This doesn't belong to you either. It is my computer software.*
Nicolas	Non, tu te trompes. Ce n'est pas le tien. C'est celui de mon copain, Claude. Le tien est sûrement bien rangé sur ton étagère.	*No, you're wrong. It is not yours. It is my friend Claude's. Yours is probably put away neatly on your shelf.*
Stéphanie	Mark, est-ce que tu veux voir des photos amusantes de Nicolas?	*Mark, do you want to see some funny pictures of Nicolas?*

A quick check

1   Replace the expressions in bold (**possessive adjectives + nouns**) with the corresponding possessive pronouns in the following sentences.

Example: C'est **leur maison**.   C'est **la leur**.

Où se trouve **votre maison**?	Où se trouve _____?
Andrew ne trouve pas **ses disques compacts**.	Andrew ne trouve pas _____.
Il prend **mes disques**.	Il prend _____.
J'oublie souvent de rendre **tes disques**.	J'oublie souvent de rendre _____.

2   Complete the following sentences with the words in the box.

> de, les nôtres, appartient, toi, eux, la leur, à, le mien, leurs, toi, leurs

C'est le dictionnaire ___ Sandy.
Ce magazine appartient ___ Sandy.
Ce livre n'est pas à ___. C'est _____.
_____ voisins sont plus aimables que _____.
Ce catalogue *La Redoute* _____ à Sandy.

«Est-ce qu'il y a des photos de ___ dans ce catalogue?»,
demande Andrew.

La voiture garée en face de la maison des Dickson est à ___.

La nouvelle Peugeot 406 n'est pas _____. C'est celle de
_____ voisins.

The next stage

1 More about possessive adjectives and pronouns

Agreement

Possessive adjectives and pronouns agree with *what is owned*
and *not* the owner. This means that some sentences can be
ambiguous in French, as it is not clear who the owner is.

This is usually made clear by the context or situation, since the
listener/reader would automatically know who the possessor
was.

Son logiciel est le même que **le sien.**	*His/her software is the same as his/hers.* = *Nicolas' friend's software is the same as Stéphanie's.*

See **The story** above.

Votre can either refer to several owners or to one owner
addressed in a formal way:

Où est **votre** voiture?	*Where is your car?*

Here again the context will show who the owner(s) is/are.

The possessive adjectives (**son, sa, ses**) and possessive pronouns
(**le sien, la sienne, les siens, les siennes**) can also be used in a
general sense to mean *one's, your* or *everyone's*:

On a besoin de **son** lecteur laser pour écouter **ses** disques compacts.	*You need your CD player to listen to your CDs.*

Clarifying ownership

To make clear who the owner is, especially in spoken French,
you can add the preposition **à** with a stressed pronoun:

Ce sont **ses** baskets **à elle**.	*These are **her** trainers.*
Mark a **son** appartement **à lui**.	*Mark has his **own** flat.*

Son dessin **à elle** a gagné le premier prix.

Her drawing won first prize.

A similar situation can arise with the possessive adjective *their* in English, and with **leur** and **leurs** in French. French can make matters clearer by using **à eux** or **à elles**.

Voici leur appartement **à eux**.

Here is their flat. (at least two people, one or both of whom are masculine)

Voici leurs photos **à elles**.

Here are their photos. (the girls')

Their/theirs

Number agreements with the possessive adjective **leur/leurs** and the possessive pronouns **le (la) nôtre / les nôtres, le (la) vôtre / les vôtres, le (la) leur / les leurs** can sometimes cause a problem for English speakers. This is because English adds an *-s* to change the adjective into the pronoun. (*your book* → *yours*; *our magazine* → *ours*, *their television* → *theirs*).

The possessive agrees with the owner in English, so you tend to think of *their* as always plural. In French, you add an **s** only when the thing owned is plural.

Possessive **adjective** + noun	Possessive **pronoun**
Voici leur platine laser et leurs disques compacts. *This is their CD player (one) and their CDs (several).*	**Voici la leur (platine laser).** *This one is theirs.* but **Ce sont les leurs (disques)?** *Are they theirs?* (several).

Les copains de Nicolas écoutent souvent **leurs** disques compacts.

Nicolas' friends often listen to their CDs.

S'ils n'apportent pas **leur** platine laser, ils peuvent se servir de **la nôtre.**

If they do not bring their CD player they can use ours.

Ils peuvent aussi écouter **les nôtres.**

They can also listen to ours. (our CDs).

2 More about possession

Possession with parts of the body

Possessive adjectives are used in English with parts of the body (*my* hand, *your* head etc.). In French the definite article is more likely especially in written and more formal French:

Elle a une bague **au** doigt.	*She's got a ring on her finger.*
Il a mal **au** pied droit.	*His right foot hurts.*
J'ai mon sac à **la** main.	*I've got my bag in my hand.*

Saying 'of mine, of yours, of his, of theirs' etc.

The preposition à followed by a stressed pronoun (**moi, toi**) or a name (**Nicolas**) is also used to express possession in this way in French. See **The main points 6**.

Ce sont des copains **à moi**.	*They are friends of mine.*
Non. Ce sont des copains **à Nicolas**.	*No. They're friends of Nicolas'.*
J'ai trouvé des livres **à toi**.	*I found some books of yours.*

Appartenir à **(to belong to)**

Ce livre **appartient** à Stéphanie.	*This book belongs to Stéphanie.*

If the object of the verb **appartenir** is a pronoun, the pronoun comes before the verb:

Il **lui** appartient.	*It is hers / belongs to her.*

See Unit 9 **The main points 3**.

08

permission and obligation

In this unit you will learn
- to say what you can do
- to give and refuse permission
- to say what needs to be done
- to give orders and instructions

Topic
- leisure activities and plans

Grammar

- Verbs followed by an infinitive: **pouvoir** (*to be able to*), **savoir** (*to know, to know how to*), **vouloir** (*to want to*), **devoir** (*to have to*)
- Impersonal expressions: **il faut** (**falloir** to *need something/to be necessary*), **il pleut** (**pleuvoir** to *rain*)
- Other verbs ending in **-oir**: **valoir** (*to be worth*), **voir** (*to see*), **recevoir** (*to receive*), **s'asseoir** (*to sit down*)
- Expressions with **avoir**

The next stage

- The difference between **savoir** and **connaître**
- **Devoir** (*to have to* or *to owe*)

Getting started

1 You have already met the structure **aimer** + infinitive (*to like doing something*) in Unit 2 **The main points 3**.

Nous **aimons jouer** aux échecs.	*We like to play chess.*
J'**aime faire** du sport.	*I like to do/I am keen on sport.*

and the immediate future **aller** + infinitive (*to be going to do something*) in Unit 6 **The main points 1**.

Je **vais acheter** des cadeaux.	*I am going to buy presents.*

In this unit you will meet similar structures, i.e. verbs followed by infinitives which are used to say what:

- you *can do / are able to*: **pouvoir** + infinitive
- you *are allowed to*: **pouvoir** + infinitive
- you *are able / have the knowledge to*: **savoir** + infinitive
- you *want to do*: **vouloir** + infinitive
- you *must do / have to do*: **devoir** + infinitive

Georges **doit** se lever tôt pour aller travailler, car il commence à 8h00.	*Georges has to get up early to go to work, because he starts at 8 o'clock.*
Il **peut** rentrer plus tôt le soir, s'il n'y a pas de travail urgent et il **peut** faire soit du ball-trap soit du jardinage pour se distraire. Il **doit** souvent travailler le samedi et	*He can come home earlier in the evening if there is no urgent work and he can enjoy either clay-pigeon shooting or gardening. He often has to work on Saturdays and*

| Isabelle ne **sait** jamais à quelle heure il va rentrer. | *Isabelle never knows at what time he is going to come home.* |
| Isabelle **sait** très bien cuisiner et fait souvent de la pâtisserie pour l'église de la Croix du Petit Dieu. Elle travaille bénévolement pour une entreprise caritative car elle **veut** aider les défavorisés. | *Isabelle is a very good cook and and often bakes cakes for the Croix du Petit Dieu church. She works on a voluntary basis for a charity, because she wants to help the underprivileged.* |

2 In this unit you will also meet the impersonal way of saying what you need, what is necessary, what must be done or has to be done:

| **Il faut** beaucoup d'adresse et de précision pour faire du ball-trap. | *You need a lot of skill and accuracy to do clay-pigeon shooting.* |
| **Il faut** beaucoup s'exercer pour gagner les premiers prix. | *You must train a lot to win the first prizes.* |

3 You will meet other -**oir** verbs which are also irregular:

| Georges aime faire les concours de ball-trap mais quand **il pleut** on ne **voit** pas très bien les assiettes et les concours sont annulés. | *Georges likes clay-pigeon shooting competitions but when it rains you cannot see the plates very well and the competitions are cancelled.* |

4 In this unit you will also learn a few set expressions with **avoir**:

| Quand Georges va à la chasse il prend de la boisson et de la nourriture pour faire un pique-nique. Quand il **a soif** ou quand il **a faim** il peut s'arrêter et casser la croûte. | *When Georges goes shooting he takes food and drink for a picnic. When he is hungry or thirsty he can stop and have a snack.* |

Say it in French

1 Saying what you can do

| Les Lemaire ne **peuvent** pas partir en vacances cette année car ils ont beaucoup de dépenses. | *The Lemaires cannot go on holiday this year because they have many expenses.* |

Ils **peuvent** se distraire dans la région car il y a beaucoup de choses à faire, des randonnées en forêt, à la campagne...
They can enjoy themselves in the area because there are many things to do, walks in the forest, in the country...

Ils **peuvent** se rendre à la mer, à Malo-les-bains ou à St Omer en un peu plus d'une heure.
They can go to the seaside to Malo-les-bains or St Omer in just over an hour.

Est-ce que Georges **peut** faire du ball-trap toute l'année?
Can Georges go clay-pigeon shooting all the year around?

Oui, mais il ne **peut** chasser que durant une période limitée.
Yes, but he can only shoot during a limited period.

2 Giving and refusing permission

Nicolas a envie d'aller faire du camping avec quelques amis.
Nicolas feels like going camping with some friends.

«Est-ce que je **peux** aller camper avec des copains?» demande-t-il à Isabelle.
"Can I go camping with some friends?" he asks Isabelle.

«Oui, tu **peux** si ton père veut bien.»
"Yes, you can if your dad agrees."

«Vous **pouvez** emprunter notre tente.»
"You can borrow our tent."

3 What needs to be done

Avant de partir, Nicolas **doit** ranger sa chambre.
Before leaving Nicolas must tidy his bedroom.

Isabelle veut aller à la mer avec Stéphanie et Mark. Georges **doit** travailler.
Isabelle wants to go to the seaside with Stéphanie and Mark. Georges has to work.

Elle **doit** préparer toutes les affaires de plage. Elle ne **doit** pas oublier le paravent.
She must prepare all the beach things. She must not forget the wind break.

Avant de partir, ils **doivent** vérifier la pression des pneus et le niveau d'huile.
Before leaving they have to check the tyre pressure and the oil level.

4 Giving orders and instructions

Nicolas, tu **dois** ranger tes affaires.
Nicolas, you must tidy your things.

Il **faut** aussi ranger tes vêtements.	*You must also tidy your clothes.*
Tu **dois** prendre soin de la tente.	*You must take care of the tent.*
Il **faut** la déplier et l'aérer avant de l'emporter.	*You have to unfold it and air it before taking it.*

The main points

1 Verbs followed by an infinitive

These are known as *modal verbs*. They are irregular and the spelling of the stem changes in the **nous** and **vous** forms.

Pouvoir

Just as in English, **pouvoir** (*to be able to*) can mean both *to have the ability to* and *to have permission to* do something. The exact meaning is indicated by the context.

pouvoir *to be able to*	
je **peux**	nous **pouvons**
tu **peux**	vous **pouvez**
il/elle/on **peut**	ils/elles **peuvent**

Stéphanie **peut** conduire la voiture de ses parents.	*Stéphanie can drive her parents' car.*

Pouvoir either means *to be able to* or *to be allowed to* in the above example. Only the context will determine the exact meaning.

Stéphanie **peut** conduire la voiture de ses parents car la voiture est assurée.	*Stéphanie is able to drive her parents' car because it is insured.*

For other examples refer to **Getting started 1**.

Stéphanie **peut** conduire leur voiture car ils savent que c'est une bonne conductrice.	*Stéphanie is allowed to drive their car because they know she is a good driver.*

See other examples in **Say it in French 2**.

Savoir or pouvoir

In French you use **savoir** and not **pouvoir** if you want to stress the fact that you *have the knowledge / the ability to* do something, and that you *know how to* do something:

savoir *to know (how to)*	
je **sais**	nous **savons**
tu **sais**	vous **savez**
il/elle/on **sait**	ils/elles **savent**

Alison **sait** cuisiner.
Stéphanie **sait** bien conduire.

Alison knows how to cook.
Stéphanie can (knows how to) drive well.

Est-ce qu'elle **sait** aussi bien conduire en Écosse? Ses parents ne le **savent** pas.

Can she drive as well in Scotland? Her parents do not know.

Vouloir

This verb forms the present tense like **pouvoir**.

vouloir *to wish/want*	
je **veux**	nous **voulons**
tu **veux**	vous **voulez**
il/elle/on **veut**	ils/elles **veulent**

Vouloir is used

• in the **present tense** to say that someone *would like* something / *would like to do* something or to ask if they *would like* something / *would like to do* something:

Nicolas, **veux**-tu venir avec nous demain? Nous allons à St Omer.
Non, je ne **veux** pas y aller.
A quelle heure **voulez**-vous partir?
Mark **veut** visiter la région.

Nicolas, would you like to come with us tomorrow? We are going to St Omer.
No, I don't want to go there.
What time do you want to leave?
Mark wants to visit the area.

• in the **conditional tense** (see Unit 18 **The main points 3**) to say that you *would like* something in a less direct and more polite way.

You have already met **vouloir** in expressions such as: **je voudrais** (*I would like*).

Refer back to Unit 4 **The main points 3**.

Mark, où **voudrais**-tu aller?   *Mark, where would you like to go?*

Je **voudrais** bien aller sur la côte.   *I'd like to go to the coast.*

Devoir

In English there is a choice between *have to* and *must* to express the necessity or the moral obligation to do something. In French there is only one verb, **devoir**.

devoir *to have to*	
je **dois**	nous **devons**
tu **dois**	vous **devez**
il/elle/on **doit**	ils/elles **doivent**

Nicolas **doit** montrer le respect à ses parents et **doit** être poli. Georges est très strict.   *Nicolas must show respect to his parents and be polite. Georges is very strict.*

Lorsque Stéphanie conduit en France elle **doit** se souvenir des priorités à droite.   *When Stéphanie drives in France she has to remember to give way on the right.*

2 Impersonal expressions

Falloir / Il faut **(one must/one has to/needs something)**

Falloir is called an impersonal verb. It is only used with the subject pronoun *il*.

It can be used in different tenses. See **Verb tables** page 254. It is used as follows

• To say that something is needed: **Il faut** is followed by a noun with a definite, indefinite or partitive article **le, la, les, un, une, des, du, de la, de l', d'**. See Unit 4 **The main points 2**.

Il faut de la nourriture pour la route, le plan de St Omer et un guide touristique.   *We need food for the road, the street map of St Omer and a tourist guide.*

• To say that you need something or that someone needs something:

Il me faut un plan de la ville.   *I need a street map of the city.*

Est-ce **qu'il vous faut** des directions précises?	*Do you need precise directions?*

In this case **il faut** is used with the indirect object pronoun, which is placed between **il** and **faut**. See Unit 9 **The main points** 3.

• To say that something *has to / must* be done. **Il faut** can also be followed by an infinitive:

Mark, **il faut** se lever de bonne heure demain matin.	*Mark, we must get up early tomorrow morning.*
Il faut partir avant l'heure de pointe.	*We must leave before the rush hour.*

Pleuvoir **(to rain)**

This is another impersonal verb used only with **il**.

Et s'**il pleut** beaucoup, qu'est-ce qu'on fait?	*If it rains a lot, what do we do?*
Stéphanie, comment dit-on: "It's raining cats and dogs" en français?	*Stéphanie, how do you say: "It's raining cats and dogs" in French?*
On dit: «Il pleut des cordes / des hallebardes.»	*You say:* «Il pleut des cordes / / des hallebardes.»

3 Other verbs ending in -*oir*

Valoir **(to be worth)**

Valoir is usually used with the third person singular or plural subject pronouns (**il/elle/ils/elles**) or with **ça/cela** (*this, that*) or with a noun:

Combien est-ce que **ça vaut**?	*How much is that worth?*
Combien **valent** ces plans de St Omer?	*How much do these street plans of St Omer cost?*
Ils **valent** €2,30 chacun.	*They cost €2,30 each.*
S'il pleut **cela** ne **vaut** pas la peine de partir.	*If it rains it's not worth going.*

Voir (to see)

This verb is conjugated like **croire**. See Unit 6 **The main points 2.**

voir to see	
je **vois**	nous **voyons**
tu **vois**	vous **voyez**
il/elle/on **voit**	ils/elles **voient**

Quand il pleut beaucoup on
ne **voit** pas bien la route et il
y a plus de risques d'accident.

*When it is raining hard you
don't see the road well and
there is more risk of an
accident.*

Other verbs, which are formed by adding a prefix to the verb
voir, have the same endings as **voir**, but alter the stem. Check
them in a good dictionary:

apercevoir	*to notice*
concevoir	*to conceive*
décevoir	*to deceive*
percevoir	*to cash in, to perceive*
recevoir	*to receive*

Stéphanie se lève et **aperçoit** des
nuages menaçants. Deux minutes
plus tard, il pleut à verse. Un tel
temps **déçoit** vraiment!

*Stéphanie gets up and
notices threatening clouds.
Two minutes later it is
pouring down. Such
weather is really
disappointing!*

Stéphanie **reçoit** souvent des
nouvelles de France.

*Stéphanie often receives
news from France.*

S'asseoir (to sit down)

The verb **s'asseoir** is a highly irregular reflexive verb which you
can see in full in the **Verb tables,** page 250.

Mark **s'assied** à côté de Stéphanie
et regarde la carte de France pour
voir où se trouve St Omer.

*Mark sits down next to
Stéphanie and looks at the
map of France to see where
St Omer is.*

4 Expressions with *avoir*

Expressions where *avoir* corresponds to 'to have' in English

- avoir rendez-vous

Isabelle **a rendez-vous** chez le coiffeur.	*Isabelle has an appointment at the hairdresser's.*

- avoir mal à la tête

Elle **a mal à la tête** et elle prend deux aspirines.	*She has a headache and takes two aspirins.*

- avoir le courage de

Georges **a le courage de** ses opinions.	*Georges has the courage of his convictions.*

Expressions where *avoir* + noun corresponds to 'to be' + adjective in English

You have already come across some phrases using **avoir** which do not mean *have* in English:

J'ai faim.	*I am hungry.*
J'ai soif.	*I am thirsty.*
J'ai 21 ans.	*I am 21.*

Other expressions:

avoir de la chance	*to be lucky*
ne pas avoir de chance	*to be unlucky/unfortunate*
avoir la chance de	*to be lucky/fortunate (enough) to*
avoir du courage	*to be courageous*
avoir peur / avoir peur de	*to be afraid / afraid of*
avoir l'habitude de	*to be used to*
avoir honte / avoir honte de	*to be ashamed / ashamed of*
en avoir marre de	*to be fed up with*
avoir sommeil	*to be tired*

Expressions where *avoir* does not mean 'to have' in English:

Stéphanie, Mark and Isabelle **n'ont pas de chance** car le temps est affreux.	*Stéphanie, Mark and Isabelle are unlucky because the weather is awful.*
Isabelle **en a marre de** ce temps variable. Elle voudrait habiter dans un pays chaud.	*Isabelle is fed up with this changeable weather. She would like to live in a hot country.*

The story

From this stage you should feel confident enough to read and understand the French in the dialogues in **The story**. If you have any problems, look up unknown words or expressions in your dictionary. If you are completely at a loss, look at the transcriptions, on pages 237–43.

In this conversation between Mark and Stéphanie, look for **verbs followed directly by an infinitive**, the modal verbs **pouvoir** and **devoir**.

Mark et Stéphanie prévoient de faire de l'équitation.

Stéphanie	Qu'est-ce que tu veux faire demain, s'il ne pleut pas? Tu veux faire de l'équitation ou des randonnées?
Mark	Je ne sais pas monter à cheval.
Stéphanie	Tu peux apprendre; ce n'est pas difficile.
Mark	Est-ce qu'il y a des centres équestres à St Amand?
Stéphanie	Il y en a plusieurs, mais je peux monter chez mon amie Monique, qui a plusieurs chevaux. Tu vois les pâtures, là-bas? Ce sont les siennes. On aperçoit les chevaux d'ici.
Mark	Il faut porter des vêtements spéciaux?
Stéphanie	Oui et non. Tu peux porter un jean et des baskets, mais tu dois porter une bombe. Mon père peut te prêter la sienne. Je vais téléphoner à Monique pour voir si nous pouvons monter demain. Au fait, quand tes parents veulent-ils venir?
Mark	Ils peuvent venir en juillet. Ils veulent visiter le nord et peut-être aller passer quelques jours à Paris.

A quick check

1 Add the missing verbs and/or expressions in the following
sentences: You will need **savoir, devoir, pouvoir, avoir envie
de, vouloir**

S Je vais demander à mes parents s'ils _____ rester chez
nous à ce moment-là. Je crois que Papa ne _____ pas
travailler le 14 juillet car c'est férié. Est-ce que tu _____
combien de temps ils _____ rester?

M Je ne _____ pas exactement. Une quinzaine de jours. Ils
_____ inviter tes parents à venir en Écosse l'année
prochaine. Est-ce que tu crois que tes parents _____ venir
à Dundee?

S Oui, j'en suis sûre. Cette année ils ne _____ pas partir en
vacances.

2 Ask questions about the following phrases using the
pronouns and verbs in brackets. Example: chanter (tu,
savoir) – Est-ce que tu sais chanter?

parler français (vous, savoir)
aller au cinéma (tu, vouloir)
rentrer tard (il, pouvoir)
ranger nos affaires (nous, devoir)

The next stage

1 The difference between *savoir* and *connaître*

These two verbs often create problems as they both mean *to
know*. **Savoir** means *to have knowledge of, to know how* to and
connaître means *to be acquainted with, to be familiar with*.

Je **connais** le chemin.	*I know (am familiar with) the way.*
Je **sais** quel chemin prendre.	*I know which way to go.*

The idea of *having the knowledge of* is introduced in this second
sentence.

You use **connaître** when talking about people:

Est-ce que Mark **connaît** les amis de Stéphanie?	*Does Mark know (is he acquainted with) Stéphanie's friends?*

2 *Devoir* (to have to, to owe)

Devoir does not always mean *to have to / must*, it can also mean *to owe*.

The meaning will only be made clear by the context. When **devoir** means *to owe*, it is not followed by an infinitive. Look at the difference between these two examples:

Isabelle **doit** acheter une bouteille de shampooing chez le coiffeur. Je vous **dois** combien, s'il vous plaît?

Isabelle must buy a bottle of shampoo at the hairdresser's. How much do I owe you, please?

09 directions, instructions and advice

In this unit you will learn
- to ask for and give directions
- to advise and tell someone to do / not to do something

Topics
- travel plans
- directions

Grammar

- Verbs to give directions: **continuer** (*to continue*), **tourner** (*to turn*), **prendre** (*to take*) and useful expressions such as **il faut, vous devez / tu dois** (*you need to / you have to*)
- Using imperatives to give directions **prenez** (*take*)
- Indirect object pronouns **me, te, lui** (*to me, to you, to her/him*)
- The pronoun **y** (*there, about this*)

The next stage

- **Aller** and **donner** in the imperative
- Functions of object pronouns
- The difference between **y** and **en**

Getting started

1 Useful verbs to give directions

The **present tense**, which you met in Units 1, 3, 5, 6, is used to give directions. Look back at these Units if you are not sure of verb endings, especially those of irregular verbs such as **prendre** (*to take*) (see Unit 6 **The main points 2**). You will also need to look back at ordinal numbers: **le premier / la première** (*the first*) etc. (Unit 3 **The main points 4**) and at prepositions of place (Unit 6 **The main points 3**) **à côté de** (*next to*), **près de** (*near*), **en face de** (*opposite*).

Vous **prenez** la première à droite.	*You take the first on the right.*
Vous **continuez** tout droit et vous **tournez** à gauche. C'**est** près d'ici.	*You go straight ahead and you turn left. It is near here.*
L'Abbaye **est** sur la place en face de l'hôtel de ville.	*The Abbey is in the market place opposite the town hall.*

The impersonal expression **il faut** (*one must / one has to / one needs to*) (Unit 8 **The main points 2**) is also useful when giving directions and telling people what to do:

Il faut tourner à droite.	*You'll need to turn right.*
Il faut prendre la quatrième rue à gauche.	*You'll need to take the fourth street on the left.*

Another useful verb for giving directions is the verb **devoir** (Unit 8 **The main points 1**):

Vous **devez** continuer tout droit, traverser la rue et continuer jusqu'à la rue de Lille.

You have to go straight ahead, cross the road and continue as far as the rue de Lille.

2 To give directions, you can use a form of the verb called the **imperative**. The imperative will be covered in Unit 12 **The main points 1**. In this Unit, you will only learn how to use some imperatives to give directions.

Prenez à droite.
Take a right-hand turn.
Prends la première à droite.
Take the first on the right.
Continuez/continue tout droit.
Go straight ahead.

3 Finally, to give directions *to someone*, you need to learn different personal pronouns. You have already met **subject pronouns** and **stressed pronouns** in Unit 1 **The main points 8**.

Je ne sais jamais donner les directions.

I never know how to give directions.

Et **toi**, tu sais donner les directions?

*Do **you** know how to give directions?*

You met **direct object pronouns** in Unit 5 **The main points 3**, answering the question *what*?:

Je **le** prends.
*I take **it**. (I take **what**?)*
Je **l'**aime.
I like him/her/it.
Je sais **les** donner.
I know how to give them (directions).

The pronouns you need to answer the question *to whom?* are called **indirect object pronouns**. You will meet these pronouns in this unit:

Je **lui** donne des directions précises.

I give him/her precise directions.

Un homme demande les directions pour aller à la gare.

A man asks the way to the station.

Stéphanie **lui** indique le chemin.

Stéphanie shows him the way.

Un couple **lui** demande le chemin pour aller à la mairie. Elle **leur** dit de continuer tout droit et de prendre la première rue à droite.

A couple asks her the way to the town hall. She tells them to go straight on and to take the first on the right.

Say it in French

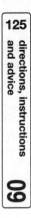

1 Asking for and giving directions

Excusez-moi, Monsieur, où se trouve le chemin de l'Empire, s'il vous plaît?	*Excuse me, where is the chemin de l'Empire, please?*
Ce n'est pas loin d'ici.	*It's not far from here.*
Vous continuez tout droit et juste après le pont vous prenez la première à gauche.	*You go straight on and just after the bridge you take the first on your left.*
Vous allez jusqu'au bout de la rue Salengro, puis vous tournez à gauche.	*You go right down to the end of the rue Salengro, then you turn left.*
Et vous êtes au chemin de l'Empire.	*And you are at the chemin de l'Empire.*
Et pour aller au gîte Le Luron?	*And to go the gîte Le Luron?*
C'est dans la forêt de St Amand.	*It is in the St Amand forest.*
Du chemin de l'Empire, prenez la première à droite. Continuez tout droit, traversez la rocade du Nord.	*From the chemin de l'Empire you take the first right. Go straight ahead, cross the northern bypass.*
Ensuite il faut continuer tout droit jusqu'au bout de la rue Basse.	*Then you'll have to go straight ahead, right to the end of the rue Basse.*
Vous arrivez place du Mont des Bruyères.	*You arrive at Mont des Bruyères square.*
Là vous continuez tout droit.	*There you go straight on.*
Prenez la rue Transvaal et vous êtes à la forêt de St Amand.	*Take the rue Transvaal and you are at the forest of St Amand.*
Le gîte Le Luron est à votre droite.	*The gîte Le Luron is on your right.*

2 Advising someone to do / not to do something

Andrew, si tu veux rester à Dundee chez un copain, tu dois être raisonnable.	*Andrew, if you want to stay at a friend's in Dundee you you must be sensible.*
Tu dois t'occuper de la maison.	*You must look after the house.*
Il faut sortir la poubelle le mardi matin.	*You must take the dustbin out on Tuesday mornings.*
Il faut te lever de bonne heure pour aller en classe.	*You must get up early to go to your classes.*

Il **ne faut pas** trop te servir du téléphone.
Si tu as des problèmes tu **dois** contacter ton oncle. Tu **lui** téléphones et tu **lui** dis de venir te chercher.
Il peut **nous** passer un coup de fil si nécessaire. Toi aussi, tu peux **nous** donner de tes nouvelles.

You must not use the telephone too often.
If you have any problems you must contact your uncle. Ring him and tell him to come and fetch you.
He can give us a ring if necessary. You can also keep in touch with us.

The main points

1 Verbs for giving directions

Irregular verbs:

aller (*to go*), **être** (*to be*) (Unit 1), **prendre** (*to take*) (Unit 6)

Regular verbs:

continuer (*to continue*), **descendre** (*to go down*), **remonter** (*to go up*), **tourner** (*to turn*), **traverser** (*to cross*)

To give information and/or advice to someone formally these verbs are used with **vous**:

Vous continuez tout droit, **vous** tournez à gauche, puis **vous** prenez la deuxième à gauche. **Vous** y êtes.

You go straight on, turn left, then you take the second on the left. You are there.

To give information to someone you know well or to direct someone in an informal way, you would use the pronoun **tu** (Unit 1 **The main points 5**):

Tu traverses la rue de Tournai et **tu** remontes le chemin du Corbeau.

You cross the rue de Tournai and go up le chemin du Corbeau.

falloir **and** *devoir*

You met both these verbs in Unit 8 **The main points 1, 2**.

• **Falloir**: The impersonal structure **Il faut** is often followed by the infinitive of a verb of direction but could also be followed by **que** + verb in the subjunctive. You will meet expressions like these in Unit 16 **The main points 2**.

Il faut tourner à droite et prendre la quatrième à gauche.

You'll need to turn right and to take the fourth on the left.

Il ne faut pas tourner à gauche
car c'est un sens interdit.

*You must not turn left, as it
is a one-way street.*

• **Devoir:** this modal verb is used to tell people what they *have
to do* to get to the place they are inquiring about. Unlike **il faut**
which cannot be used with other pronoun subjects, **devoir** can
be used with any of the subject pronouns. (See Unit 8 **The main
points 1**).

Vous devez vous arrêter aux
feux, puis vous tournez à gauche.
Tu dois remonter la rue de Condé
jusqu'au rond-point.

*You must stop at the traffic
lights, then you turn left.
You have to go back up the
rue de Condé as far as the
round-about.*

Nous devons prendre un bus
sur la place?

*Do we have to catch a bus
in the market place?*

2 Using imperatives to give directions

This is the easiest and the most frequent way of giving
directions. You just use the verbs *without* a subject pronoun, i.e.
instead of saying *you continue* **vous continuez**, you just say
continue **continuez**. Instead of saying **tu continues**, you just say
continue.

For -**er** verbs, including the verb **aller**, you drop the -s when **tu**
is the subject:

Continuez tout droit, **prenez**
à gauche, **passez** devant la mairie
et c'est à votre gauche.
Continue, prends à droite, **va** un
peu plus loin et c'est à droite.

*Go straight ahead, turn
left, pass the town hall and
it is on your left.
Go straight on, go right, go
a bit further and it is on the
right.*

Here are the imperative forms of the verbs to give directions:

Tu form	**Vous** form	
va	**allez**	aller
continue	**continuez**	continuer
descends	**descendez**	descendre
passe	**passez**	passer
prends	**prenez**	prendre
remonte	**remontez**	remonter
tourne	**tournez**	tourner
traverse	**traversez**	traverser

Prenez la première à gauche. **Allez** jusqu'au carrefour. Au carrefour **continuez** tout droit jusqu'aux feux et **prenez** la première à droite.

Take the first on the left. Go to the crossroads. At the crossroads go straight ahead to the traffic lights and take the first right.

If you are speaking in an informal or friendly way you say:

Prends la première à gauche. **Va** jusqu'au carrefour. Au carrefour **continue** tout droit jusqu'aux feux et **prends** la première à droite.

3 Indirect object pronouns

Here is a list of the **personal pronouns** you have already met:

- subject pronouns   Unit 1 **The main points 1**
- reflexive pronouns   Unit 3 **The main points 2**
- direct object pronouns   Unit 5 **The main points 3**

In the fourth column below you will find **indirect pronouns** – the pronouns used to answer the question *to whom?* Where the direct and indirect objects are different, they are in italic:

subject	reflexive	direct object	indirect object
je	me	me	me
tu	te	te	te
il/elle/on	se	*le/la*	*lui*
nous	nous	nous	nous
vous	vous	vous	vous
ils/elles	se	*les*	*leur*

As you can see, object pronouns only differ in the third person singular (**il/elle/on**) and plural (**ils/elles**). With indirect pronouns, you use **lui** and **leur** whether you are speaking about a male or a female person:

Les Dickson demande les directions pour aller chez les Lemaire.

The Dicksons ask for directions to go to the Lemaires'.

Mark va **leur** donner un plan de St Amand à son retour.

Mark is going to give them a street-map of St Amand on his return.

Il va aussi **leur** écrire pour confirmer qu'ils sont les bienvenus chez les Lemaire. Les Dickson vont venir en juillet. Isabelle demande à Georges si cela **lui** convient.	*He is also going to write to them to confirm that they are welcome at the Lemaires'. The Dicksons are going to come in July. Isabelle asks Georges if this is all right with him.*
Stéphanie **lui** explique que les Dickson souhaitent venir le 7 juillet.	*Stéphanie explains to him that the Dicksons wish to come on the 7th of July.*

You will find out about the use of two object pronouns in Unit 12 **The main points 6.**

Verbs which take indirect object pronouns:

appartenir à quelqu'un Cela **m'**appartient.	*to belong to someone* *This belongs to me.*
apporter quelque chose à quelqu'un Le facteur **nous** apporte le courrier à 7h. **donner quelque chose à quelqu'un**	*to bring someone something / to bring something to someone* *The postman brings us the mail / the mail to us at 7 a.m.* *to give someone something / to give something to someone*
Il **te** donne beaucoup de cadeaux.	*He gives you a lot of presents.*
écrire à quelqu'un Il **lui** écrit souvent.	*to write to someone* *He often writes to her/him.*
envoyer quelque chose à quelqu'un Il **vous** a envoyé un mel? **expliquer quelque chose à quelqu'un** Il **leur** explique la situation clairement.	*to send someone something / to send something to someone* *Did he send you an E-mail?* *to explain something to someone* *He explains the situation clearly to them.*
montrer quelque chose à quelqu'un *someone* Il **lui** montre le chemin.	*to show someone something / to show something to someone* *He shows him the way.*
offrir quelque chose à quelqu'un	*to present someone with something*

Mark **lui** offre des fleurs.   *Mark presents her with some flowers.*

poser des questions à quelqu'un   *to ask someone questions*
Elle **me** pose souvent la même   *She often asks me the same*
question.   *question.*

4 The pronoun *y*

This pronoun means *there* in examples such as: Vous y êtes.
(See **The main points 1**)

Vous y allez quand?   *When are you going there?*

Y also means *about this/it*.

J'y pense souvent.   *I often think about it.*

Y comes before the verb except when the verb is in the
imperative.

Restez-y.   *Stay there.*

For **y** with other pronoun objects, see page 166.

The story

From this discussion about Mark's parents and their visit to
France, make a list of the **instructions** and identify the **indirect
object pronouns**.

**Mark demande à Stéphanie si ses parents peuvent venir en
juillet.**

Mark   Stéphanie, ma mère vient de me demander si elle et
papa peuvent venir chez vous le 7 juillet. Est-ce que
cela convient à tes parents?

Stéphanie   Je vais leur poser la question tout de suite et tu peux
lui retéléphoner plus tard pour lui donner la
réponse.

Stéphanie appelle sa mère et elle lui donne la nouvelle.

Stéphanie   Maman, est-ce que les parents de Mark peuvent
venir chez nous le 7 juillet? Ils aimeraient passer
trois ou quatre jours chez nous, puis visiter la
région et aussi Paris.

Isabelle	Bien sûr, avec plaisir. Ton père peut peut-être prendre quelques jours de congé. Comment vont-ils voyager?
Stéphanie	Ils vont prendre l'avion de Glasgow à Paris et louer une voiture à l'aéroport. Mark va leur donner une carte routière et un plan de St Amand pour les aider.

Voici les instructions que Mark va donner à ses parents:

Vous arrivez à l'aéroport Roissy-Charles de Gaulle et vous prenez l'autoroute du nord, la A1, jusqu'à Péronne.

Ensuite prenez la A2 jusqu'à la sortie Cambrai/Valenciennes. Quittez la A2 à Valenciennes et continuez jusqu'à la Sentinelle. Là, vous devez prendre la A23 jusqu'à la sortie St Amand / Lille.

Quittez la A23 à l'entrée de St Amand et prenez la voie rapide jusqu'à la forêt de Raismes. Au deuxième rond-point, tournez à gauche et vous êtes au chemin de l'Empire.

A quick check

1 Mark's instructions at the end of **The story** are given in the **vous** form as he is talking to his parents. Give them in the **tu** form.

2 Make up 4 instructions using the **vous** forms of the imperative and the vocabulary given below. The verbs are in bold.

For example: **Passez devant la mairie.**

tourner	à	la première	**continuer**	Lille
droite	**prendre**	à	gauche	
tout	devant	droit	**passer**	
descendre	la	jusqu'	mairie	
au	coin	de	rue	

3 Replace the expressions in bold below with the appropriate pronouns.

a Tu dis **à tes parents** que c'est d'accord.
b Tu téléphones **à Andrew** pour dire quand tu vas revenir.
c Tu donnes les directions **à Alison et Patrick**.
d Patrick demande les directions exactes **à Mark**.

The next stage

1 *Aller* and *donner* in the imperative

For -**er** verbs, including **aller,** in the imperative you drop the -s from the **tu** form. **Va vite!** (*Go quickly!*) However you retain the -s before vowels or vowel sounds to make it easier to pronounce:

Vas-y!   *Go!* (there).
Donnes-en un peu!   *Give a bit / some of it!*

2 Functions of object pronouns

Reflexive and object pronouns

If you look back to indirect pronouns in **The main points 3,** you can see that **me, te, nous, vous** can serve different functions. They can be used as **reflexives, direct objects** or **indirect objects**:

Je **me** pose des questions.   *I am asking **myself** questions.* (to myself)
Il **me** regarde.   *He is looking at / watching **me**.* (me)
Il **me** pose des questions.   *He is asking **me** questions.* (to me)

To identify what type of pronoun it is, you ask the following questions:

- Are the subject and the object the same person? (= reflexive)
- Does the pronoun answer the question *who (whom) / what* (= direct object)
- Does the pronoun answer the question *to whom?* (= indirect object)

Use of indirect object pronouns

Learners often have difficulty in using **indirect object pronouns** in French because English and French verbs are sometimes different. See Unit 12 **Getting started 3.** Be particularly careful with the following verb structures:

demander à   *to ask*
téléphoner à   *to phone*

Nous **leur** demandons les directions. *We ask them for directions.*

Il **leur** téléphone. *He rings them up.* (telephones to them)

You can choose the correct pronoun by identifying the verb and asking *who (whom) / what?* or to *whom?* after it. In the sentence je *le* **donne,** le answers the question *what?*:

verb = **donne; donne** *what?* → **le;** so le is a **direct object.**

In je *lui* **donne,** lui answers the question *to whom?*:

verb = **donne; donne** *to whom?* → **lui;** therefore **lui** is an **indirect object.**

3 The difference between *y* and *en*

They can both mean *of this* but **y** replaces **à** + noun.

J'**y** pense souvent. = Je pense **à cela.** *I often think of/about this.*

whereas **en** (Unit 5 **The main points 3**) replaces **de** + *noun.*

J'**en** mange = Je mange **de cela.** *I eat some (of it).*

10

describing a sequence of events

In this unit you will learn
- to describe and ask about a process that involves several stages
- to describe and ask about a series of actions and events
- to ask and say why something happened

Topic
- planning a visit

Grammar

- Expressions of time: **hier** (*yesterday*), **aujourd'hui** (*today*), **demain** (*tomorrow*)
- Structuring adverbs: **d'abord** (*first*), **ensuite** (*then*), **finalement** (*finally*)
- Time prepositions: **pendant** (*during*), **avant** (*before*), **après** (*after*), **depuis** (*since*)
- Cause and effect: **parce que** (*because*), **donc** (*so*), **car** (*for*)

The next stage

- More about time expressions
- Speaking impersonally:
  - impersonal expressions: **Il faut** (*It is necessary*), **Il est important** (*It is important*), **Il est difficile** (*It is difficult*)
  - the present passive: **ils sont invités par...** (*they are invited by...*), **l'invitation est envoyée par...** (*the invitation is sent by...*)

Getting started

1 To talk or write about a series of events or actions, you use words such as **d'abord** (*first*), **ensuite** (*then*), **finalement** (*finally*). These words are adverbs of time (you have already met some of them in Unit 6) and they are used to make the sequence of events clear:

D'abord, tu organises le voyage, **ensuite** tu achètes les billets. **Puis** tu prépares les valises et **enfin** tu prends un taxi pour aller à l'aéroport.	*First you plan the trip, next you buy the tickets. Then you pack and finally you get a taxi to go to the airport.*

2 You can also express the idea of a sequence of events using a preposition + a noun: **avant l'aube / 6 heures** (*before dawn / 6 o'clock*), **après le coucher du soleil / 19 heures** (*after sunset / 7p.m.*), **pendant l'après-midi** (*during the afternoon*). See prepositions of time in Unit 6 **The main points 3**.

These expressions let you write and speak about things which usually take place in an established order.

3 Events are sometimes related by a process of cause and effect, rather than by time. To show this kind of relationship between events or stages in a process you need to use conjunctions, words such as **parce que** (*because*), **donc** (*so*), **car** (*for*).

La famille Dickson va en France **parce qu'**ils veulent rencontrer la famille de la copine de leur fils Mark. Ils pensent que Mark et Stéphanie vont bientôt se fiancer, **donc** ils veulent rencontrer ses parents et voir son pays. Les parents de Mark sont un peu inquiets, **car** ils ne connaissent pas bien Stéphanie.

The Dickson family is going to France because they want to meet the family of their son Mark's girlfriend. They think that Mark and Stéphanie are going to become engaged soon so they want to meet her parents and see her country. Mark's parents are a bit worried, since they don't know Stéphanie well.

4 If you want to know how events are related to one another, you will need to be able to ask questions.

• For time relationships, you can use **quand?** (*when*) or questions such as **Qu'est-ce qui se passe d'abord/ensuite?** (*What happens first/then?*) with the adverbs you have already learned (Unit 6 **The main points 4**).

Quand souhaitent-ils y aller?

When do they wish to go there?

Qu'est-ce qui se passe d'abord?

What happens first?

• For cause and effect, you can use questions beginning with **Pourquoi?** (*Why?*).

Pourquoi veulent-ils aller en France?

Why do they want to go to France?

Say it in French

1 Asking about several stages

Qu'est-ce qui se passe d'**abord** à l'agence de voyage?
Premièrement je dis que nous voulons aller en France.
Et **ensuite / après / puis?**
Il faut **ensuite** leur dire combien de personnes, l'âge de chacun et à quelle période nous voulons y aller.
Puis tu te renseignes sur les prix et les horaires et **finalement** tu fais la réservation.

What happens first at the travel agency?
First of all I say that we want to go to France.
And then?
Then I'll have to explain how many of us there are, how old we are and when we want to go.
Then you get information on prices and times and finally you make the booking.

2 Asking about a series of actions or events

Comment pouvez-vous vous payer des vacances en France?

How can you afford a holiday in France?

En décembre dernier nous avons gagné un peu d'argent à la loterie. Ta mère a **aussi** donné plusieurs cours particuliers **en février et en mars**. Ce mois-ci nous n'allons pas au restaurant et nous limitons les sorties coûteuses, **donc** nous faisons des économies. **De plus, le mois prochain** mon patron va me donner une augmentation. Pas de problème donc pour payer le billet!

Last December we won a bit of money on the lottery. Your mother also gave several private lessons in February and March. This month we aren't eating out and we're cutting down on expensive outings, so we're saving money. In addition, next month my boss is going to give me a pay rise. So, no trouble paying the fare!

3 Asking why something happened

Pourquoi est-ce que les Lemaire veulent rencontrer les Dickson à l'aéroport?

Why do the Lemaires want to meet the Dicksons at the airport?

Parce qu'il est très difficile de conduire à Paris en raison de la circulation intense.

Because it is very difficult to drive in Paris due to the heavy traffic.

Pour quelle raison les Dickson veulent-ils aller en France?

Why (For what reason) do the Dicksons want to go to France?

Ils veulent y aller pour faire la connaissance des Lemaire.

They want to go there to make the acquaintance of the Lemaires.

Pourquoi est-ce qu'ils veulent les rencontrer cet été?

Why do they want to meet them this summer?

Mark et Stéphanie vont peut-être se fiancer cette année. **Par conséquent** ils pensent qu'il est important de les rencontrer le plus vite possible.

Mark and Stéphanie are maybe going to get engaged this year. So they think it is important to meet them as soon as possible.

Comme il y a de la place chez les parents de Stéphanie, les Dickson vont y rester quelques jours.

As there is room at Stéphanie's parents', the Dicksons are going to stay there for a few days.

Puisqu'ils ont envie de connaître la région, ils vont aussi visiter différents endroits.

Since they are keen to know the area, they are also going to visit different places.

The main points

1 Expressions of time

To say when one thing happened in relation to another, you need to be able to use time expressions such as **hier** (*yesterday*), **aujourd'hui** (*today*), **demain** (*tomorrow*), the adjectives **dernier** (*last*) and **prochain** (*next*) and the demonstrative adjectives – **ce, cet, cette, ces** (See Unit 2 **The main points 5**). You will learn the tenses you need to use with these time expressions in Units 11, 13 and 14.

		past	present	future
matin	*morning*	**hier matin**	**ce matin**	**demain matin**
après-midi	*afternoon*	**hier après-midi**	**cet après-midi**	**demain après-midi**
soir	*evening*	**hier soir**	**ce soir**	**demain soir**
nuit	*night*	**la nuit dernière**	**cette nuit**	**la nuit prochaine**
semaine	*week*	**la semaine dernière**	**cette semaine**	**la semaine prochaine**
mois	*month*	**le mois dernier**	**ce mois-ci**	**le mois prochain**
été	*summer*	**en été dernier**	**cet été**	**l'été prochain**
année	*year*	**l'année dernière**	**cette année**	**l'année prochaine**

L'année dernière Stéphanie a débuté son stage en Écosse. **Cette année** la famille Dickson va en France et **l'année prochaine** les parents de Stéphanie passeront les vacances d'été chez les Dickson.

Last year, Stéphanie started her work placement in Scotland. This year the Dickson family is going to France and next year Stéphanie's parents will spend the summer holidays at the Dicksons'.

See also **Say it in French 2.**

2 Structuring adverbs

Verbs show whether they refer to the present, past or future by their form:

Mark **rencontre** Stéphanie.	*Mark meets Stéphanie.*
Mark **a rencontré** Stéphanie.	*Mark met / has met Stéphanie.*
Mark **va rencontrer** Stéphanie.	*Mark is going to meet Stéphanie.*
Mark **rencontrera** Stéphanie.	*Mark will meet Stéphanie.*

To show more precisely where the verb comes in a series of events, you can use an **adverb of time**. Adverbs usually tell us more about verbs so they are often found near verbs: **Je la rencontre souvent** (*I often meet her*). You can change the word order depending on what you want to emphasise:

Je vais **d'abord** l'inviter à prendre un café.	*I'll invite her first of all to have coffee.*
D'abord, je vais l'inviter à prendre un café.	*First I'll invite her to have coffee.*
Je vais l'inviter à prendre un café, **d'abord.**	*I'll ask her to have a coffee first.*

Other time adverbs or adverbial phrases which can be used to structure a series of events are:

d'abord	**pour commencer**	**en premier lieu**	*first*
ensuite	**deuxièmement**	**en deuxièmement lieu**	*second/next*
après	**puis / alors**	**en 3ème/4ème … lieu**	*then/after that*
enfin	**finalement**	**en dernier lieu**	*finally*

See also **The main points 1** and **The story**.

3 Time prepositions

To explain where in a sequence an event occurs, occurred or will occur, you can use a **time preposition** plus a noun:

Après les examens je vais aller plus souvent au cinéma.	*After the exams, I will go to the cinema more often.*
Avant les vacances, nous sommes toujours fatigués. **Pendant** les vacances nous nous reposons et **après** notre retour à la maison nous sommes en pleine forme.	*Before the holidays we are always tired. During the holidays we rest and after coming home we are in top form.*
Je dois étudier sérieusement **avant** les vacances.	*I have to study seriously before the holidays.*

Prepositions showing the order of a series of events (**avant, après, jusqu'à**) can be followed by the time instead of a noun:

Je téléphone souvent à mes parents **après 9 heures** et nous parlons **jusqu'à 10h**.
I often phone my parents after 9 o'clock and we talk until 10 o'clock.

L'avion de Londres arrive **avant 18 heures**, puis il part pour Berlin.
The London plane arrives before 6 o'clock, then it leaves for Berlin.

Sandy travaille **jusqu'à 10 heures**. Ensuite elle se couche.
Sandy works until 10 o'clock. Then she goes to bed.

4 Cause and effect

Events can also be related through the effects they produce. The simplest way to show this is by using the expression **parce que** (*because*). You can ask a question to find out about cause and effect using **pourquoi?** (*why?*).

Pourquoi choisissez-vous de prendre l'avion?
Why do you choose to go by plane?

Parce que c'est plus rapide.
Because it's quicker.

Other **linking expressions** can be used to show the effect or the result of something:

L'avion va plus vite que le train, **donc** nous le prenons pour aller en France.
The plane goes quicker than the train, so we will take it to go to France.

Comme l'avion est plus rapide que le train, nous avons décidé de le prendre pour aller en France.
Since the plane is faster than the train, we decided to fly to France.

C'est parce que l'avion est plus rapide que le train, **que** nous avons décidé de le prendre pour aller en France.
It's because the plane is faster than the train that we decided to fly to France.

Puisque l'avion va plus vite que le train, nous avons décidé d'aller en France en avion.
As the plane is faster than the train, we decided to go to France by plane.

See also **Say it in French 3**.

The story

Look particularly for **structuring adverbs** and **expressions of cause and effect**.

Les Lemaire se préparent à recevoir les Dickson.

Isabelle   Comment les choses vont-elles se passer? D'abord ils vont louer une voiture à l'aéroport. Ensuite il y a deux heures de route avant d'arriver chez nous. Puis il faut dîner,...

Georges   Qu'est-ce qu'on fait d'habitude quand on a des invités? On leur montre la ville et puis on visite un peu la région. Les Dickson vont sûrement s'intéresser aux environs de St Amand. On peut donc les conduire en forêt et à Valenciennes. Et on peut aussi leur présenter nos amis.

Isabelle   Oui, bien sûr, mais on prend des vacances pour se reposer! Il faut leur laisser le temps de se détendre et ne pas essayer de faire trop de choses. D'ailleurs, comme c'est la première fois qu'ils viennent en France, il faut leur montrer ce qui est typiquement français.

Georges   Il est difficile de décider ce qui est intéressant pour des Écossais parce que nous ne connaissons pas l'Écosse.

Isabelle   Il est préférable donc de leur demander ce qu'ils veulent voir – la campagne, la mer, les villes,...

Georges   Et puis, il est important de leur présenter des amis de Stéphanie car ils veulent sûrement mieux la connaître.

A quick check

1 Check **The main points 1, 2, 3, 4** and identify the expressions of time, and of cause and effect in the extracts below. Then put the 10 elements in the correct order to make a brief story entitled **Les vacances**.

- nous essayons de nous lever le plus tard possible.
- Il est donc midi et nous n'avons pas pris une décision.
- car nos parents commencent à se fâcher.
- Pendant les vacances, nous voulons nous reposer, mais nos parents préférent être très actifs.
- Après avoir mangé, il faut accepter de sortir…
- Finalement, tout le monde est prêt, et nous pouvons enfin partir.
- Puis nous prenons une douche et nous nous habillons très lentement.
- C'est pour cette raison que …
- Alors nous discutons interminablement le programme du jour.
- D'abord nous mangeons un petit déjeuner copieux.

The next stage

1 More about time expressions

Expressions such as **avant** (before), **après** (*after*), **pendant** (*during*) (see **The main points 3**), are not only found in sentences where the present tense is used. They are also used when talking about past, recently past and future events.

Avant mon stage en Grande-Bretagne je ne m'intéressais pas à l'histoire écossaise.	*Before my work experience in Great Britain, I wasn't interested in Scottish history.*
J'ai téléphoné à Stéphanie ce matin **après** 9h et nous nous sommes rencontrés **avant** 10h.	*I phoned Stéphanie after 9 o'clock and we met before 10 o'clock.*
Pendant notre séjour nous ferons beaucoup de randonnées en forêt.	*During our stay we'll take a lot of walks in the forest.*

Exception: **depuis**

To indicate how long something has been going on, or when it started, you can use: **depuis** (*for/since*).

Les Lemaire **attendent** les Dickson depuis plus de deux heures.	*The Lemaires have been waiting for the Dicksons for more than two hours.*

| Depuis 1990 nous **allons** tous les ans à Annecy en juillet. | *We've been going to Annecy in July every year since 1990.* |

The verb tenses in English and French are different here – in French the present is used (see Unit 15 **The next stage** for more information on **depuis**).

2 Speaking impersonally

It is useful to be able to speak about events without necessarily using the personal forms of the verb. There are two main ways of doing this:

• using **impersonal expressions** and
• using a form of the verb called the **passive**. The passive is based on the verb **être** (see Unit 1 **The main points 2**).

Impersonal expressions

Some of these were used in earlier sections of this unit in **The story**:

> il faut dîner...
> Il faut leur laisser le temps de se détendre.
> il faut leur montrer ce qui est typiquement français.
> Il est difficile de décider...
> Il est préférable donc de leur demander...
> Il est important de leur présenter...

Il faut (*It is necessary*) is followed directly by an infinitive:

| **Il faut apprendre** le français avant les vacances. | *We'll have to (it is necessary to) learn French before the holidays.* |

See Unit 8 **Say it in French 2, The main points 2**.

Other impersonal expressions are followed by **de** and an infinitive:

Il est difficile de comprendre Nicolas, car il parle très vite.	*It's hard to understand Nicolas because he speaks very fast.*
Il est préférable de prendre vos vacances en été.	*It's better to take your holidays in the summer.*
Il est facile de voir pourquoi Mark aime Stéphanie.	*It's easy to see why Mark likes Stéphanie.*
Il est important de connaître les parents de Stéphanie.	*It's important to know Stéphanie's parents.*
Il est ridicule de refuser de parler français.	*It is stupid to refuse to speak French.*

The present passive

Another way of speaking impersonally or indirectly is to say that something *is done by someone*. This is called the **passive voice**. You need to be able to use **être** + the past participle of another verb, followed by the preposition **par** (*by*):

Les Dickson **sont accueillis par** les Lemaire.

The Dicksons are welcomed by the Lemaires.

Les valises **sont faites par** Alison parce que les autres n'aiment pas les faire.

The packing is done by Alison because the others don't like doing it.

Notice that the past participle acts like an adjective and agrees with the person(s) or thing(s) it is telling you about:

Les Dickson (masc. plural) sont accueillis.
Les valises (fem. plural) sont faites.

-er verbs		**-ir** verbs		**-re** verbs	
infinit.	past part.	infinit.	past part.	infinit.	past part.
donner	**donné**	**accueillir**	**accueilli**	**vendre**	**vendu**
inviter	**invité**	**atterrir**	**atterri**	**rendre**	**rendu**

The past participles of regular verbs are formed in the following way:

For more information on past participles, see Unit 13 **The main points 1** and **The next stage 1**.

Here are some examples of the use of the **present passive** (for the past tenses of the passive, see Unit 15 **The main points 4**).

Je **suis** toujours **accueilli** à la gare par mes parents.

I'm always collected at the station by my parents.

Tu **es invité(e)** par mes parents à venir dîner à la maison demain.

You are invited by my parents to come and have dinner at home tomorrow.

Il **est** très **attiré** par Stéphanie.

He is very attracted by Stephanie.

Cette voiture **est louée** par nos amis écossais.

This car is hired by our Scottish friends.

Nous **sommes invités** par les Lemaire.

We are invited by the Lemaires.

Vous **êtes** souvent **photographié** par votre copine.

You are often photographed by your girlfriend.

Les Dickson **sont invités** par les Lemaire à passer leurs vacances en France.

The Dicksons are invited by the Lemaires to spend their holidays in France.

Les valises **sont faites** par Alison.

The packing is done by Alison.

11

future plans
and events

In this unit you will learn
- to speak and write about the future
- to ask about future events
- to talk about your hopes and plans

Topic
- hopes for the future

Grammar

- Regular verbs in the future tense (**le futur**)
- Common irregular verbs in the future
- Irregular verbs in -**er**: the future: **manger** (*to eat*), **appeler** (*to call*), **acheter** (*to buy*)
- Time expressions and the future
- Relative pronouns **qui** and **que**

The next stage

- The future: differences between French and English
- Other time expressions and the future
- Relative pronouns after **de**: **dont** (*of which/whom*)
- Relative pronouns referring to people, after other prepositions: **avec qui, pour qui**
- Relative pronouns referring to things, after other prepositions: **lequel** etc.

Getting started

1 When you are speaking, you can often choose to use the present tense to refer to something you are going to do. If you do this, you will usually need to use a time expression as well, to show that you are referring to the future:

Je vais en France **cet été**.	*I'm going to France this summer.*
Tu vas au cinéma **ce soir?**	*Are you going to the cinema this evening?*
Il arrive demain matin à 8 **heures**.	*He's arriving tomorrow morning at 8 o'clock.*

2 You have already learned (Unit 6 **The main points 1**) how to use **aller** (*to go*) with an infinitive to speak about the immediate future.

Je **vais acheter** un dictionnaire français-anglais.	*I'm going to buy a French-English dictionary.*
Mes parents **vont téléphoner** à Madame Lemaire ce soir.	*My parents are going to phone Madame Lemaire this evening.*
La semaine prochaine Mark **va commencer** à travailler sur une plate-forme Shell.	*Next week, Mark is going to start working on a Shell platform.*

Go back to Unit 6 and make sure you can use this form without any difficulty.

3 As well as learning to use the future tense in this unit, you will also learn some of the time expressions you need so that you can talk about and ask questions about the future. Some of them you have already learned in Unit 10 **The main points 1, 2.** In the examples in **1** (above), these expressions are in bold. Locate the two time expressions in **Getting started 2.**

4 The irregular verbs you have already covered

avoir	*to have*	**vouloir**	*to wish/want*
être	*to be*	**pouvoir**	*to be able*
aller	*to go*	**savoir**	*to know*
venir	*to come*	**devoir**	*to be obliged / have to*
faire	*to make/do*	**falloir**	*to be necessary*

use the same future endings as the regular verbs, but have an irregular stem.

Say it in French

1 Speaking and writing about the future

Les parents de Mark **arriveront** à l'aéroport Roissy-Charles-de-Gaulle. Là, ils **loueront** une voiture.	*Mark's parents will arrive at Roissy-Charles-de-Gaulle airport. There they will hire a car.*
Les Lemaire les **rencontreront** à l'aéroport et les Dickson les **suivront** en voiture.	*The Lemaires will meet them at the airport and the Dicksons will follow them in the car.*
Ils **arriveront** à St Amand deux heures plus tard.	*They will arrive in St Amand two hours later.*
Je leur **préparerai** un bon repas français.	*I will prepare them a good French meal.*
Je leur **ferai** une bonne mousse au chocolat.	*I will make them a nice chocolate mousse.*
Ils n'**auront** peut-être pas faim à cette heure-là.	*Perhaps they won't be hungry at that time.*

2 Asking about future events

À ton avis, qu'est-ce qu'ils **feront** durant leur séjour?	*What do you think they will do during their stay?*
Qu'est-ce qu'on leur **montrera**?	*What shall we show them?*

Seront-ils intéressés? **Voudront**-ils
visiter St Amand et ses environs?

Will they be interested?
Will they want to visit
St Amand and its
surroundings?

Souhaiteront-ils rencontrer des
amis de Stéphanie?

Will they want to meet
some of Stéphanie's friends?

Peut-être **auront**-ils déjà des
plans précis.

Perhaps they'll already have
specific plans.

Nous leur **demanderons** ce qu'ils
veulent faire.

We'll ask them what they
want to do.

Ce **sera** la meilleure solution.

That'll be the best way.

3 Talking about your hopes/your plans

J'espère qu'ils se **plairont**
chez nous.

I hope (that) they'll enjoy
being here.

Nous **ferons** tout notre possible
pour les mettre à l'aise.

We'll do our best to put
them at their ease.

Je ne sais pas comment nous
communiquerons, mais nous
ferons de notre mieux.

I don't know how we will
communicate, but we'll
do our best.

J'**achèterai** un bon dictionnaire
demain ou bien j'**emprunterai**
celui de Nicolas.

I'll buy a good dictionary
tomorrow or I'll borrow
Nicolas'.

J'espère que Nicolas nous
aidera.

I hope that Nicolas will
help us.

Nous **pourrons** toujours nous
faire comprendre par des
gestes et nous **demanderons** à
Nicolas d'être interprète.

We'll always be able to
make ourselves understood
with gestures and we'll ask
Nicolas to be our interpreter.

Stéphanie **reviendra** peut-être en
France à ce moment-là.

Stéphanie will perhaps come
back to France at that time.

The main points

1 Regular verbs in the future tense

For regular verbs, and many irregular verbs, the stem for this
tense is the infinitive – **aimer** (*to love*), **finir** (*to finish*). Regular
verbs ending in -**re** – **entendre** (*to hear*), **apprendre** (*to learn*),
vendre (*to sell*) – drop the e (**entendr**-, **apprendr**-, **vendr**-) before
adding the endings. The endings are the same for all French
verbs.

Subject pronoun	Stem (= infinitive)	Endings
je/j'	aimer-	**AI**
tu	finir-	**AS**
il	apprendr-	**A**
elle	visiter-	**A**
on	rencontrer-	**A**
nous	vendr-	**ONS**
vous	partir-	**EZ**
ils	grossir-	**ONT**
elles	entendr-	**ONT**

J'aimerai Stéphanie toute ma vie.
I'll love Stéphanie all my life.

Tu finiras avant moi.
You'll finish before me.

Il apprendra à faire de la planche à voile.
He'll learn to windsurf.

Isabelle **visitera** le musée avec les Dickson.
Isabelle will visit the museum with the Dicksons.

On les **rencontrera** à l'aéroport.
We'll meet them at the airport.

Nous vendrons la BMW à notre retour.
We'll sell the BMW when we get back.

Vous partirez tôt le matin.
You'll leave early in the morning.

Ils grossiront s'ils mangent trop.
They'll get fat if they eat too much.

Elles entendront de la musique française.
They'll hear some French music.

See **Say it in French 1, 2, 3.**

2 Common irregular verbs in the future

The stem of the future tense of the following verbs is very irregular and has to be learned in each case:

avoir *to have,* **être** *to be,* **aller** *to go,* **venir** *to come,* **faire** *to make/do,* **vouloir** *to wish/want,* **pouvoir** *to be able,* **savoir** *to know,* **devoir** *to be obliged / have to,* **falloir** *to be necessary.*

Bonus: the same stem is used for the conditional tense – see Unit 18 **The main points 1** and **Verb tables** page 250.

Although the stems are not the infinitives, they all end in **-r**.

Infinit.	Stem	
avoir	**aur-**	aurai, auras, aura, aurons, aurez, auront
être	**ser-**	serai, seras, sera, serons, serez, seront
aller	**ir-**	irai, iras, ira, irons, irez, iront
venir	**viendr-**	viendrai, viendras, viendra, viendrons, viendrez, viendront
faire	**fer-**	ferai, feras, fera, ferons, ferez, feront
vouloir	**voudr-**	voudrai, voudras, voudra, voudrons, voudrez, voudront
pouvoir	**pourr-**	pourrai, pourras, pourra, pourrons, pourrez, pourront
savoir	**saur-**	saurai, sauras, saura, saurons, saurez, sauront
devoir	**devr-**	devrai, devras, devra, devrons, devrez, devront
falloir	**faudr-**	il faudra
voir	**verr-**	verrai, verras, verra, verrons, verrez, verront

Stéphanie

En l'an 20.., j'**aurai** mon diplôme.	*In 20.., I will have my degree.*
Est-ce que j'**aurai** d'autres examens à passer?	*Will I have other exams to take?*
Non. Je ne **serai** plus étudiante et j'**irai** en Grande-Bretagne chercher du travail.	*No, I will no longer be a student and will go to Great Britain to look for work.*
Mark **viendra** me voir quand il ne **sera** pas sur la plate-forme de forage.	*Mark will come and see me when he is not on the oil-rig.*
Ferons-nous des promenades ensemble?	*Will we go for walks together?*
Nous **ferons** peut-être du sport.	*Perhaps we will take up sport.*
Il ne **voudra** pas m'accompagner à mes cours d'équitation mais on **pourra** aller à des matchs de foot ensemble.	*He will not want to go with me to my horse--riding lessons, but we will be able to go to foot ball matches together.*

You can also use the future in the **negative**: Il ne **voudra** pas; je ne **devrai** pas and in the **interrogative**: Est-ce que j'**aurai** … ? Ferons-nous … ?

Look for the irregular verbs in **Say it in French 1, 2, 3**.

3 Irregular verbs in -er in the future

Verbs spelt like **manger, appeler, acheter** follow the spelling rules you learned for the present tense (Unit 1 **The next stage 2**; **Verb tables** page 250).

Quand nous serons en France,   *When we are in France,*
nous **mangerons** peut-être des   *maybe we'll eat some snails.*
escargots.

(The **g** in **manger** remains soft because it is followed by **e**)

Je t'**appellerai** chez toi ce soir.   *I'll ring you at your place*
tonight.

(To avoid two neutral **e**'s following one another, the consonant **l** is doubled.)

Mon père m'**achètera** le billet et je   *My father will buy me the*
viendrai te voir en Écosse.   *ticket and I'll come and see*
you in Scotland.

(To avoid two neutral **e**'s following one another, a grave accent is added to the **e** in the second last syllable of the verb)

4 Time expressions and the future

When you use a verb in the future tense, you are referring, either explicitly or implicitly, to a period of time after the moment when you are speaking or writing.

Prepositions with time

In **2** (above) Stéphanie is talking about some years ahead (**En l'an 20..**). As well as dates, you will find it useful to be able to use the names of days and months and expressions for telling the time (see Unit 2 **Say it in French 3** and Unit 3 **The main points 4**).

Note the **prepositions** used in the time expressions in bold below:

En 3000 le monde fêtera le   *In 3000 the world will*
commencement du quatrième   *celebrate the start of the*
millénaire.   *fourth millennium.*
En été nous irons à la plage, mais   *In summer we shall go to*
au printemps nous serons dans   *the beach, but in spring*
le Massif central.   *we'll be in the Massif central.*
Elle viendra nous voir **en janvier**.   *She will come and see us in*
January.

| Nos amis les Dickson arriveront **lundi**. | *Our friends the Dicksons will arrive on Monday.* |
| Leur avion atterrira à **13 h 15**. | *Their plane will land at 1.15 p.m.* |

Prochain

You can also use the adjective **prochain** (*next*) (see Unit 10 **The main points 1**) with the names of months or days:

| Vendredi **prochain** je terminerai mon stage et je rentrerai chez moi. | *Next Friday I'll finish my work placement and I'll go home.* |

The future with *dans* and *en*

The prepositions **dans/en** are both used for future time. **Dans** is used in speaking about a point of time in the future:

Dans quinze jours mon patron sera en vacances et nous pourrons travailler plus calmement.	*In a fortnight's time my boss will be on holiday and we'll be able to work more calmly.*
Nous nous verrons **dans** huit jours et je te raconterai tout.	*We'll see one another in a week and I'll tell you everything.*
Je serai chez toi **dans** 10 minutes.	*I'll be at your place in ten minutes time.*

En is used to say how long it will take to do something:

| Il viendra **en** moins de dix minutes. | *He'll come in less than ten minutes.* (i.e. it will take him less than 10 minutes) |
| Elle finira son doctorat **en** 4 ans. | *She'll finish her doctorate in four years.* (i.e. it will take her four years) |

5 Relative pronouns *qui* and *que*

Relative pronouns are useful to make your French more polished. Like other pronouns (e.g. personal pronouns, Unit 1 **The main points 1** and Unit 5 **The main points 3**), they also make it possible for you to avoid repetition and to construct longer sentences. They are particularly useful in writing.

Qui

Qui is a **subject** pronoun. It can replace people (*who*):

Mon chef, **qui** travaille souvent en France, sera très content de vous rencontrer.	*My boss, who often works in France, will be very pleased to meet you.*
Est-ce que tu connais le directeur **qui** m'a interviewée?	*Do you know the director who interviewed me?*

or things (*which/that*):

Je veux vous parler de votre CV **qui** m'intéresse beaucoup.	*I should like to talk to you about your CV which interests me very much.*
Vous travaillerez dans le bureau **qui** se trouve à côté du mien.	*You'll be working in the office (that is) beside mine.*

Que

Que is an **object** pronoun which can replace people (*whom*):

J'ai attendu dans le bureau de la secrétaire **que** j'ai rencontrée la semaine dernière.	*I waited in the office belonging to the secretary (whom) I met last week.*

or things (*which/that*):

Je suis très content(e) de l'ordinateur **que** j'utilise pour mon travail.	*I'm very happy with the computer (that) I use for my work.*

In English, the relative pronoun is often not expressed:

the office (that is) beside mine
the secretary (whom) I met last week
the computer (that) I use for my work

Some verbs are always followed by a preposition

téléphoner à quelqu'un (*to phone someone*)
demander à quelqu'un (*to ask someone*).

Where verbs like this are followed by a relative pronoun, **qui** (*whom*) is used for people:

M. Monnoury est le nom de la personne **à qui** j'ai téléphoné ce matin.	*Mr Monnoury is the person (whom) I phoned this morning.*

The story

In this passage, look for the **verbs in the future tense**, the **time expressions** and the **relative pronouns**.

Qu'est-ce que tu fais? Stéphanie, Mark, Alison et Georges parlent de leur travail et de leurs projets d'avenir.

Stéphanie Le travail que je fais actuellement ne m'intéresse pas beaucoup, mais après mon stage je pourrai trouver un emploi quand je rentrerai en France. C'est mon chef, Mr Williams, qui m'encourage à apprendre l'anglais et à me perfectionner en informatique. «Vous utiliserez toujours l'anglais et l'informatique» me dit-il.

Mark A présent le poste que j'occupe m'oblige à passer beaucoup de temps sur plate-forme. Mais j'aurai besoin de cette expérience du forage en mer. C'est l'expérience pratique qui sera nécessaire si je veux avoir plus tard un poste de cadre.

Alison Le travail d'un professeur devient de plus en plus dur. Pendant les vacances, qui passent toujours beaucoup trop vite pour moi, on ne se repose pas. Il faut préparer les cours car il est difficile de trouver le temps qu'il faut pendant le trimestre. Ce soir, comme d'habitude, je corrigerai des copies et je préparerai des polycopies que j'utiliserai demain.

Georges Un plombier ne dort jamais tranquille car à tout moment le téléphone peut sonner. Il faut toujours dépanner des gens qui ont des problèmes – des problèmes qui n'arrivent que la nuit ou pendant le week-end. J'espère que mon fils aura un emploi qui lui permettra de bien dormir et de ne pas travailler à des heures impossibles.

A quick check

Change the **verbs** and the **time expressions** in the following passages to the future:

Stéphanie	Aujourd'hui je travaille au bureau. Je tape des lettres pour mon chef et j'assiste à une réunion des membres du département de ressources humaines. Est-ce que tu viens me chercher à 17 heures 30? On achète de quoi manger à *Marks et Spencer*.
Mark	Ce soir je mange avec Stéphanie. Mardi je ne suis pas ici car je prends l'hélicoptère et je recommence à travailler sur une plate-forme BP. Je règle l'appareil de forage et je le contrôle par ordinateur. Nous sommes sur plate-forme pour trois semaines. Je ne vois pas Stéphanie et elle me manque beaucoup.
Alison	Aujourd'hui à 4 heures nous avons une réunion de tous les enseignants. Elle dure au moins deux heures et demie et je ne rentre pas avant 19 heures 30. Vous préparez vous-mêmes le dîner - et il ne faut pas oublier de faire la vaisselle!
Georges	Est-ce que nous pouvons manger à 21 heures ce soir? La réparation de la tuyauterie chez Madame Vincent n'est pas terminée et je dois aussi remplacer les robinets dans sa salle de bains.

The next stage

1 The future: differences between French and English usage

Using the future in place of the present

After: **quand** *when*, **lorsque** *when*, **aussitôt que** *as soon as*, **dès que** *as soon as* French uses a verb in the future: Quand vous **arriverez**... but in English we use a verb in the present: *When you arrive...*

Nous les **accueillerons** quand ils **arriveront**.	*We'll welcome them when they arrive.*
Lorsque Mark **partira**, Stéphanie se **sentira** très triste.	*When Mark leaves, Stéphanie will feel very sad.*

Accueillir follows the same pattern as the verb **cueillir**. See **Verb tables** page 258.

The future perfect

In French a tense called the **future perfect** (Quand j'**aurai terminé** mon travail) is used where in English you would use a past tense. This emphasizes that one action will come after the other:

Je te téléphonerai quand
j'**aurai terminé** mon travail.

I'll ring you when I've finished work.

Dès que j'**aurai réparé** le tuyautage
de Madame Vincent, je rentrerai
à la maison.

As soon as I've repaired Madame Vincent's pipes, I'll come home.

2 Other time expressions and the future

Some useful expressions are found in the table in Unit 10 **The main points 1**. In addition, you may need:

après-demain *the day after tomorrow*
le lendemain *the following/next day*
demain en huit *a week tomorrow/tomorrow week*
mercredi en quinze *a fortnight on Wednesday*

3 Relative pronouns after *de*: *dont*

If you want to use a relative pronoun:

- with expressions which always include the preposition **de**:
  avoir besoin de *to need*, **avoir peur de** *to be afraid of*
- with verbs which can be followed by **de**: **parler de** *to speak about / of*, **rêver de** *to dream about*

the relative pronoun **dont** replaces **de** + **qui** (*of whom; of which*):

Les employés **dont** nous avons
besoin sont difficiles à trouver
dans cette région de l'Écosse.

The employees we need are hard to find in this part of Scotland.

Les résultats **dont** il a peur seront
publiés la semaine prochaine.

The results he's afraid of will be published next week.

Je ferai ce soir les exercices **dont**
le professeur nous a parlé.

This evening, I'll do the exercises the teacher spoke about.

La carrière en marketing **dont**
je rêve me permettra de voyager
partout en Europe.

The career in marketing I dream of will allow me to travel all over Europe.

The word order with **dont** is important.

noun		subject	verb
les employés	**dont**	nous	avons besoin
les résultats	**dont**	il	a peur
les exercices	**dont**	le professeur	a parlé
la carrière	**dont**	je	rêve

4 Relative pronouns referring to people, after prepositions

La collègue **avec qui** je viens au bureau habite près de chez moi.
Le client **pour qui** je fais des recherches veut améliorer ses logiciels.

The colleague I come to work with (with whom I come to work) lives near me.
The client I'm doing research for (for whom I'm doing research) wants to improve his software.

5 Relative pronouns referring to things, after prepositions

When they follow a preposition, relative pronouns referring to **things** have the following form. They agree with the word they replace in number and gender:

	Masculine	Feminine
Singular	lequel	laquelle
Plural	lesquels	lesquelles

As-tu vu l'ordinateur **sur lequel** je travaille? (ordinateur: masc. sing. → **lequel**)

Have you seen the computer I work on (on which I work)?

Les compagnies pétrolières **avec lesquelles** nous traitons sont rarement françaises. (compagnies: fem. plur. → **lesquelles**)

The oil companies we work with (with which we work) are rarely French.

Les salles de bain **dans lesquelles** je travaille sont tres révelatrices de la vie des gens. (salles de bain: fem. pl. → lesquelles)

The bathrooms I work in (in which I work) reveal a lot about people's lives.

12

orders and instructions

In this unit you will learn
- to ask someone to do or not to something
- to give orders and instructions

Topic
- money
- the bank

Grammar

- The imperative of regular verbs
- The imperative of irregular verbs
- The present tense for giving instructions
- The infinitive and giving instructions
- Giving negative instructions
- Two pronoun objects
- The imperative with two pronoun objects

The next stage

- Other ways of giving orders
- Polite requests

Getting started

1 The imperative form of the verb is used for giving instructions (see Unit 9 **The main points** 2). To do this, you use parts of the present (indicative) tense. By now, you should have a secure knowledge of the present tense of regular and some irregular verbs. Check these in Units 1, 2, 5, 6, 8 and 9 and in your notebook.

2 In this unit you will learn how to use verbs which have more than one pronoun object. You learned about direct pronoun objects in Unit 5 **The main points** 3, and indirect pronoun objects in Unit 9 **The main points** 3. You should revise them before beginning this unit.

Alors, est-ce que tu **les** prends ou est-ce que tu ne **les** prends pas?	*Well, are you taking them or are you not taking them?*
Stéphanie laisse tomber son carnet de chèques et Mark **le** ramasse.	*Stéphanie drops her cheque book and Mark picks it up.*
Mark **leur** téléphonera et **leur** dira que les Lemaire les **rencontreront** à l'aéroport.	*Mark will phone them and tell them that the Lemaires will meet them at the airport.*

3 The distinction between direct and indirect objects is sometimes difficult for English speakers. See Unit 9 **The next stage** 2. You can identify the **direct object** by asking *what?* or *whom?* after the verb:

I gave the teller the cheque. → verb = *gave* → *gave **what?*** → *the cheque*

'*cheque*' is the **direct object**.

The **indirect object** is not related directly to the verb, but to a preposition, usually *to*. Because the preposition is often not expressed in English, it can take a moment to work out what is the indirect object.

You can decide whether an object is indirect by asking the question *to / for whom?* after the verb:

I gave the cheque → to / for whom? → *(to) the teller.*
'teller' is the **indirect object**.

Study the following examples and ensure that you can recognize the difference between the two types of object in English.

Give him the money! → *'money'* = direct object: *'him'* = indirect object.
Give it to George!
Let's buy them this book!
I'll give him the money.
Sandy brought her a cup of tea.

4 If you use the imperative without some kind of accompanying polite expression, it can be a very direct way of telling someone to do something or getting something done. For polite requests, you can use set expressions with **vouloir** (*to wish/want*). Some of the expressions given in Unit 4 **The main points 1** will help.

Say it in French

1 Asking someone to do something

Est-ce que nous pouvons nous arrêter à la banque? J'ai besoin de retirer de l'argent.	*Can we stop at the bank? I need to draw some money.*
Arrête s'il te plaît, car je voudrais acheter un petit cadeau pour Madame Lemaire.	*Please stop, because I would like to buy a small gift for Madame Lemaire.*
N'oublie pas les conseils de notre prof de français pour demander à quelqu'un de répéter quelque chose.	*Don't forget our French teacher's advice for asking someone to repeat something.*
Pourriez-vous répéter s'il vous plaît?	*Could you repeat please?*

Pouvez-vous parler plus lentement s'il vous plaît?	*Can you speak more slowly please?*

2 Giving orders

Andrew, **occupe-toi** bien de la maison.	*Andrew, look after the house well.*
Sors la poubelle le mardi matin.	*Put the bin out on Tuesday mornings.*
Ne te lève pas trop tard.	*Don't get up too late.*
Toi et tes amis, **n'utilisez pas** trop le téléphone.	*You and your friends must not use the phone too much.*
Contacte ton oncle si tu as des problèmes.	*Contact your uncle if you have any problems.*
Suivons les conseils de Mark.	*Let's follow Mark's advice.*
Il ne **faudra** pas rouler pas trop vite car il est important de lire les panneaux routiers.	*We mustn't drive too fast, as it is important to read the road signs.*
Insérer la carte bancaire, taper le numéro personnel. **Choisir** le montant.	*Insert you bank card, key in your personal number. Select the amount.*
Retirer la carte avant d'obtenir l'argent.	*Take your card out before the money is issued.*

The main points

1 The imperative of regular verbs

The verbs you have studied so far have been in the **indicative** (or standard) **mood**. It is used for making statements. See Unit 9 **The main points 2**. The **imperative mood** is used for giving instructions or orders. In French, there are three forms of the imperative, depending on the situation the speaker is in:

- speaking to a friend
- speaking to someone you don't know well or to a group of people
- speaking to a group of people in which you are included

Look back at **Say it in French** and see if you can find examples of the first two.

In each of the three situations described you can use part of the present tense of the verb (without a subject) to give an instruction:

• speaking to a friend, use the **tu** form of the verb:

Donne cet argent à ton frère!	*Give that money to your brother!*
Finis tes devoirs!	*Finish your homework!*
Viens ici!	*Come here!*

For -**er** verbs only, the **s** of the **tu** form is dropped in the imperative: **Donne!** (*Give!*), **Achète!** (*Buy!*), **Chante!** (*Sing!*).

• speaking to someone you don't know well or to a group of other people, use the **vous** form of the verb:

Insérez votre argent dans la fente à droite!	*Insert your money in the slot on the right!*
Protégez votre carte des regards indiscrets!	*Hide your card from prying eyes!*
N'**oubliez** pas votre carte de crédit!	*Don't forget your credit card!*

• speaking to a group of people in which you are included (*Let's do something* in English), use the **nous** form of the verb:

Allons à la banque ce matin!	*Let's go to the bank this morning!*
Essayons ma carte bancaire!	*Let's try my bank card!*
Apprenons à mieux parler français!	*Let's learn to speak French better!*

The **tu** and **vous** forms are more common than this form which, although it expresses a suggestion rather than an order, is thought of as an imperative in French.

In the boxes below, the imperative forms are in bold:

jouer *to play*	**finir** *to finish*	**rendre** *to give back*
je joue	je finis	je rends
tu **joue(s)**	tu **finis**	tu **rends**
il/elle/on joue	il/elle/on finit	il/elle/on rend
nous **jouons**	nous **finissons**	nous **rendons**
vous **jouez**	vous **finissez**	vous **rendez**
ils/elles jouent	ils/elles finissent	ils/elles rendent

Ne joue pas avec Pierre!	*Don't play with Pierre!*
Jouons le concerto No 3 ce soir!	*Let's play the Concerto No 3 tonight!*

Jouez dans le jardin!	*Play in the garden!*
Finis tes devoirs!	*Finish your homework!*
Finissons le gâteau!	*Let's finish the cake!*
Ne **finissez** pas tout aujourd'hui!	*Don't finish the lot today!*
Rends ton amie heureuse!	*Make your friend* (f) *happy!*
Rendons grâce à Dieu!	*(Let's) give thanks to God!*
Rendez ce livre à Andrew, s'il vous plaît.	*Give this book back to Andrew please.*

2 The imperative of irregular verbs

Avoir **and** *être*

Some irregular verbs such as **avoir** and être have special forms in the imperative:

avoir	Aie!	Ayons!	Ayez!
être	Sois!	Soyons!	Soyez!

Irregular *-er* verbs

Irregular -er verbs (Unit 1 **The next stage 2**) have an irregular **tu** form (see **Verb tables** page 262):

Achète trois kilos de cerises!	*Buy three kilos of cherries!*
Appelle ce numéro à 8 heures!	*Phone this number at 8 o'clock!*
Jette ce papier dans la poubelle!	*Throw that paper in the bin!*
Lève-toi et marche!	*Arise and walk!*
Répète ce que je dis!	*Repeat what I say!*

Some of the irregular verbs in **-er**, e.g. **manger** (*to eat*), **placer** (*to place/put*), are also irregular in the **nous** form, if the pronunciation of the consonant becomes hard before the vowel **o**. This is avoided by inserting an **e** before the ending for verbs ending in **-ger** (e.g. **manger**) or by adding a cedilla to the **c** for verbs ending in **-cer** (e.g. **placer**):

Mangeons cette tarte!	*Let's eat this tart!*
Plaçons notre argent en lieu sûr!	*Let's invest our money in a safe place!*

Other irregular verbs

aller	Va!	Allons!	Allez!
faire	Fais!	Faisons!	Faites!
savoir	Sache!	Sachons!	Sachez!

3 The present tense for giving instructions

When you are speaking, you can use the present tense (including the subject – **tu** or **vous**) to give a direct order:

Tu ouvres un compte et **tu** y verses l'argent.	*You open an account and you put the money in.*
Tu prépares le terrain et **tu plantes** les fraises.	*You prepare the soil and you plant the strawberries.*
Tu tonds le gazon avant de sortir.	*(You) mow the lawn before you go out.*
Vous chantez tous ensemble.	*You all sing together.*
Vous rangez les bicyclettes et **vous nettoyez** vos baskets.	*(You) put the bikes away and (you) clean your trainers.*

4 The infinitive for giving instructions

In formal situations, where written instructions are given, the infinitive is sometimes used to issue a direct instruction:

Composer votre numéro personnel.	*Type in your PIN.*
Demander une liste de nos services bancaires.	*Ask for a list of our banking services.*
Retirer votre carte et votre argent.	*Take your card and your money.*
Se munir d'une pièce d'identité.	*Provide yourself with some ID.*

See **Say it in French 2**.

5 Giving negative instructions

The negative of the imperative is formed, as for the indicative, by using **ne** and **pas** (see Unit 1). As in other tenses, **ne** precedes the verb and **pas** follows it:

Ne mettez **pas** vos cartes de crédit dans votre porte-monnaie!	*Don't put your credit cards in your purse!*
Ne gaspillez **pas** votre argent!	*Don't waste your money!*
Ne dépensons **pas** sans réfléchir!	*Let's not spend without thinking about it!*

For negative commands using the infinitive (**4**, above), both **ne** and **pas** come before the verb:

| **Ne pas utiliser** la carte après la date d'expiration! | *Do not use the card after the expiry date!* |

6 Two pronoun objects

You learned how to use direct pronoun objects in Unit 5 **The main points 3,** and indirect pronoun objects in Unit 9 **The main points 3.** A verb can sometimes have both a direct and an indirect object. See above, **Getting started 3.**

| Je donnerai **un chèque** (direct object) **à Mark** (indirect object). | *I'll give a cheque to Mark.* (*I'll give Mark a cheque.*) |

If both the objects are pronouns, they both go before the verb:

| Je **le** (the cheque) **lui** (to Mark) donnerai. | *I'll give it to him.* |

There is a fixed order when two object pronouns are used. It is not related to whether the pronouns are direct or indirect objects – you have to learn the order in which the pronouns are used in French.

The grid overleaf, which looks a bit like the placings for a football team, shows you the order to follow, from left to right, when you are using two pronoun objects. The most usual combinations are from columns 1 and 2:

| Je **vous les** envoie. | *I'll send them to you.* |

and from columns 2 and 3:

| Mark **le lui** achète. | *Mark buys it for him/her.* |
| Les Dickson **les** (les cadeaux) **leur** (aux Lemaire) apportent. | *The Dicksons take them* (the gifts) *to them* (the Lemaires). |

subject	object pronouns					verb
	1	**2**	**3**	**4**	**5**	
	me					
	te					
Je	se	le	lui			envoie
Mark	nous	la	leur	y	en	achète
Les Dickson	vous	les				apportent
	se					

7 The imperative with two pronoun objects

Using two pronoun objects with the direct imperative is simple. The objects follow the verb (as they do in English) and the direct object comes before the indirect object. The indirect object pronouns are: **moi, toi, lui, nous, vous, leur**, the same forms (except for **leur**) as the stressed pronouns (see Unit 1 **The main points** 8). The verb and the pronouns are joined by hyphens:

Envoie-**le-lui**!	*Send it to him/her!*
Apportons-**les-leur**!	*Let's take them to them!*
Achetez-**la-moi**!	*Buy it for me!*

If the imperative verb is in the negative, the rules for order given in **6**, above, apply:

Ne **le lui** envoyez pas!	*Don't send it to him/her!*
Ne **les leur** apportons pas!	*Let's not take them to them!*
Ne **me** l'achetez pas!	*Don't buy it for me!*

The story

In the conversation below, pick out the **verbs in the imperative** and the **object pronouns**.

Nicolas, son père et sa mère essaient de calculer comment il peut se permettre d'aller en Grande-Bretagne l'année prochaine.

Georges   Tu devrais changer complètement tes habitudes. Tu mets de l'argent de côté, tu ouvres un nouveau compte en banque, tu y verses au moins 150 euros par mois et tu ne dépenses rien!

Nicolas   C'est facile pour toi! Fais ceci! Fais cela! Ne fais pas ceci! Tu commandes et moi j'obéis. Mais pour moi, ce n'est pas facile. Imagine un peu! Je me prive de sorties, de vêtements, de livres, de cinéma. Pense à l'effet que tout cela aura sur moi!

Isabelle Oui, écoute Georges! Aide-le! Ne lui donne pas d'ordres! Donne-lui plutôt des conseils!

Georges C'est ce que j'essaie de faire. Je veux l'aider. Ne me le reprochez pas! D'ailleurs j'allais suggérer qu'on lui donne l'argent que nous avons mis de côté pour la nouvelle voiture. Donnons-le-lui! Il en a vraiment besoin.

Isabelle Alors là, non! Ne nous affolons pas! Il a une année pour trouver cet argent. Il faut imaginer d'autres solutions parce que moi, je veux une nouvelle voiture!

Nicolas Ne vous fâchez pas! Restons calmes. Je vous en prie, n'imaginez pas que je suis complètement stupide. Je me trouverai un petit boulot, je ferai du baby-sitting et bientôt j'aurai l'argent qu'il me faut.

A quick check

1 Choose one word from each of the three lists below. Put the verb (Column 1) into the imperative (**tu** form) and make a list of five instructions for a friend going to France.

verbs	nouns	places
utiliser	**une carte bancaire**	**la banque**
acheter	**une carte Visa**	**les restaurants**
changer	**vos euros**	**les magasins**
	des devises	**un grand magasin**
	une ceinture porte-monnaie	

Exemple: **Achetez une ceinture porte-monnaie dans un grand magasin!**

2   In the same way, make a second list of five negative instructions using the imperative (**vous**) form:

verbs	nouns	places
ouvrir	**votre porte-monnaie**	**le métro**
changer	**votre carte de crédit**	**l'hôtel**
laisser	**votre argent**	**votre chambre**
mettre	**votre passeport**	

Exemple: **Ne laissez pas votre argent dans votre chambre!**

3   Look at the pronouns in bold in the following sentences, and imagine the nouns they might be replacing:

Exemple: Mark **les lui** achète → **Mark achète des roses à Stéphanie.**

Tu **nous le** donnes.
Il **la lui** apporte.
Nous **te les** offrons.

4   Answer the following questions, using two pronoun objects in your answer:

Exemple: **Mark, offre-t-il les fleurs à Stéphanie?** → Oui, il **les lui** offre.

Est-ce que tu donnes cet argent à notre fils?
Ces cadeaux, vous les apportez aux Lemaire?
Nous recommandons cet hôtel à nos amis?

The next stage

1 Other ways of giving orders

As well as using the imperative, you can also give instructions using some impersonal expressions such as **il faut** and **il est nécessaire/essentiel de** followed by an infinitive. (See Unit 9 **The main points 1** and Unit 10 **The next stage 2**.)

Il faut épargner quand on est jeune.	*You have to save when you are young (It is necessary to save ...)*

| Il est nécessaire d'encaisser le chèque cette semaine. | *You have to pay the cheque in this week. (It is necessary to pay ...)* |

See **Say it in French 2.**

2 Polite requests

If you want to make a polite request, rather than give an order, you can use set expressions based on the conditional tense of the verb **vouloir** (for more information on the conditional see Unit 18 **The main points 1, 3**).

| **Voudriez-vous** fermer la fenêtre? | *Would you close the window please?* |
| **Voudrais-tu** me prêter quelques euros? | *Would you lend me a few euros please?* |

To make an order or an instruction even more polite, you can add an expression which makes it less direct:

n'est-ce pas?	Tu partages cet argent avec ton frère, n'est-ce pas?	*You're sharing that money with your brother, aren't you?*
s'il vous plaît **s'il te plaît**	Rends ce livre à Andrew, s'il te plaît.	*Give that book back to Andrew, please.*
je vous en prie **je t'en prie**	Je vous en prie, ne parlez pas de la crise économique!	*Please (I beg you), don't talk about the economic crisis!*

See **Say it in French 1.**

13 talking about past events

In this unit you will learn
- to talk and write about past events
- to talk and write about a series of events that happened in the past
- to say that things took place over a period of time
- to present events that happened in the recent past

Topic
- travel preparations
- arrivals

Grammar

- The past participle
- The perfect tense with **avoir**
- The perfect tense with **être**
- The immediate past: **venir de**
- Other time expressions for sequencing events in the past

The next stage

- Agreement of the past participle
- Uses of **il y a** (*ago*)

Getting started

1 To form the perfect tense of most verbs, you use the present tense of **avoir** (Unit 1 **The main points 2**) plus a past participle (**2** below). Notice the use of the present tense of **avoir** in the following examples:

Mark **a** rencontré Stéphanie à Aberdeen.	*Mark met Stéphanie in Aberdeen.*
Stéphanie **a** présenté Mark à ses parents.	*Stéphanie introduced Mark to her parents.*
Nous **avons** rendu visite aux Lemaire en France.	*We visited the Lemaires in France.*

2 To speak about the past, you will need to know the past participle of each verb. In earlier units you learned a number of infinitives – the basic form of the verb – such as **donner**, **finir**, **vendre**. The past participle is formed from the infinitive:

donner	Il a **donné** un cadeau à sa mère.	*He gave his mother a gift.*
finir	Nous avons **fini** de dîner.	*We've finished eating.*
vendre	Vous avez vendu votre maison.	*You've sold your house.*

Check the irregular verbs you learned in Units 1, 5, 6, 8, 11, and those you have in your notebook. Sometimes the past participle of these verbs is irregular too:

pouvoir → **pu**
vouloir → **voulu**
savoir → **su**
dire → **dit**

3 A small number of verbs do not use the present tense of **avoir**, but of **être**, to form the perfect tense. You have learned the present tense of **être** (Unit 1 **The main points 2**, so you will easily recognize it when you find it as part of the perfect tense:

Nicolas **est** sorti à 20 heures.	*Nicolas went out at 8 o'clock.*
Il **est** allé voir son copain Pierre.	*He went to see his friend Peter.*
Ils **sont** montés dans la chambre de Pierre.	*They went up to Peter's room.*

4 In many ways past participles function as adjectives and follow the same rules for agreement.

• If they are used with a noun, they agree with it in number and gender:

un rendez-vouz manqué (m. sing.)	*a missed meeting*
une lettre tapée (fem. sing.)	*a typed letter*
des bureaux partagés (m. plural)	*shared offices*
des réunions chargées (fem. plural)	*packed meetings*

• If past participles are used with **avoir** or **être** to form the perfect tense, there are rules about agreement as these examples show:

J'ai rencontré votre secrétaire. Je l'ai rencontrée la semaine dernière. Elle s'est excusée et nous avons parlé du problème.	*I met your secretary. I met her last week. She apologized and we talked about the problem.*

You will gradually learn more about agreement of past participles.

5 In Unit 6 **The main points 1**, you saw how the present tense of **aller** + infinitive can be used to show that something is going to happen in the immediate future. In a similar way, the present tense of **venir** + **de** + an infinitive can be used to describe something in the immediate past – something which *has just* happened. (You learned the present tense of **venir** in Unit 6 **The main points 2**.)

Nicolas **vient de** rentrer. Il est 23 heures.	*Nicolas has just come in. It is 11 o'clock.*
Georges **vient de** se réveiller. Il n'est pas content. Isabelle **vient de** se coucher.	*Georges has just woken up. He isn't happy. Isabelle has just gone to bed.*
Ils **viennent de** se rendre compte que Nicolas grandit.	*They have just realized that Nicolas is growing up.*

6 In Unit 11, **The main points 4**, you met a set of time prepositions which are used to talk about the future. Similarly, there are prepositions – some of them the same – which are frequently used in speaking about the past:

Après le déjeuner, j'ai pris le bus pour aller en ville.
After lunch, I got the bus to go to town.

Avant le commencement du film, j'ai acheté des bonbons.
Before the film started, I bought some sweets.

Pendant le film, je me suis endormi.
During the film, I went to sleep.

7 Just as there are time expressions which are associated with the future (Unit 11 **The main points 4**), there are time expressions which you will find useful for speaking about the past:

Nicolas? Je l'ai vu **hier**. Il m'a téléphoné **avant-hier** et **hier soir** je l'ai vu au cinéma.
Nicolas? I saw him yesterday. He phoned me the day before yesterday and last night I saw him at the cinema.

La semaine dernière je l'ai rencontré en ville et nous sommes allés au parc.
Last week I met him in town and we went to the park.

Say it in French

1 Past events

Les Lemaire **ont décidé** d'aller accueillir les Dickson à l'aéroport.
The Lemaires decided to go and meet the Dicksons at the airport.

L'avion **a atterri**! ... Les voilà! Dis donc! Ils **ont apporté** beaucoup de bagages! ...
The plane has landed! ... There they are! Goodness! They've brought a lot of luggage! ...

Comment allez-vous?
How are you?

Avez-vous **fait** bon voyage?
Did you have a good trip?

Très bien, merci. Nous **n'avons pas eu** trop de problèmes.
Fine, thank you. We didn't have too many problems.

Vous **êtes arrivés** à l'heure. Nous **avons laissé** la voiture dans le parking, car souvent l'avion est en retard.
You arrived on time. We've left the car in the car park, because the plane is often late.

2 A series of events in the past

Avant le départ de l'avion, nous **avons pris** un café. Ensuite, nous **avons suivi** les indications pour la salle de départ. Là nous **avons attendu** quelques minutes, et finalement ils **ont annoncé** le départ de l'avion.	*Before the plane left, we had a coffee. Then we followed the signs to the departure lounge. We waited there a few minutes, and finally they announced the departure of the flight.*

3 Events that took place over a period of time

Le voyage **a demandé** beaucoup de préparation. Entre décembre et mars je **suis allée** plusieurs fois à l'agence de voyage. J'**ai téléphoné** souvent aussi. Mon mari **s'est occupé** de l'argent.	*The trip needed a lot of preparation. Between December and March I went to the travel agency several times. I phoned often as well. My husband looked after the money.*
Quand on lui a expliqué comment fonctionne la carte Cirrus, il a décidé de ne pas acheter beaucoup d'euros.	*When they explained how the Cirrus card works, he decided not to buy a lot of euros.*

4 Events in the recent past

Le vol a été assez intéressant...	*The flight was quite interesting...*
L'avion **vient de** décoller, quand un passager **se lève, sort** un pistolet, et **commence** à menacer l'hôtesse.	*The plane has just taken off, when a passenger gets up, gets out a gun, and starts threatening the stewardess.*

The main points

1 The past participle

The past participle is used as part of the **perfect tense** in both French and English. Examples in English are: I have **given,** they have **brought,** it has **landed,** we have **waited.**

Regular verbs

For all regular French verbs, and for some irregular verbs such as **aller** (*to go*), **sortir** (*to go out*), **partir** (*to leave*), the past participle is formed from the infinitive, the part of the verb that ends in -er, -ir, -re:

apporter	*to bring*	→	**apporté**	*brought*
atterrir	*to land*	→	**atterri**	*landed*
attendre	*to wait*	→	**attendu**	*waited*

See also Unit 10, **The next stage 2**.

Irregular verbs and the past participle

For irregular verbs, you will have to learn the past participles, just as you learned them for irregular verbs in English: **gone, hung, ate** for example.

You should keep a list of irregular past participles in your notebook. Here are some of the most common, to add to those you have already noted in **Getting started** above. You will find a more complete list of irregular verbs at the back of the book.

Infinitive		Past participle	Infinitive		Past participle
avoir	*to have*	**eu**	**prendre**	*to take*	**pris**
écrire	*to write*	**écrit**	**suivre**	*to follow*	**suivi**
faire	*to make/do*	**fait**	**venir**	*to come*	**venu**
mettre	*to put*	**mis**	**voir**	*to see*	**vu**

As you have seen (**4** above), there are rules about the agreement of past participles with subjects or objects. Some of the rules for agreement are given in **The next stage 1**.

See also the present passive, Unit 10 **The next stage 2**.

2   The perfect tense with *avoir*

Look back at **Say it in French**. The verbs in the perfect tense are in bold.

The perfect tense is used to speak about events that happened in the past. It is a **compound tense**. That means it is composed of more than one verb: the present tense of **avoir** (the **auxiliary verb**) and the past participle of a second verb (the **main verb**).

Most verbs in French form the perfect tense using the appropriate part of the present tense of **avoir** (Unit 1 **The main points** 2) and the past participle.

Since you can already use the present tense of **avoir**, the formation of the perfect tense is not difficult:

J'**ai** acheté les billets.	*I (have) bought the tickets.*
Tu **as** préparé les valises.	*You did the packing.*
Elle **a** envoyé une lettre.	*She (has) sent a letter.*
Nous **avons** fini les préparatifs.	*We've finished the preparations.*
Vous **avez** choisi quelle agence de voyage?	*Which travel agency did you choose?*
Ils **ont** attendu l'arrivée de l'avion.	*They waited for the arrival of the plane.*

Now look again at the examples in **Getting started 1** and **2** and **Say it in French 1** and **2**.

The negative

If you are using this tense in the **negative**, you put **ne** after the subject and **pas** after the auxiliary verb (the present tense of **avoir**):

Mon mari **n'a pas** acheté les billets.	*My husband hasn't bought the tickets.*
Nous **n'avons pas** téléphoné à Stéphanie.	*We didn't ring Stéphanie.*

Inversion

To ask more formal questions with inversion, reverse the order of the subject and the auxiliary verb (**avoir**):

As-tu envoyé la lettre?	*Did you send the letter?*
Pourquoi **ont-ils** attendu l'arrivée de l'avion?	*Why did they wait for the plane to arrive?*

3 The perfect tense with *être*

There are two groups of verbs which *do not* use **avoir** to form the perfect tense.

Verbs which express a change of state or movement

aller	*to go*	**je suis allé(e)**
entrer	*to enter*	**tu es entré(e)**
arriver	*to arrive*	**elle est arrivée**
monter	*to go up*	**on est monté**
tomber	*to fall*	**nous sommes tombé(e)s**
naître	*to be born*	**ils sont nés**
venir	*to come*	**elle est venue**
sortir	*to go out*	**tu es sorti(e)**
partir	*to leave*	**il est parti**
descendre	*to descend*	**elle est descendue**
rester	*to remain*	**vous êtes resté(e)s**
mourir	*to die*	**ils sont morts**

The negative and question forms are the same as those shown above for **avoir**:

Nicolas, **tu n'es pas arrivé** à l'heure.
Nicolas, you didn't arrive on time.

Est-elle arrivée avec ses parents?
Did she arrive with her parents?

Reflexive verbs

(See Unit 3 **The main points 2.**)

All reflexive verbs form the perfect tense with **être**:

s'habiller	**ils se sont habillés**	*they got dressed*
se lever	**nous nous sommes levé(e)s**	*we got up*
se promener	**je me suis promené(e)**	*I went for a walk*

The negative and question forms of these verbs are the same as for the other verbs, but because of the reflexive pronoun object, they look different:

Nous **ne nous sommes pas levé(e)s** pour le déjeuner.
We didn't get up for breakfast.

Se sont-ils habillés chaudement avant de sortir?
Did they dress warmly before going out?

Agreements

As you can see from these examples, and from those in **Getting started**, when the perfect tense is formed with **être** as the auxiliary verb, the past participle agrees in *number* and in *gender* with the *subject*. Check the examples above, and in **The story**, for this new type of agreement.

Avoir and *être* form the perfect tense with *avoir*:

Isabelle n'**a** pas **eu** le temps de nettoyer la cuisine.	*Isabelle did not have time to clean the kitchen.*
Patrick **a été** surpris quand Alison a commencé à parler français.	*Patrick was surprised when Alison started to speak French.*

The position of adverbs with the perfect tense

Short adverbs can go between the auxiliary verb and the past participle:

Ils l'ont **vite** fait.	*They did it quickly.*
Il a **rarement** voyagé.	*He has seldom travelled.*
Il a **vraiment** été surpris.	*He was really surprised.*

Longer adverbs (Unit 6 **The main points 4**) normally go after the past participle:

Ils ont préparé leur voyage **méticuleusement**.	*They prepared their trip carefully.*
Ils ont appris les bases de la grammaire française **remarquablement vite**.	*They have learnt the basics of French grammar remarkably quickly.*

4   The immediate past: *venir de*

The present tense of **venir** (Unit 6 **The main points 2**) followed by **de** and an infinitive is used to say that something has just happened or has just been done:

Je **viens de descendre** de l'avion.	*I've just got off the plane.*
Nous **venons de rencontrer** les Lemaire.	*We have just met the Lemaires.*
Georges et Isabelle **viennent de** nous **accueillir**.	*Georges and Isabelle have just greeted us.*

Look back at **Say it in French 4** for another example.

5   Other time expressions

To say when you did something in the past, you need to be able to use expressions to show when you did it. See Unit 10 **The main points 1**:

| avant-hier
*the day before
yesterday* | hier
yesterday
hier matin
yesterday morning
hier soir
yesterday evening | aujourd'hui
today |

Hier matin nous sommes allés à Lille.

Yesterday morning we went to Lille.

The story

In this conversation, identify the **verbs in the perfect tense** (with both **avoir** and **être**). Make a list of the **past participles** and add any that are new to your list.

Isabelle raconte à une amie, Chloé, l'arrivée des Dickson à l'aéroport.

Isabelle Nous avons essayé d'apprendre un peu d'anglais. Heureusement que les Dickson ont appris le français avant d'arriver.

Chloé Est-ce qu'ils ont parlé français tout de suite?

Isabelle Non. Ils ont commencé par quelques mots en anglais, mais après, ils se sont souvenus de leurs cours de français.

Chloé Mais qu'est-ce que tu as fait? Vous ne vous êtes pas sentis un peu gênés?

Isabelle Si, Si. J'ai trouvé la situation très difficile. Des gens qu'on n'a jamais rencontrés, et des étrangers en plus. Et il ne faut pas oublier que Stéphanie a beaucoup insisté sur l'importance de cette visite! Quand ils sont descendus de l'avion, j'ai eu peur.

Chloé Je t'admire vraiment! Je n'ai jamais pu parler avec des gens que je ne connais pas, et comme je n'ai jamais appris l'anglais...

Isabelle Le commencement n'a pas été facile. Mais avec de la bonne volonté on a réussi à communiquer. Ce sont peut-être les futurs beaux-parents de notre fille, après tout. Et ils ont été charmants avec elle. Ils l'ont accueillie chez eux et Alison, surtout, l'a beaucoup aidée. Nous nous sommes bien entendus finalement.

A quick check

1 Imagine that you are Georges Lemaire. Write five sentences about what happened when you went to meet the Dicksons at the airport. (You will find some suggestions in **The story**.)

2 Fill in the appropriate auxiliary verb (**avoir** or **être**) in the following sentences:

Quel voyage! D'abord le taxi n'_____ pas arrivé à l'heure. Nous _____ téléphoné à la compagnie et ils _____ envoyé un autre taxi, mais nous _____ arrivés à la gare deux minutes avant le départ du train. Nous _____ couru et nous _____ attrapé le train de justesse. Avec des valises très lourdes et tous les paquets des enfants, nous _____ eu du mal à trouver des places. Finalement, nous nous _____ assis dans un wagon fumeurs. Naturellement ça m'_____ donné la migraine!

3 Write answers to the following questions:

Q Vous êtes parti(e)s en vacances A Oui, nous…
   cette année?
Q Où êtes-vous allé(e)?   A Nous…
Q Qu'est-ce que vous avez vu?   A Nous…
Q Tu as acheté des souvenirs?   A Non, je…
Q Et ta soeur, elle en a acheté?   A Bien sûr que oui! Elle…

The next stage

1 Agreement of the past participle

When the perfect tense is formed with **avoir**, the past participle agrees with the **direct object** if the object *comes before* the verb:

J'ai acheté les billets. (Direct object = **les billets**.
                           No agreement – it *follows* the verb.)

Je **les** ai achetés.   (Direct object = **les**, replacing **les billets**.
                           It comes *before* the verb, so the past
                           participle agrees.)

Où sont les valises? (fem. plural)   *Where are the cases?*
Mark les a mises dans la voiture.   *Mark put them in the car.*
Et les passeports? (masc. plural)   *And what about the passports?*

Tu ne les as pas perdus, j'espère!   *You haven't lost them, I hope!*

Mais non! Quelle idée! Je les ai fourrés dans mon sac avec toutes les choses que nous avons préparées pour le voyage.

Of course not! What an idea! I shoved them in my handbag with all the other things we got ready for the trip.

2 Use of *il y a* (ago)

To say how long ago something happened, you can use **il y a** (*ago*).

Ils sont arrivés **il y a** huit jours.
They arrived a week ago.

Nous sommes allés à Lille **il y a** cinq jours.
We went to Lille five days ago.

Stéphanie a téléphoné **il y a** trois heures.
Stephanie phoned three hours ago.

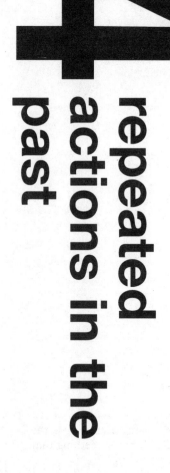

14

repeated actions in the past

In this unit you will learn
- to talk and write about past habits/things you used to do regularly
- to discuss situations in the past which lasted for some time
- to discuss single events set in the past
- to say how often you did things, or how frequently things were done

Topic
- memories

Grammar

- The imperfect tense
- Time expressions used with the imperfect
- Using the perfect and the imperfect together

The next stage

- Other time expressions used with the imperfect
- More about the perfect and the imperfect used together
- The use of the imperfect in direct and indirect (reported) speech

Getting started

1 In Unit 13, you learned how to use the perfect tense. French has another past tense – the imperfect – which is used to express other aspects of the past:

Quand il **était** jeune, Patrick **travaillait** à Londres. Tous les jours il **prenait** le métro.	*When he was young, Patrick worked in London. Every day he took the tube.*

2 The imperfect is used with some of the same time expressions as the perfect tense (Unit 13 **The main points 5**). There are other time expressions which show that something was done frequently (**tous les week-ends**) or that a situation in the past lasted some time (**pendant cette période**). The imperfect is the correct tense to use after these expressions:

Avant son mariage, Patrick ne s'intéressait pas au bricolage. **Pendant cette période,** il habitait un petit appartement désagréable. **Tous les week-ends** il faisait du sport. **A cette époque-là,** il sortait beaucoup et **le samedi** il allait toujours au match de foot.	*Before he got married, Patrick wasn't interested in DIY. During that time, he lived in a horrible little flat. Every weekend he played sport. At that time he went out a lot and on Saturdays, he always went to the football match.*

3 Sometimes when you are speaking about the past, you have to choose whether to use the perfect or the imperfect, depending on what kind of past event you want to speak about. For single events (**s'est marié, est né, a cessé**) use the perfect (Unit 13 **The main points 1, 2, 3**). For something that happened frequently (**il voyageait**) use the imperfect:

Patrick s'**est marié** avec Alison en 1977. Au début, il **voyageait** beaucoup, mais, quand Mark **est né**, il **a cessé** de voyager.

Patrick got married to Alison in 1977. At first, he used to travel a lot, but, when Mark was born, he stopped travelling.

4 When you are talking about the past, you use the imperfect for things which happened often. There are a number of time expressions you can use to show how frequently something happened:

Tous les jours Patrick allait à son travail. **Le samedi,** il allait au match de foot. **Deux fois par mois,** il emmenait Mark et Alison au zoo. **Une fois par an,** ils prenaient des vacances.

Every day Patrick went to work. On Saturdays, he went to the football match. Twice a month, he took Alison and Mark to the zoo. Once a year they went on holiday.

Say it in French

In the following passages, you will find examples of when to use the structures in **Getting started**. Note particularly the time expressions that are followed by the imperfect.

1 Past habits/things you used to do regularly

Après la naisssance de Nicolas, nous n'**allions** plus au cinéma. **Le samedi,** nous **prenions** le bus pour aller chez mes parents et **le dimanche** nous nous **promenions** dans le parc près de chez nous. **Le vendredi soir,** mes parents **gardaient** Nicolas, et Georges et moi, nous **faisions** les courses.

After Nicolas was born, we didn't go to the cinema any more. On Saturdays we used to get the bus to go to my parents' place and on Sundays we went for a walk in the park near our house. On Friday evenings, my parents looked after Nicolas, and Georges and I did the shopping.

2 Situations in the past which lasted for some time

Je me souviens des années 70. Nous n'**avions** pas beaucoup d'argent mais nous **étions** fous de

I remember the seventies. We didn't have much money but we were mad on rock

musique rock. Il n'**était** pas facile
d'acheter les disques que nous
voulions à St Amand, et nous ne
pouvions pas aller tous les
week-ends à Lille.

music. It wasn't easy to
buy the records we wanted
in St Amand and we
couldn't go to Lille every
weekend.

3 Single events in the past set against a background

Oui, la vie n'**était** pas facile
à cette époque-là, et comme
nous **voulions** acheter une voiture,
il **fallait** faire des économies.
Quand nous nous **sommes mariés**,
mes parents nous **ont donné** de
l'argent et c'est cet argent qui
nous **a permis** d'acheter notre
première maison.

Yes, life wasn't easy then,
and as we wanted to buy a
car, we had to save money.
When we got married, my
parents gave us some
money and it was that
money that made it
possible for us to buy our
first house.

4 Talking about how often you did things

Vous vous souvenez? Nous allions
tous les ans à St Omer. Oui,
c'était **chaque année**, en août,
pendant les vacances scolaires.
Il faisait beau **tous les jours** et
le matin, nous allions nous
promener sur la plage de bonne
heure. Après, nous allions toujours
nous baigner **plusieurs fois**
par jour. Une fois par semaine il y
avait un vieux film au cinéma.
C'était **toujours** débile, mais on y
allait quand même.

Do you remember? We
used to go to St Omer
every year. Yes, every year,
in August, during the
school holidays. The
weather was good every
day and in the morning we
used to go for a walk on
the beach early. Afterwards,
we always went for a swim
several times a day. Once a
week there would be an
old film at the cinema. It
was always pathetic, but
we used to go just the same.

The main points

1 The imperfect tense

The imperfect tense of the verb is a single word, formed from a
stem. You form the stem by taking the **vous** form (the second

person plural) of the present tense (Unit 1). You take off the **-ez** ending:

avoir	vous avez	→	**av-**
parler	vous parlez	→	**parl-**
finir	vous finissez	→	**finiss-**
prendre	vous prenez	→	**pren-**
Exception: **être**		→	**ét-**

To the stem, you add the following endings:

-ais, -ais, -ait, -ions, -iez, -aient:

Quand nous étions petits je te **détestais**.	*When we were little I hated you.*
Tu ne **cessais** pas de pleurer.	*You wouldn't stop crying.*
Notre père (il) **t'aimait** mieux que moi.	*Our father liked you better than me.*
Maman (elle) te **donnait** tout ce que tu voulais.	*Mum gave you everything you wanted.*
Toi et Papa (vous) **étiez** toujours ensemble.	*You and dad (you) were always together.*
Maman et moi (nous) **faisions** souvent la cuisine.	*Mum and I (we) were often doing the cooking.*
Nos parents (ils) ne **savaient** pas que tu me **frappais**.	*Our parents didn't know that you used to hit me.*

The imperfect is used for:

• repeated actions or habits in the past

Tu me battais **tous les jours**.	*You used to hit me every day.*
Je me plaignais **souvent** à nos parents.	*I often used to complain to our parents.*

• situations which lasted a long time, or an indefinite time, in the past:

Nous partagions une chambre.	*We used to share a room.*
Nos parents n'avaient pas beaucoup d'argent.	*Our parents didn't have much money.*

Look back at **Say it in French** and decide why the imperfect was used in each case.

2 Time expressions with the imperfect

Since this tense is used for things which were done frequently in the past, it is found with time expressions showing how often things were done:

souvent	*often*
fréquemment	*frequently*
tous les jours	*every day*
tous les mois	*every month*
tous les ans	*every year*
le samedi	*every Saturday /on Saturdays*
deux fois par jour	*twice a day*
cinq fois par trimestre	*five times a term*

Le samedi nous allions au cinéma.	*On Saturdays, we used to go to the cinema.*
J'allais **souvent** voir mes parents.	*I often went to see my parents.*
Tous les jours Patrick allait à son travail.	*Every day Patrick went to work.*
Il fallait passer un contrôle continu **deux fois par trimestre.**	*There was continuous assessment twice a term.*

The imperfect is also used with time expressions which refer to long periods or situations which lasted a long or indefinite time in the past. Look for some of these in **Say it in French**.

A cette époque, nous étions plutôt pauvres.	*At that time, we were rather poor.*
Avant la naissance de ma soeur, mes parents pouvaient continuer à jouer au golf.	Before my sister was born, my parents could still play golf.
Tout le monde portait des vêtements bizarres **pendant les années 70.**	*Everyone wore weird clothes in the seventies.*

à cette époque	*at that time*
avant cet événement	*before that happened*
pendant cette période	*during that time*

3 Using the imperfect and the perfect together

Both the perfect and the imperfect are used when talking about past time. Often you will need to make a choice between the two tenses. In the examples in **Getting started 3** and in **The story**, you will find the two tenses used together.

Sometimes the imperfect is used to set the scene in the past, while the perfect is used for a single action or a series of actions (**Say it in French 3, The story**):

Oui! Je me souviens! Tu **étais** horrible. Tu **pleurais** tout le temps et Maman s'**occupait** de toi toute la journée. Je te **détestais**. Puis Andrew **est né** et tout **a changé**.

Yes, I remember! You were awful. You cried all the time and Mum looked after you the whole day long. I hated you. Then Andrew was born and everything changed.

Sandy:

Je n'**étais** pas horrible! Tu ne **voulais** pas jouer avec moi et tu **prenais** tous mes jouets. Quand tu **as commencé** à l'école, tu **as cessé** de m'embêter.

I was not awful! You didn't want to play with me and you used to take all my toys. When you went to school, you stopped bothering me.

See also **The next stage 2**.

The story

Make a list of all the **verbs in the imperfect** and another one of the **verbs in the perfect**. Can you explain why each one was chosen?

Isabelle parle à Alison de la jeunesse de Stéphanie

Isabelle   Elle était très calme quand elle était petite et elle a appris à parler et à marcher plus tôt que Nicolas. Elle avait trois ans quand elle est allée à l'école maternelle et elle ne l'aimait pas beaucoup. Même très petite, elle chantait toujours juste et je n'ai pas été surprise quand, plus tard, elle a décidé de chanter avec la chorale *Les Quatre Vents*. Avant d'aller en Écosse, elle chantait avec la chorale deux fois par semaine.

Tous les enfants font des dessins à l'école, mais, pour Stéphanie, le dessin était très important. Elle adorait les couleurs vives et pour son anniversaire et à Noël elle demandait toujours des crayons ou des peintures à l'eau. Et elle aimait beaucoup les musées d'art. On allait assez souvent voir des expositions, au moins deux ou trois fois par an. Je me souviens d'une exposition des impressionnistes à Paris, quand elle avait 12 ans. Elle a tant insisté que je suis allée à Paris avec elle, et nous avons vu l'exposition trois fois!

A quick check

1 Using the verbs in the imperfect below, write five or six sentences about your childhood (real or imagined).

Nous habitions...
J'aimais...
Je n'aimais pas...
Mon père était...
Nous n'avions pas de...
Mes frères et mes soeurs étaient...
Ce qui nous amusait, c'était...

2 In the following paragraph, Nicolas is speaking about his memories of childhood. Identify the two time expressions which should be followed by the imperfect and the two usually followed by the perfect. Fill in the blanks with the appropriate tense (imperfect or perfect). See **The main points 3**.

Nicolas: Tu te souviens, Stéphanie? Moi, j'(**être**) toujours plus petit que toi et pendant mon enfance, j'(**avoir**) honte, parce que ma soeur (**être**) plus grande que moi. Et puis, un jour, je (**remarquer**) que je (**mesurer**) quelques centimètres de plus que toi. Ce jour-là, je (**faire**) la fête!

The next stage

1 Other time expressions used with the imperfect

- **de** (date) **à** (date)   *from* (date) *to* (date)

De 1995 à 1999, Stéphanie allait au collège.   *From 1995 to 1999, Stéphanie was at college.*

- **entre** (date) **et** (date)

Nicolas était membre d'un club cinéma **entre septembre 1999 et juin 2000.**

between (date) *and* (date)

Nicolas was a member of a film club between September 1999 and June 2000.

2 More about the perfect and the imperfect used together

See above, **The main points 3.**

To say what the situation was, or what was going on, when something else happened, you use the imperfect for the background situation and the perfect for a single event:

Quand Stéphanie **est allée** à Aberdeen, elle **avait** 20 ans.

When Stephanie went to Aberdeen, she was 20.

Je lui **ai offert** de l'argent, parce qu'elle **était** sans le sou.

I gave her some money because she didn't have a penny.

Nous lui **avons ouvert** un compte en banque, car elle ne **savait** pas organiser ses finances.

We opened a bank account for her, because she didn't know how to organize her money.

Un soir, elle **a téléphoné** pendant que j'**étais** absente. Elle **voulait** me raconter ses problèmes. Elle **a rappelé** plus tard.

One evening, she phoned while I was out. She wanted to talk to me about her problems. She phoned back later.

3 The imperfect in direct and indirect (reported) speech

Notice how the tenses change when direct speech (the actual words spoken by the person) is reported and becomes indirect speech:

	Direct speech	Indirect speech
Georges	J'aime beaucoup le ball-trap mais je déteste l'équitation.	Georges a dit qu'il **aimait** beaucoup le ball-trap mais qu'il **détestait** l'équitation.

I like clay pigeon shooting very much but I hate horse-riding.

Nicolas Tous les soirs je m'amuse avec mon ordinateur. J'ai des amis partout dans le monde et on corrrespond par courrier électronique.

Every evening I play with my computer. I have friends all over the world and we correspond by e-mail.

Georges said that he liked clay pigeon shooting very much but (that) he hated horse-riding.
Nicolas m'a assuré qu'il **s'amusait** avec son ordinateur tous les soirs. Il a expliqué qu'il **avait** des amis partout dans le monde, et qu'ils **correspondaient** par courrier électronique.
Nicolas told me that he played with his computer every evening. He explained that he had friends all over the world and that they corresponded by e-mail.

15 going back in the past

In this unit you will learn
- to relate various past events to one another
- to say that something happened before or after something else
- to write an account of past actions and events
- to say that something was done by someone else

Topic
- travel memories
- First World War battle sites

Grammar

- The pluperfect tense
- Conjunctions of time
- Complex sentences
- The perfect passive

The next stage

- Other ways of expressing the passive
- Saying how long something has been going on
- Using the perfect infinitive
- The infinitive after **avant de** (*before*)

Getting started

1 If you want to go further back in time than the immediate past, you need to be able to use the pluperfect tense. This works just like the similar tense in English where we use the auxiliary verb *had*:

Before I began to learn French, I **had** already **learned** Spanish.

To form this tense, you will need to use the imperfect of **avoir** (Unit 14 **The main points** 1) and use the appropriate past participles (Unit 13 **The main points** 1).

Mon père m'a offert un téléphone portable pour mon anniversaire. Malheureusement, **j'avais** déja **vu** un portable que j'aimais et je **l'avais acheté** avant mon anniversaire. Mon père était déçu.	*My father gave me a mobile phone for my birthday. Unfortunately I had already seen a mobile that I liked and I had bought it before my birthday. My father was disappointed.*

2 To use longer sentences explaining when one event happened in relation to another, and if you want to write more formal French, you will find there are a number of useful words which join parts of a sentence together. In Unit 10 (**The main points** 4) you learned some conjunctions expressing cause and effect. Here you will learn some you can use in time sequences.

Nicolas et moi, nous avons décidé de nous connecter à l'Internet **après que** son professeur en avait parlé. Le soir, Nicolas envoyait des mels **pendant que** moi, je	*Nicolas and I decided to get the Internet connection after his teacher had spoken about it. In the evening Nicolas used to send*

regardais la télé. Il est vite devenu expert et demande maintenant un nouvel ordinateur.

e-mails while I was watching TV. He quickly became an expert and now he's asking for a new computer.

3 You have already met the present passive in Unit 10, **The next stage 2**. In this unit, you will learn how to use the passive form when you are speaking about the past, to say that something *was done by someone*.

L'ordinateur **a été acheté** par Georges pour Nicolas, et à Noël beaucoup de jeux informatisés lui **ont été offerts**. Les logiciels de base ont été développés par Microsoft.

The computer was bought for Nicolas by Georges, and at Christmas he was given lots of computer games. The basic software was developed by Microsoft.

Say it in French

1 Relating various past events to one another

Isabelle L'année où nous sommes allés en Belgique – c'était en été 2000?
Non, c'était avant. Nicolas **avait gagné** le prix au club cinéma en mars 1999 et c'est cette année-là que nous y sommes allés.
Georges Non. C'était l'année après, 2000, qu'il a gagné le prix et il a décidé d'aller à Paris pour visiter les studios de France 2. La Belgique, c'était donc en 1999.

The year we went to Belgium - was that in summer 2000?
No, it was before. Nicolas had won the prize at the film club in March 1999 and that's the year we went. No. It was the year after, 2000, that he won the prize and he decided to go to Paris to visit the France 2 studios. So Belgium was in 1999.

2 Something happened before or after something else

Isabelle Je me souviens d'un concert de la chorale de Stéphanie, *les Quatre Vents*, à Lille. Nous **avions réservé** une chambre à l'hôtel bien avant la date du concert. **Puis** ils ont changé la date.

I remember a concert given by Stéphanie's choir, les Quatre Vents, in Lille. We had reserved a hotel room well before the date of the concert. Then they changed the date.

Georges Non, tu n'**avais pas réservé** la chambre avant l'annonce de la nouvelle date! Tu **avais fait** la réservation au restaurant **d'abord. Ensuite,** ils ont annoncé le changement de date et nous avons eu du mal à trouver une chambre d'hôtel.

No, you hadn't booked the hotel room before the new date was announced! You had made the restaurant booking first. Then they announced the change of date and we had trouble finding a hotel room.

3 Writing about past actions and events

Devoir d'Alison pour la classe de français – *Notre visite en France* (*Alison's homework for her French class* – Our trip to France)

En septembre nous **avions décidé** d'aller visiter les Lemaire en France. J'ai donc écrit à Isabelle Lemaire pour lui demander de nous suggérer des dates. Nous **avions commencé** nos cours de français en octobre et au Nouvel An, nous **avions commencé** à préparer le voyage. Au commencement du mois de février j'ai écrit encore une fois à Isabelle Lemaire pour lui confirmer les dates de notre visite.

In September we had decided to visit the Lemaires in France. So I wrote to Isabelle Lemaire to ask her to suggest some dates. We had started our French classes in October and at the New Year, we had started to make preparations for the trip. At the beginning of February I wrote again to Isabelle Lemaire to confirm the dates of our visit.

4 Something was done by someone else

Les cours de français **ont été organisés** par le conseil de la ville. Une salle **a été réservée** au lycée et les manuels et les dictionnaires français-anglais **ont été achetés** par le professeur.

The French classes were organized by the town council. A room was booked in the secondary school and the textbooks and the French-English dictionaries were bought by the teacher.

The main points

1 The pluperfect tense

This is the tense of the verb you use to say that something **had** already happened before another event in the past, or to say that you **had** already done one thing before you did something else.

Like the perfect (Unit 13 **The main points 1, 2, 3**), it is made up of two words, an auxiliary verb (**avoir** or **être**) and a past participle:

• the auxiliary verb is in the imperfect (Unit 14 **The main points 1**)

| avoir | → | **j'avais** (+ past participle) |
| être | → | **j'étais** (+ past participle) |

• the past participles are the same as the ones you learned for the perfect (Unit 13 **The main points 1**).

Avant d'aller en France:

J'	**avais écrit**	à Isabelle Lemaire.
Tu	**avais fait**	des économies.
Il (Georges)	**avait essayé**	d'apprendre l'anglais.
Nous	**avions appris**	le français.
Vous (G & I)	**aviez préparé**	votre itinéraire.
Ils (les enfants)	**avaient promis**	d'être sages.

2 Conjunctions of time

In order to be able to tell a story, or speak or write about a number of past events, you need to use linking words called **conjunctions**. See also Unit 10 **The main points 4**. These words allow you to situate the different happenings in relation to one another.

Some of the most useful conjunctions of time are:

quand	when
après que	after
pendant que	when/while
puis/ensuite	then

Quand Mark nous a parlé de Stéphanie, nous avons compris que c'était sérieux.

When Mark spoke to us about Stéphanie, we realized that it was serious.

Après que nous avions décidé de visiter les Lemaire, nous avons commencé à apprendre le français.

After we had decided to visit the Lemaires, we started to learn French.

Mark perfectionnait son français
pendant qu'il parlait à
Stéphanie.

Mark was improving his
French when he was talking
to Stéphanie.

3 Complex sentences

When you are speaking or, more particularly if you are writing, about a series of events, you will need to be able to link different events and experiences together into longer sentences.

To do this, you use a variety of other conjunctions:

Simple link	Time	Reason/purpose	Opposition
et *and*	**après que** *after* **pendant que** *while* **quand** *when*	**parce que** *because* **car** *because/for* **donc** *thus*	**mais** *but* **pourtant** *however / and yet* **cependant** *however*

J'ai commencé à apprendre le français **et** Patrick veut l'apprendre aussi.

I started learning French and Patrick wants to learn too.

Nous avons acheté les cadeaux **après que** Stéphanie nous avait parlé de ses parents.

We bought the presents after Stéphanie had spoken to us about her parents.

La visite en France a été organisée **parce que** notre fils Mark a une partenaire française.

The trip to France was organized because our son Mark has a French partner.

Georges et Isabelle ne parlent pas anglais, **pourtant** nous avons réussi à communiquer avec eux.

Georges and Isabelle don't speak English, nevertheless we managed to communicate with them.

4 The perfect passive

In Unit 10 **The next stage 2,** you learnt how to use the present passive (present tense of **être** + the past participle).

You will also need the passive to talk or write about past events. To do this, you use the perfect of **être**, followed by a past participle:

La visite en France **a été suggérée** par Mark.

The visit to France was suggested by Mark.

Les cours de français **ont été donnés** par un professeur du lycée.

The French classes were taken by a secondary teacher.

Les plans de St Amand et de sa région nous **ont été envoyés** par les Lemaire.

The maps of St Amand and the region were sent to us by the Lemaires.

The story

While you are reading this letter, make a note of the **verbs in the pluperfect tense** and the **conjunctions** or **linking words** Alison uses.

Alison écrit à son professeur de français en Écosse.

Cher Alain,

Vous m'aviez demandé de vous écrire pendant notre séjour en France. J'avais donc commencé une lettre le jour de notre arrivée, mais nous avions trop de choses à faire et tout était si intéressant que je n'ai pas pu écrire plus tôt.

Nous avions prévu de passer quelques jours chez les Lemaire et de visiter ensuite la région de St Amand. Plusieurs suggestions de choses à voir nous ont été offertes par Georges et Isabelle Lemaire, et nous allons maintenant quitter St Amand et visiter les sites des batailles de la première guerre mondiale dans le nord de la France. Nous irons ensuite à Paris.

Pendant que Patrick parlait à Georges, Isabelle et moi avons bavardé de nos enfants, de sorte que je comprends mieux Stéphanie maintenant.

Je n'y avais pas pensé, mais ma formation de professeur d'histoire et de géographie est très utile pour un voyage à l'étranger. Je me suis renseignée sur la situation géographique de St Amand et parce que j'ai lu plusieurs livres sur l'histoire de la France et de la première guerre mondiale, le nord de la France m'intéresse beaucoup.

Nous vous remercions des excellents cours de français et nous espérons que vous passez des vacances très agréables. A bientôt!

Avec notre meilleur souvenir,

Alison Dickson

A quick check

1 In the following paragraph, the verbs are in bold. Re-write the paragraph one stage further back in the past, putting the verb in the perfect tense into the pluperfect and the verbs in the present tense into the perfect:

Avant la première guerre mondiale, les Allemands **ont** bien **préparé** leurs armées, de sorte que les armées des alliés **perdent** des millions d'hommes dans des batailles dans le nord de la France. A Verdun, des millions de soldats **meurent** et les Allemands **traversent** facilement la ligne Maginot.

2 Using the conjunctions given, connect the sentences below into a single complex sentence:

a Dans le nord de la France la terre est très plate.
Le paysage est quelquefois monotone.
Les villages sont agréables à voir.
Conjunctions: donc, mais

b Les coquelicots poussent dans les champs de la Flandre.
On achète des coquelicots ce jour-là en Grande-Bretagne.
La guerre a cessé le 11 novembre.
On célèbre le jour de l'Armistice le 11 novembre.
Conjunctions: car, et, parce que

The next stage

1 Other ways of expressing the passive

In French, the passive form of the verb (être + past participle) is used less often than in English. There are two other ways of expressing the passive (something being done to someone / something by someone / something else) in French:

Using *on* as the subject of the sentence

On nous a priés de ne pas prendre de photos dans le musée.
Quand nous avons visité les cimetières de guerre, **on** nous a expliqué la construction de la Ligne Maginot.

*We **were asked** not to take photos in the museum.
When we visited the war cemeteries, the construction of the Maginot Line **was explained** to us.*

Using a reflexive verb

Le guide a commencé par nous dire: «**Je m'appelle** Henri. Mon grand-père est mort à Verdun.»

*The guide began by saying: "I **am called** Henri. My grandfather died at Verdun"*

Le nombre de morts dans ces batailles **s'explique** par le manque de préparation des troupes alliées.

*The number killed in these battles **is explained** by the lack of preparation of the allied troops.*

Des livres d'histoire et des plans des sites intéressants **se vendent** en librairie.

*History books and maps of the interesting sites **are sold** in bookshops.*

2 To say how long something had been going on

In French you use the word **depuis** (*since*, *for*), with the imperfect, to say that something *had been going on* for a certain time when something else happened:

J'attendais **depuis une heure** quand Stéphanie a enfin téléphoné.

*I **had been waiting for an hour** when Stéphanie finally phoned.*

Quand Nicolas est né, nous étions à St Amand **depuis** cinq ans.

*When Nicolas was born we had been in St Amand **for** five years.*

3 Using the perfect infinitive

To say that you did something after (**après**) something else, you can use **après** with a perfect infinitive. This is made up of the past participle of the main verb, with the infinitive form of **avoir** before it:

Après avoir quitté St Amand, nous avons visité le nord de la France.

***After leaving** St Amand, we visited the north of France.*

Après avoir acheté un ordinateur, Georges a commencé à s'intéresser à l'Internet.

***After buying** a computer, Georges started to get interested in the internet.*

4 The infinitive after *avant de*

You can use an infinitive after **avant de** to say something happened before something else:

Avant de quitter St Amand, nous avons remercié les Lemaire.

***Before leaving** St Amand, we thanked the Lemaires.*

Georges s'est renseigné auprès d'un ami, **avant d'acheter** un ordinateur.

*Georges asked a friend for advice **before buying** a computer.*

16 wishes, probability and possibility

In this unit you will learn
- to talk about what you want and what you wish for
- to say what is probable or possible
- to construct longer and more complex sentences

Topic
- visiting Paris

Grammar

- Using the subjunctive
- Forming the present subjunctive: regular verbs
- The subjunctive of irregular verbs
- Verb 'signals' for the subjunctive
- Other verb signals followed by the subjunctive: *wishing, wanting, fear, regret*
- Impersonal expressions followed by the subjunctive: *necessity, importance, pity*
- Relative pronouns ce **qui** and ce **que**

The next stage

- Probability and the subjunctive
- Other verbs followed by the subjunctive
- The subjunctive to express the future
- **Lequel, laquelle** after the preposition **de**

Getting started

1 There is another very useful form of the verb in French called the **subjunctive**. You have to use it in some common contexts. You will soon learn to recognize the most frequent ones:

Ma femme **veut que** nous **allions** à Paris, mais, avant d'y aller, **il faut que** nous **fassions** une réservation à l'hôtel.	*My wife wants us to go to Paris, but before we go, we'll have to reserve a hotel room.*

2 The subjunctive is used after certain expressions which function as 'signals'. Different signals are used to express wishes, to show doubt or approval and to give orders:

Les Lemaire **veulent que** nous passions la nuit à Arras.	*The Lemaires want us to spend the night in Arras.*
Ils **doutent que** nous trouvions un hôtel à Amiens.	*They doubt we'll find a hotel in Amiens.*
Ils **sont contents** que nous allions ensuite à Paris.	*They are glad that we're going to to Paris afterwards.*
Georges **insiste** que Patrick prenne la carte Michelin.	*Georges insists that Patrick takes the Michelin map.*

3 You have already learned a number of impersonal expressions in Unit 10 **The next stage 2**. In this unit you will learn some to express probability and possibility:

Patrick n'a pas l'habitude de conduire en France. **Il est possible** qu'il ait des problèmes, mais **il est probable qu'**il s'y habituera facilement.

Patrick is not used to driving in France. It is possible that he will have some problems, but probably he will easily get used to it.

4 In Unit 11 **The main points 5**, you met the relative pronouns **qui** and **que**. In this unit, you will learn how to write more polished sentences using other relative pronouns:

Ce qui attire Alison, c'est surtout l'histoire de la Révolution française. Patrick et Alison visiteront le musée Carnavalet **dont** la section sur la Révolution est très connue.

What interests Alison especially is the history of the French Revolution. Patrick and Alison will visit the Carnavalet Museum whose section on the French Revolution is well known.

La Révolution est la période pendant **laquelle** les institutions politiques de la France moderne ont été créées.

The Revolution is the period during which the political institutions of modern France were created.

Say it in French

1 What you want or wish for

Je veux que nous **visitions** le Musée Carnavalet et **j'aimerais que nous allions** aussi au Musée de l'Histoire de France. Patrick **souhaite** qu'on **ait** le temps de voir des stades de sport.

I'd like us to visit the Carnavalet Museum and I'd like us to go to the Musée de l'Histoire de France too. Patrick hopes we have time to visit some sports stadiums.

2 Envisaging possibilities

Avant d'arriver à Paris, **il est possible qu'**on **voie** la cathédrale à Beauvais.
Penses-tu que nous **puissions** nous y arrêter?
Je ne crois pas que nous **ayons** le temps de nous arrêter en route.

*Before we get to Paris, we could see the cathedral at Beauvais.
Do you think we could stop there?
I don't think we'll have time to stop on the way.*

3 Longer and more complex sentences

Les touristes à Paris ont un grand choix. Les grands monuments **dont** on parle dans tous les guides, les musées dans **lesquels** on trouve des expositions magnifiques, les attractions pour **lesquelles** la ville est connue, voilà **ce qu'**il faut voir!

Tourists in Paris have a great choice. The big monuments all the guide books talk about, the museums in which there are magnificent exhibitions, the attractions for which the city is famous, that's what they have to see!

The main points

1 Using the subjunctive

Most of the verbs you know how to use are in what is called the **indicative mood** (all tenses in Units 1–15; see also Unit 12 **The main points 1**). This is the mood for statements and comments. There are two other important moods:

• to express *commands* and *instructions*, you use the **imperative mood.** (Unit 12)
• to express some feelings: *wishing, wanting, approval, disapproval, regret, doubt* etc. you use the **subjunctive mood.** (Units 16, 17)

The **subjunctive mood** (*If only he **were** here; Intelligent though she **be** etc*) has virtually disappeared from English but it is very frequently required in French.

Its use is always signalled by a word or expression (the 'signal') which comes before it in the sentence. There are two stages in learning to use it:

• learning how to form the subjunctive (stem + endings)
• learning to recognize the various 'signals' (Units 16, 17 and 18)

Look back at **Getting started 1** and **2** and **Say it in French 1** and **2**, and see if you can identify some of the 'signals'.

2 Forming the present subjunctive

The present subjunctive of both regular and irregular verbs is formed from the **ils/elles** (3rd person plural) part of the present tense. You are already familiar with this form (Unit 1).

To get the stem, you remove the **-ent** ending:

ils parlent	→	**parl-**
ils choisissent	→	**choisiss-**
ils mettent	→	**mett-**

To the stem you add the endings (you have met similar endings already in the present and the imperfect): **-e, -es, -e, -ions, -iez, -ent.**

Avant de visiter Paris,

il faut	que	je		**lise**	un livre d'histoire.
	que	tu		**apprennes**	à conduire plus vite.
	qu'	il	nous	**prête**	un plan.
		(*Georges*)			
	que	nous		**trouvions**	un hôtel.
	que	vous	nous	**donniez**	des conseils.
		(*Georges et Isabelle*)			
	qu'	ils		**téléphonent**	à l'hôtel pour nous.
		(*Les Lemaire*)			

Virtually all the 'signals' of the subjunctive end in **que** (**il faut que, je veux que**) so, in grammar books, the forms of the subjunctive are always written with **que** (**que je lise, qu'ils téléphonent**) to remind you that **que** is part of the signal.

Que also has many other functions in French. It is only followed by the subjunctive when it is part of one of the special subjunctive signals.

Although the subjunctive of **-er** verbs looks very like parts of the present tense (**prête, téléphonent**) or the imperfect tense (**trouvions, donniez**), you can recognize that the subjunctive is being used once you are aware of the signalling expressions.

3 The subjunctive of irregular verbs

The verbs **être**, **avoir** and **aller** are irregular in the subjunctive:

être	**avoir**	**aller**
que je **sois**	que j'**aie**	que j'**aille**
que tu **sois**	que tu **aies**	que tu **ailles**
qu'il **soit**	qu'il **ait**	qu'il **aille**
que nous **soyons**	que nous **ayons**	que nous **allions**
que vous **soyez**	que vous **ayez**	que vous **alliez**
qu'elles **soient**	qu'elles **aient**	qu'elles **aillent**

Other irregular verbs: **faire, savoir, pouvoir,** have an irregular stem which is the same for all parts of the subjunctive:

infinitive	stem	
faire	**fass-**	fasse, fasses, fasse, fassions, fassiez, fassent
savoir	**sach-**	sache, saches, sache, sachions, sachiez, sachent
pouvoir	**puiss-**	puisse, puisses, puisse, puissions, puissiez, puissent

4 Verb 'signals' for the subjunctive

The subjunctive *must be used* after a number of easily recognized 'signals'. The most common ones are verbs. The two most frequently used 'signals' are:

> **il faut que** (see **The main points 2** above)
> **vouloir que:**

Alison **veut que** Patrick l'**accompagne** au musée.	*Alison wants Patrick to go with her to the museum.*
Nous **voulons que** Mark **réfléchisse** avant de se marier.	*We want Mark to think carefully before he gets married.*
Sandy et son frère **veulent que** leurs parents **reviennent**.	*Sandy and her brother want their parents to come home.*

5 Other verb 'signals' for the subjunctive

There are other groups of French verbs, usually expressing an *emotion* or a *condition*, which are followed by the subjunctive:

Verbs for saying you wish or want something:

In addition to **vouloir que** (**The main points 4**, above), this group includes:

> **désirer que**
> **souhaiter que**
> **aimer que** (especially in the conditional tense – see Unit 18):

Je **désire**
Je **souhaite que**... } que tu m'accompagnes au musée.
J'**aimerais que**...

I want you to come to the museum with me.

Verbs expressing fear: *avoir peur que, craindre que*

Patrick **a peur que** les musées (ne) soient ennuyeux.	*Patrick is afraid the museums will be boring.*

Il **craint qu'**Alison (ne) passe trop de temps dans la section sur l'Occupation.	*He fears Alison will spend too much time in the section on the Occupation.*

Note that in formal French, there is a **ne** before the subjunctive which follows verbs expressing fear (**Il craint qu'Alison ne passe …**). This **ne** has no negative meaning and in informal French it is sometimes omitted.

Verbs expressing regret: *regretter que, être désolé(e) que*

Patrick **regrette** qu'elle n'accepte pas de l'accompagner au Musée de l'Automobile.	*Patrick is sorry that she will not agree to go to the Musée de l'Automobile with him.*
Il **est désolé que** le Musée des Arts et Métiers soit fermé.	*He is disappointed that the Musée des Arts et Métiers is closed.*

6 Impersonal expressions and the subjunctive

Some impersonal expressions, such as **il** + verb + **que**, are followed by the subjunctive. The main ones are used to say that you feel something is *necessary*, *important*, or that it is *a pity*:

il faut/faudra que (see above, **The main points 1**)
il vaut mieux que   it will be better if
il est préférable que   it is preferable that
il est important que   it is important that
il est dommage que   it is a pity that

Il vaut mieux qu'Alison aille seule au Musée de la Libération à Montparnasse.	*It will be better for Alison to go to the Museum of the Liberation at Montparnasse by herself.*
Il est important qu'elle encourage Patrick à aller au Musée du Sport au Parc des Princes.	*It is important that she should encourage Patrick to go to the Museum of Sport at the Parc des Princes.*
Il est dommage qu'ils ne s'intéressent pas aux mêmes musées!	*It is a pity they are not interested in the same museums!*

7 The relative pronouns *ce qui* and *ce que*

When you are writing an account of events, or giving a formal oral presentation, you will find relative pronouns useful to help you to express yourself in a more structured way. See Unit 11 **The main points 5, The next stage 3**.

In addition to the relative pronouns you met in Unit 11, there are others you can use to give what you say or what you write a denser and more tightly knit structure, or to emphasize a particularly important point.

Ce qui and **ce que** (what/which) which refer only to *things*, can be used to emphasize a particular word or expression in the sentence.

- **ce qui** is the **subject** of the verb in the clause it is in:

Ce qui intéresse Alison, c'est surtout l'histoire de la France.

What Alison is specially interested in is the history of France.

- **ce que** is the **object** of the verb:

Ce qu'elle veut voir, c'est les musées historiques.

What she wants to see is the historical museums.

The story

In this passage, you should be able to find examples of various **'signals'** with **following subjunctive verbs**. Make a list of them and compare your list with **The main points 1–6**.

Voici une description du quartier du Louvre, qu'Alison et Patrick ont visité à Paris.

Ce qui est remarquable dans ce quartier, c'est le grand nombre de monuments qui s'y trouvent. Il faut que les touristes voient non seulement le musée, mais aussi la Cour carrée, la Colonnade, la Pyramide et l'Arc de Triomphe du Carroussel.

Le Palais du Louvre, dont l'architecture est très variée, a été aggrandi par Louis XIV. Il est peut-être dommage que la Pyramide, dont on a terminé la construction dans les années 80, soit si différente du reste du Palais.

C'est le président François Mitterrand qui a ordonné qu'on construise une extension moderne au Louvre. Il a insisté que l'architecte soit de renommée internationale.

Certains Français regrettent qu'il ait choisi un architecte étranger. Ils craignent que le contraste entre les bâtiments historiques et la Pyramide ne soit trop choquant. Il faut cependant que les gens s'habituent à de tels développements, s'ils veulent que les bâtiments historiques continuent à servir dans le monde moderne.

A quick check

1 Identify the 'signals' and the accompanying verbs in the subjunctive in the following sentences:

Patrick est sûr qu'il faut qu'ils soient à l'aéroport à 7 heures du matin.
Sandy a peur que ses parents ne manquent l'avion, mais Nicolas a insisté qu'elle se calme.
Alison veut que Patrick soit assis à côté d'elle dans l'avion.

2 Complete these sentences, using an appropriate verb in the subjunctive:

Comme je veux apprendre le français, il faut que je...
Pour bien parler français, il est important que tu...
Je voudrais aller au cinéma ce soir, mais mon père insiste que nous...
Ma mère va au supermarché demain. Qu'est-ce que tu veux qu'elle...?

3 Put the words in the groups below in the correct order to form sentences:

- Paris, visiter, femme, Tout, ma, musées, que, les, faire, ce, de, est, veut, c'
- différence, Louvre, qui, Pyramide, est, Palais, intéressant, et, c', la, Ce, entre, le, la, est, du
- que, faut, voir, il, Musée, c', du, le, Louvre, est, Ce

The next stage

1 Probability and the subjunctive

There is a group of expressions used to talk about various degrees of probability.

The expressions which tell us that something is likely or almost certain to happen are followed by the **indicative**. See above, **The main points 1**:

il est clair que
    certain que
    sûr que   + verb in the indicative
    probable que

Il est probable qu'Alison ira au Musée Carnavalet.   *Alison will probably go to the Musée Carnavalet.*

The expressions which mean that an event may not happen, or that it is doubtful, are followed by the **subjunctive**:

il est possible que
    douteux que
    peu probable que   + verb in the subjunctive
    impossible que

Parce que Patrick n'aime pas la musique, **il est peu probable qu'**ils **aillent** au Musée de la Musique à la Villette.   *Since Patrick doesn't like music, they are unlikely to go to the Musée de la Musique at La Villette.*

Patrick et Alison ne passent que trois jours à Paris; **il est** donc **douteux qu'**ils **voient** tous les monuments intéressants.   *Patrick and Alison are only spending three days in Paris, so it is doubtful if they will see all the interesting monuments.*

2   Other verbs with the subjunctive

There are two other groups of verbs which signal a subjunctive in the following verb:

Verbs you use to give orders or to make demands:

vouloir que	*to wish/want that* (see **The main points 3**)
ordonner que	*to command that*
exiger que	*to demand that*
insister que	*to insist that*

Patrick et Alison **veulent que** Sandy et Andrew **fassent** le ménage pendant leur absence. Patrick **a ordonné que** la pelouse **soit tondue** et Alison **a exigé que** les enfants **nettoient** la maison une fois par semaine. Sandy et Andrew **ont insisté** qu'Alison leur **prépare** des repas congelés.

Patrick and Alison want Sandy and Andrew to do the housework while they are away. Patrick instructed them to mow the lawn and Alison demanded that they clean the house once a week. Sandy and Andrew insisted that Alison prepare frozen meals for them.

Verbs you use to say that you are pleased about something, or that you are sorry:

être content(e) que	*to be happy that*
être ravi(e) que	*to be delighted that*
regretter que	*to be sorry that*

Sandy et Andrew **sont contents que** leurs parents **reviennent.**

Sandy and Andrew are happy that their parents are coming home.

Patrick **regrette qu'**il n'**ait** pas de billet pour le match au Parc des Princes.

Patrick is sorry that he hasn't got a ticket for the match at the Parc des Princes.

3 The subjunctive to express the future

In this unit you have learned how to form and use the present tense of the subjunctive. Although there is a past tense of the subjunctive (Unit 17), there is no future. The present tense of the subjunctive can be used to talk about future time:

Je suis contente que vous **preniez** l'avion du matin. Il est possible que je **vienne** à l'aéroport mais je ne pense pas qu'Andrew **puisse** venir.

I am glad you'll be taking the morning plane. It is possible that I'll come to the airport, but I don't think Andrew will be able to come.

4 *Lequel/laquelle* **after the preposition** de

Although **dont** (Unit 11 **The next stage 3**) is usually used when a relative pronoun follows **de**, there are some circumstances where it is replaced by **de** + **lequel** / **laquelle** to speak about things, or **de** + **qui** if you are speaking about people.

This happens if the noun which the relative pronoun replaces (the **antecedent**) comes after a preposition:

Nous avons décidé de téléphoner à l'hôtel **duquel** les Lemaire nous avaient parlé.

We decided to phone the hotel the Lemaires had spoken to us about.

Quand vous serez à Paris, vous pourrez téléphoner **aux** amis **de qui** nous avons parlé.

When you are in Paris, you can phone the friends we spoke about.

7 how you feel about something

In this unit you will learn
- to say what you intend to do and why
- to restrict what people can do
- to express your doubts
- to talk about your hopes and fears

Topic
- opinions, hopes and fears

Getting started

1 In Unit 16 (**The main points 2, 3, 4, 5**), you learned some of the 'signals' for the subjunctive. You should make sure that you can form the present subjunctive and use these signals before continuing with this unit. It is particularly important to be able to use **il faut que** and **vouloir que** (Unit 16, **The main points 2**):

Georges, **il faudra** absolument **que** tu répondes aux questions dans ce sondage! Je **voudrais que** tous les membres de la famille y répondent. Comme ça, nous nous comprendrons mieux.

Georges, you'll absolutely have to answer the questions in this questionnaire! I'll want all the members of the family to reply. That way, we'll understand one another better.

2 The various ways of expressing doubt also involve the use of the subjunctive. You should now revise the present tense of **croire** and **dire** from your list of irregular verbs. These verbs will help you with saying you are doubtful about something:

Je ne crois pas que les réponses soient utiles. **Je ne dis pas que** ce soit une perte de temps, mais...

I don't think the answers are useful. I'm not saying it's a waste of time, but..

3 Some aspects of the subjunctive in this unit depend on your having a clear understanding of the difference between the indicative mood (all verbs in Units 1–15) and the subjunctive mood (Units 16 and 17). This is explained in Unit 16 **The**

main points 1. You will also need to be quick at identifying the subject of a verb and be able to use the infinitive.

4 Since you will meet the perfect subjunctive in this unit, you should revise the perfect (Unit 13 **The main points 1, 2, 3**) and the present subjunctive of **avoir** and être (Unit 16 **The main points 3**):

Georges croit qu'il a déjà répondu à ces questions, mais Isabelle doute qu'il **ait donné** toutes les réponses.	*Georges thinks he has already responded to these questions, but Isabelle doubts if he has answered all of them.*

Say it in French

1 What you intend to do and why

Isabelle: Je vais demander à tous les membres de la famille de répondre aux questions, **pour que** je **sache** ce qui les trouble et ce qu'ils attendent. Je répondrai moi-même d'abord **de sorte qu**'ils **voient** que ce n'est pas difficile et **afin qu**'ils **puissent** voir que je n'ai rien à cacher.	*I'm going to ask all the members of the family to answer the questions, so that I'll know what worries them and what they expect to happen. I'll answer myself first so that they see it's not difficult and that I've got nothing to hide.*

2 Restricting what people can do

J'attendrai d'analyser les réponses **jusqu'à ce que** tout le monde ait répondu. **Bien que** les questions semblent faciles, il faut du temps pour y répondre. **Pourtant**, **à moins qu**'il n'y ait un problème, tout le monde aura terminé avant la fin de la semaine. Nous analyserons les réponses ensemble – **pourvu que** tout le monde soit d'accord.	*I'll wait to analyse the answers until everyone has replied. Although the questions seem easy, they'll need time to reply. However, unless there's a problem, everyone will have finished by the end of the week. We'll analyse the answers together – provided everyone agrees.*

3 Expressing doubt

Tu sais, **je ne suis pas sûr que** ce sondage nous aide. **Je doute que** la personne qui l'a préparé soit sérieuse. **Penses-tu** vraiment qu'on puisse résoudre nos problèmes de cette façon? **Il est peu probable que** les enfants répondent de façon sérieuse et, de toute façon, **je ne trouve pas que** les questions soient intéressantes.

You know, I'm not sure that this questionnaire will help us. I doubt that the person who prepared it was serious. Do you really think that we can solve our problems in this way? It is unlikely that the children will answer seriously and, in any case, I don't think the questions are interesting.

4 Talking about hopes and fears

Georges replies to the question about the future of the family:

J'aimerais que les enfants restent dans la région et qu'ils ne quittent pas St Amand. **Je préfère qu'**ils soient près de nous, car, **je suis sûr que, quoi qu'**il arrive, on a toujours besoin de ses parents.

I'd like the children to stay in the area and not to leave St Amand. I prefer them to be close to us because I am sure that, whatever happens, you always need your parents.

Je préférerais que Stéphanie revienne en France après avoir terminé son stage, car **je doute qu'**elle puisse s'adapter à la vie en Écosse. **Je ne pense pas que** Mark ait trop de difficultés à s'habituer à la vie en France.

I'd prefer Stéphanie to return to France when she has finished her work placement, because I doubt that she will be able to adapt to life in Scotland. I don't think Mark would find it too difficult to get used to life in France.

The main points

1 Conjunctions followed by the subjunctive

Unit 16 gave you examples of some of the verbs and impersonal expressions which are 'signals' for the subjunctive.

There is another important group of 'signals' – certain types of **conjunctions,** joining parts of a sentence together. They are all followed by **que.** Here are some of the most common:

bien que	*although*	**afin que**	*in order that*
pourvu que	*provided that*	**sans que**	*without*
pour que	*so that*	**à moins que**	*unless*

Identify the **verb in the subjunctive** that follows the **'signal'** in this passage:

Bien que Stéphanie aime l'Écosse, elle sera contente de revenir en France. Elle aimerait se marier avec Mark, **pourvu qu'**ils puissent vivre en France. Elle a l'intention de chercher un emploi à Paris ou à Lille **pour qu'**ils aient de quoi vivre **sans que** Mark soit obligé de trouver un travail immédiatement. **Bien que** son père **veuille** qu'elle revienne à St Amand, elle n'a aucune intention de le faire.

Although Stéphanie likes Scotland, she will be happy to return to France. She would like to marry Mark, provided they can live in France. She intends to look for a job in Paris or Lille so that they have enough to live on, without Mark having to find a job immediately. Although her father wants her to come back to St Amand, she has no intention of doing so.

2 More 'signals' followed by the subjunctive

Some verbs for expressing opinions are followed by the subjunctive when they are used the negative: **croire que** *to believe that,* **penser que** *to think that,* **trouver que** *to think that.* See also **Getting started 2** and **Say it in French 3.**

Nicolas répond à la question sur l'avenir:

Je ne crois pas que les matières que j'étudie à l'école **soient** très utiles pour ma carrière dans le cinéma. Mes parents **ne pensent pas** qu'une telle carrière **soit** sérieuse, et mes professeurs **ne trouvent pas qu'**on **puisse** déjà, à mon âge, choisir son métier.

I don't believe that the subjects I am studying at school are very useful for my career in the cinema. My parents don't think that such a career is serious and my teachers don't think you can already, at my age, choose your job.

Another group of expressions can also signal the subjunctive.
These involve *time* and *expectation*:

attendre que	*to wait until*
s'attendre à ce que	*to expect that*
jusqu'à ce que/en attendant que	*until*
avant que (ne)	*before*

Identify the **verbs in the subjunctive** in the following sentences:

Isabelle **attendra que** Stéphanie
soit revenue pour analyser les
réponses.

*Isabelle will wait until
Stéphanie has come home
to analyse the answers.*

Elle **s'attend à ce que** les réponses
de Stéphanie reflètent son
indépendance, maintenant qu'elle
a fait son stage en Écosse.

*She expects that Stéphanie's
replies will reflect her
independence, now that
she has done her work
placement in Scotland.*

Stéphanie restera en Écosse
jusqu'à ce qu'elle ait terminé
son rapport de stage.

*Stéphanie will stay in
Scotland until she has
finished the report on her
work placement.*

Elle ne reviendra pas à St Amand
avant que Mark (n')ait promis de
passer ses vacances en France.

*She will not go back to St
Amand before Mark has
promised to spend his
holidays in France.*

3 The subjunctive or the indicative?

To help you decide if a verb is followed by the subjunctive or
not, look at these two lists:

• These verbs express *facts*, *certainty* and *probability*. They are
followed by the **indicative**:

Isabelle...
  observe que
  remarque que les questions sont faciles.

Georges ...
  croit que
  pense que les questions sont stupides.

Nicolas ...
  dit que
  déclare que sa mère l'ennuie.

- These verbs express *wishes*, *fears*, *commands* and *things which may never happen*. They are followed by the **subjunctive**:

Elle...
  souhaite que
  désire que
  aimerait que les autres répondent sérieusement.

Isabelle...
  a peur qu'
  craint qu'il (ne) réponde pas.

Nicolas...
  veut que
  aimerait que sa mère n'insiste pas.

Inversion to form a question

The verbs **croire que, penser que, trouver que** (**2,** above) are also followed by the subjunctive if they are **inverted to form a question**:

Georges...
  pense que
  croit que
  trouve que le sondage est stupide.

Pense-t-il que le sondage soit sérieux?

Probability and possibility

- Expressions of probability (**il est clair/certain que** i.e. likely to happen) are followed by the **indicative**:

Il est...
  clair que
  certain que Georges n'aime pas parler de lui.
Il est **probable** qu'il refusera de répondre.

- Expressions of **possibility** (**il est peu probable que,** i.e. uncertain) are followed by the **subjunctive**:

Il est ... **peu probable** que Georges **veuille** parler de lui.
Il est **possible** qu'il **réponde** par des mensonges.

Espérer que

Note that **espérer que** is *always* followed by the **indicative**:

Isabelle espère qu'il n'y **aura** pas de conflit entre ses projets et ceux de Georges.	*Isabelle hopes that there will not be a conflict between her plans and Georges'.*

4 The subjunctive or an infinitive?

The subjunctive is usually used in compound sentences – sentences with at least two verbs. One is the 'signal'; the other is the verb in the subjunctive.

If the **subjects** of the two verbs are *different*, the **subjunctive** is used:

Georges (subject 1) regrette qu'Isabelle (subject 2) lui **ait demandé** de répondre aux questions du sondage.	*Georges is sorry that Isabelle has asked him to reply to the questions.*

If the **subject** is the same in each case, you use an **infinitive**:

Georges ne veut pas **répondre**.	*Georges doesn't want to reply.*
Isabelle a peur de **tomber** malade.	*Isabelle is afraid she will fall ill.*
Nicolas préférerait **étudier** le cinéma.	*Nicolas would prefer to study the cinema.*

5 Subjunctive: the present and the perfect

The subjunctive is most often used in its present tense form. Sometimes, however, if you are talking about a situation in the past, you need to use a past tense subjunctive – the perfect subjunctive. This is made up of the present subjunctive of the auxiliary verb (**avoir, être,** see Unit 16 **The main points** 3) and a past participle (Unit 13 **The main points** 1):

Isabelle a peur que Stéphanie **ait décidé** de rester en Écosse.	*Isabelle is afraid that Stéphanie may have decided to stay in Scotland.*
Bien qu'elle ne **soit allée** à Aberdeen que pour faire un stage, il est possible qu'elle **ait promis** à Mark d'y rester.	*Although she only went to Aberdeen for a work placement, (it is possible that) she may have promised Mark that she will stay there.*

The story

In this text from the questionnaire published in the magazine, identify the **seven verbs in the subjunctive** and their **'signals'**.

Le sondage du mois!

**Vos voeux? Vos craintes? Vos projets?
Répondez à nos questions pour y voir plus clair!
Comparez vos réponses avec celles de vos proches!
Peut-être serez-vous surpris?**

Les questions dans notre sondage ont été préparées pour que vous puissiez analyser vous-mêmes les problèmes que vous affrontez. Bien que vous ayez une vie de famille réussie, il est possible que vos projets et ceux de vos proches ne soient pas compatibles.

Vous ne croyez pas qu'un tel conflit puisse se produire? Nous espérons que vous avez raison, et pourtant ... N'attendez pas que les problèmes vous accablent!

• La première section du sondage concerne vos voeux. Vous voulez voyager? Vous souhaitez changer d'emploi? Vous aimeriez déménager? Qu'en pensent les autres?

• Dans la deuxième section, vous allez faire face à vos cauchemars. Avez-vous peur que la pollution nous tue? Craignez-vous de prendre l'avion? Et pour vos amis, vos collègues, votre famille? Pensez-vous que l'avenir leur réserve de mauvaises surprises?

• Finalement, nous vous donnons la possibilité de penser sérieusement à vos projets d'avenir. Qu'est-ce que vous pouvez faire afin de surmonter vos craintes et préparer un avenir rose?

Ne dites pas que ce soit trop difficile!

Il est certain que, si vous répondez sérieusement, vous pourrez envisager avec sérénité les petits malheurs que la vie peut vous réserver.

A quick check

1 Write two sentences about your hopes (**espérer que** + the indicative) and two about your fears (**avoir peur que, craindre que** + the subjunctive) for someone else (two different subjects, see **The main points 4**).

Examples: J'espère que mon collègue sera promu.

J'ai peur que mon ami(e) aille vivre à l'étranger.

2 Write the same sentences, this time about yourself (both subjects the same, **The main points 4**).

Examples: J'espère être promu(e).

J'ai peur d'aller vivre à l'étranger.

3 Imagine that you are going to change your job. What are the possible problems? Think of three and write three sentences based on the model below, using the conjunction **bien que**:

Bien que le traitement soit modeste, je vais changer d'emploi.

4 After answering the questionnaire, you have decided it would be a good idea to have a big family reunion. What could be a suitable occasion for doing this?

Imagine that you are announcing three of the possible occcasions to the rest of the family. Use the expressions **afin que**, **pour que** and **de sorte que** followed by the subjunctive (see **The main points 1**):

Example: J'ai décidé de vous inviter à une grande réunion familiale **afin que** nous **puissions** fêter l'anniversaire de grand-père.

The next stage

1 The subjunctive after superlatives

You have learned how to say something is *the most* or *the least* in Unit 6 **The main points 8**. In some situations, you may need to follow a superlative by the subjunctive:

C'est le sondage **le plus stupide** que j'**aie** jamais **vu**. | *It's the stupidest questionnaire I've ever seen.*
La discussion sur les réponses au sondage est **la plus intéressante** que nous **ayons** jamais **eue**. | *The discussion about the answers to the questionnaire is the most interesting one we've ever had.*

2 The subjunctive after expressions of time

Events that have not yet taken place

Some time expressions are used to speak about events that have not yet taken (or may never take) place. They are followed by the subjunctive:

J'**attends que** ta soeur **soit** là pour discuter les réponses aux questions.

I'll wait until your sister is here to discuss the answers to the questions.

Nous attendrons **jusqu'à ce qu'**elle **soit revenue,** pour lui poser des questions sur ses projets.

We'll wait until she comes back to ask her questions about her plans.

S'attendre à ce que...

The expression **s'attendre à ce que** (*to expect that*) is also followed by the subjunctive:

Georges **s'attend à ce que** Stéphanie **décide** de se marier.

Georges expects that Stéphanie will decide to get married.

Avant que, après que

While **avant que** is followed by the **subjunctive** (an event which has not yet happened), **après que** (an event which has happened and is now over) is followed by the **indicative:**

Avant que Stéphanie (ne) **revienne,** il faudra peindre sa chambre.

Before Stéphanie comes home, we'll have to paint her bedroom.

Après que Stéphanie **est partie,** je me suis sentie très seule.

After Stéphanie left, I felt very lonely.

3 The past historic tense

In formal written texts, you may meet, as well as the perfect and the imperfect, another past tense called the past historic. It is made up of only one word – it is not a compound tense like the perfect.

The past historic is used only in written French, to recount events in the past which do not appear to have an on-going effect in the present. Like the perfect, it is used with (and in contrast to) the imperfect (Unit 14 **The main points 3**).

The stem is usually formed from the infinitive, and endings are added as shown below:

donner → donn-	
je donn-	**ai**
tu donn-	**as**
il/elle donn-	**a**
nous donn-	**âmes**
vous donn-	**âtes**
ils/elles donn-**èrent**	

finir → fin-	
je fin-	**is**
tu fin-	**is**
il/elle fin-	**it**
nous fin-	**îmes**
vous fin-	**îtes**
ils/elles fin-**irent**	

vendre → vend-	
je vend-	**is**
tu vend-	**is**
il/elle vend-	**it**
nous vend-	**îmes**
vous vend-	**îtes**
ils/elles vend-**irent**	

The past historic of irregular verbs may be difficult to recognize, but the endings – apart from the vowel **a**, **i** or **u** – are always the same:

avoir	j'eus	**pouvoir**	je pus
être	je fus	**vouloir**	je voulus

Find the examples of the two tenses in this extract from Stéphanie's **Rapport de stage** (a formal, written report on her work placement):

Je **pris** l'avion avec tous les stagiaires qui allaient en Écosse, et nous **arrivâmes** à Aberdeen à 15 heures 30. Mon Directeur de stage, M. Robertson, m'**accueillit** et nous **allâmes** directement à l'entreprise où m'attendait Madame Wilson. Elle m'**expliqua** le travail que j'avais à faire et m'**emmena** ensuite chez Madame Rushton qui a plusieurs chambres qu'elle loue aux étudiants.

I caught the plane with all the other students who were going to Scotland and we arrived in Aberdeen at 3.30 p.m. My supervisor, Mr Robertson welcomed me and we went straight to the office where Mrs Wilson was waiting for me. She explained the work I had to do and then took me to the home of Mrs Rushton who has several rooms which she lets to students.

4 The imperfect subjunctive

Another tense you will only need for reading and formal writing is the imperfect subjunctive.

In speaking, you usually use the present subjunctive or, less often, the perfect subjunctive. In formal writing, however, you will sometimes see the imperfect subjunctive.

The stem, and the main vowel, of this increasingly rare tense are found in the second person singular (the **tu** form) of the past historic (above, **The next stage 3**):

donner	→	**donnas**	→	**donn-**
finir	→	**finis**	→	**fin-**
vendre	→	**vendis**	→	**vend-**

Although you are unlikely to meet all the forms of the imperfect subjunctive, you should be able to recognize them if necessary:

donner		**finir**		**vendre**	
que je donn-	**asse**	que je fin-	**isse**	que je vend-	**isse**
que tu donn-	**asses**	que tu fin-	**isses**	que tu vend-	**isses**
qu'il donn-	**ât**	qu'il fin-	**ît**	qu'il vend-	**ît**
que nous donn-	**assions**	que nous fin-	**issions**	que nous vend-	**issions**
que vous donn-	**assiez**	que vous fin-	**issiez**	que vous vend-	**issiez**
qu'ils donn-	**assent**	qu'ils fin-	**issent**	qu'ils vend-	**issent**

Avoir and **être**, as usual, are very irregular. The past historic will help you:

avoir	que j'**e-usse**	**être**	que je **f-usse**

In formal writing, the imperfect subjunctive **must** be used after certain tenses: the imperfect, the past historic and the conditional (Unit 18):

Madame Rushton **voulait que** ses locataires **payassent** le loyer au commencement de la semaine.

Mrs Rushton wanted her lodgers to pay the rent at the beginning of the week.

Monsieur Robertson **insista que** je **fusse** dans mon bureau à neuf heures moins le quart.

Mr Robertson insisted that I be (subjunctive in English) in my office at a quarter to nine.

18 imagining what could happen

In this unit you will learn
- to say what would happen if…
- to say what would need to happen before something else could happen
- to imagine how you would react to new or unknown circumstances
- to say what you thought would happen

Topic
- wedding plans

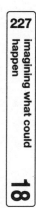

Grammar

- The formation of the conditional tense
- The conditional with **si**
- The polite use of the conditional

The next stage

- The conditional to make suggestions
- The conditional in reported speech
- The conditional perfect
- Giving doubtful information

Getting started

1 Forming the conditional is like forming the future. Check back to Unit 11 **The main points 1, 2, 3,** for the stem of the future tense, especially of irregular verbs:

Stéphanie: Si mes parents sont d'accord, nous **pourrons** (future) nous marier au printemps.

If my parents agree, we'll be able to get married in the spring.

Si mes parents étaient d'accord, nous **pourrions** (conditional) nous marier au printemps.

If my parents were in agreement, we could get married in the spring.

You should also check Unit 14 **The main points 1,** for the endings of the imperfect.

2 You have already met some frequently used parts of the verbs **vouloir** and **aimer** in the conditional. Check back to Unit 4 **Say it in French 1** (**voudrais**) and Unit 4 **The main points 1,** Unit 16 **The main points 5** (**aimerais**).

Remember that these verbs are often followed by the subjunctive:

Les Dickson **voudraient** que Mark et Stéphanie **puissent** vivre en Écosse.

The Dicksons would like Mark and Stéphanie to live in Scotland.

Mark **aimerait** que ses parents **sachent** que les Lemaire l'ont tout de suite accepté.

Mark wants his parents to know that the Lemaires accepted him straight away.

Say it in French

1 Saying what would happen if...

Stéphanie Si mes parents pouvaient visiter l'Écosse, ils **comprendraient** vite pourquoi je l'aime. Mon père n'aime pas voyager, mais je suis convaincue que, s'il acceptait de venir en Grande-Bretagne, il **oublierait** qu'il n'aime pas les étrangers. D'ailleurs, il a vite accepté Mark – si seulement il pensait à moi, plutôt qu'à lui-même, il n'y **aurait** pas de problème!

If my parents could visit Scotland, they would soon understand why I like it. My father doesn't like travelling, but I am convinced that, if he agreed to come to Britain, he would forget that he doesn't like foreigners. In any case, he quickly accepted Mark – if only he thought of me, rather than himself, there would be no problem!

2 What would have to happen first?

Isabelle Pour que le mariage ait lieu au printemps, il **faudrait** vraiment que je commence à m'organiser. Si on n'invitait pas tous les membres de la famille, on **pourrait** envisager une cérémonie intime. On n'**inviterait** pas tous les cousins germains et on **expliquerait** que seulement la famille proche de Mark pourra venir.

So that the wedding can take place in spring, I'll really have to start getting myself organized. If we didn't invite all the members of the family, we could have a small wedding. We wouldn't invite all the second cousins and we would explain that only Mark's close family will be able to come.

3 How would you react in unknown circumstances?

Nicolas Si ma copine voulait se marier avec moi, je lui **dirais** tout de suite que je ne me marierai jamais. Je lui **expliquerais** qu'on n'a pas besoin de se marier pour vivre heureux. Je lui **demanderais**: «**Aimerais**-tu

If my girlfriend wanted to marry me, I'd tell her straight away that I'll never get married. I'd explain to her that you don't need to get married to be happy. I'd ask her: "Would you

passer toute ta vie avec la même personne? Ne t'**ennuierais**-tu pas?» Je la **convaincrais** que la vie d'un couple marié manque de surprises et nous **continuerions** à vivre ensemble, heureux mais pas mariés.

like to spend your whole life with the same person? Wouldn't you be bored?" I'd convince her that the life of a married couple has no surprises and we'd keep on living together, happy but not married.

4 What did you think would happen?

Sandy Je croyais que Mark **choisirait** une fille écossaise. Je n'avais jamais pensé qu'il **rencontrerait** une Française et **déciderait** de se marier avec elle. Qui **aurait** cru qu'il **préférerait** la France à la Grande-Bretagne? Mes parents pensaient qu'il **continuerait** à travailler sur des plate-formes dans la mer du nord.

I thought Mark would choose a Scottish girl. I had never thought that he would meet a French girl and decide to marry her. Who would have thought that he would prefer France to Britain? My parents thought he would continue working on oil platforms in the North Sea.

The main points

1 The conditional tense

The conditional is a simple (one word / not compound) tense. It is made up of the same stem you use for the future (Unit 11) and the endings you learnt for the imperfect (Unit 14): **-ais, -ais, -ait, -ions, -iez, -aient**

For nearly all verbs, the stem is the infinitive (or, for **-re** verbs, the infinitive with the final -e removed):

se marier	
je me marier-	**AIS**
tu te marier-	**AIS**
il/elle se marier-	**AIT**
nous nous marier-	**IONS**
vous vous marier-	**IEZ**
ils/elles se marier-	**AIENT**

choisir	
je choisir-	**AIS**
tu choisir-	**AIS**
il choisir-	**AIT**
nous choisir-	**IONS**
vous choisir-	**IEZ**
elles choisir-	**AIENT**

attendre	
j'attendr-	**AIS**
tu attendr-	**AIS**
elle attendr-	**AIT**
nous attendr-	**IONS**
vous attendr-	**IEZ**
ils attendr-	**AIENT**

Remember the future stems of the irregular verbs:

aller → **ir-**	pouvoir → **pourr-**
avoir → **aur-**	recevoir → **recevr-**
devoir → **devr-**	savoir → **saur-**
faire → **fer-**	venir → **viendr-**
falloir → **faudr-**	voir → **verr-**
mourir → **mourr-**	vouloir → **voudr-**

2 The conditional with *si*

This tense is mainly used when in English you use *would* or *could*. It is frequently used in sentences where you imagine something:

Si Stéphanie m'invitait à son mariage, j'**accepterais** avec plaisir.	*If Stéphanie invited me to her wedding, I'd accept with pleasure.*

In sentences like this, where **si** is used, there are strict rules about the tenses you are allowed to use:

The conditional after *si* + imperfect tense

If the tense used after **si** is the **imperfect** (as in the example above):

> Si Stéphanie m'**invitait** à son mariage...

the tense in the main clause must be the **conditional**:

> j'**accepterais** avec plaisir.

Si Mark **voulait** vivre en France, il **faudrait** qu'il trouve un emploi.	*If Mark wanted to live in France, he'd have to find a job.*
Si les Lemaire **organisaient** le mariage, ils **voudraient** une cérémonie à l'église, après le mariage civil.	*If the Lemaires were organizing the wedding, they would want a ceremony in the church after the civil marriage.*
Si le repas **avait** lieu dans un restaurant, il y **aurait** plusieurs plats et beaucoup de vins.	*If the wedding breakfast were in a restaurant, there would be several courses and a lot of wines.*

The future after *si* + present tense

If the tense after **si** is in the **present**:

> Si Stéphanie m'**invite** à son mariage...

the tense in the main clause must be the **future**:

> j'**accepterai** avec plaisir.

Si Mark **veut** vivre en France, il **faudra** qu'il trouve un emploi.	*If Mark wants to live in France, he'll have to find a job.*
Si Stéphanie se **marie**, elle ne **voudra** pas cesser de travailler.	*If Stéphanie gets married, she won't want to stop working.*
Le mariage civil **aura** lieu vendredi, s'ils se **marient** à l'église samedi.	*The civil ceremony will take place on Friday if they are married in the church on Saturday.*

3 The polite use of the conditional

The conditional tense is used in French, especially with the verbs **vouloir**, **aimer** (**mieux**) and **préférer**, to make a statement less direct, or less brusque, than it would be if the present tense were used:

Georges **veut que** Stéphanie reste à St Amand.	*Georges wants Stéphanie to remain in St Amand.*

Georges **voudrait que**
       aimerait mieux que
       préférerait que
Stéphanie reste à St Amand.
	Georges would like Stéphanie to remain in St Amand.

The verb **devoir** can also be used in the conditional to make what you say more polite:

Tu **dois** inviter Tante Alice au mariage.	*You must invite Aunt Alice to the wedding.*
Tu **devrais** inviter Tante Alice au mariage.	*You ought to invite Aunt Alice to the wedding.*
Selon la tradition britannique, les parents du marié **doivent** payer les boissons.	*According to the British tradition, the groom's parents have to pay for the drinks.*
Selon la tradition britannique, les parents du marié **devraient** payer les boissons.	*According to the British tradition, the groom's parents should pay for the drinks.*

A similar distinction can be made with **falloir**:

Il **faut** célébrer les fiançailles en Écosse et en France.	*The engagement must be celebrated in Scotland and in France.*
Il **faudrait** célébrer les fiançailles en Écosse et en France.	*The engagement should be celebrated in Scotland and in France.*
Tu **dois** te marier dans une robe très simple.	*You must get married in a very simple dress.*
Tu **devrais** te marier dans une robe très simple.	*You should get married in a very simple dress.*

The story

In this letter, Stéphanie uses many **verbs in the conditional**. Identify at least ten of them, with their **subject**.

Lettre de Stéphanie à sa cousine Jeannette:

Ma chère petite Jojo,

Il faudrait que tu t'assoies! Qu'est-ce qui t'étonnerait le plus? Pourrais-tu imaginer ta grande cousine mariée – et avec un étranger? Que dirais-tu d'un mariage au printemps?

Tu serais une des demoiselles d'honneur et l'autre serait ... une Écossaise! Car je me marie avec Mark, un Écossais que j'ai rencontré pendant mon stage.

Je sais que tu pensais que je ne me marierais jamais, car je voudrais poursuivre ma carrière. Je commence à penser qu'on pourrait faire les deux. On ne devrait pas accepter de rester à la maison, simplement parce qu'on est mariée. Je compte bien continuer à travailler – à quoi bon avoir fait ce stage en Écosse, si je ne peux pas profiter de tout ce que j'ai appris?

As-tu jamais pensé à faire un stage à l'étranger? Je t'assure que tu profiterais énormément de l'expérience – et peut-être rencontrerais-tu quelqu'un d'aussi merveilleux que Mark. Je pensais que je m'ennuyerais et que je trouverais très difficile de me séparer de ma famille, mais je me suis vite habituée à la vie et au travail dans un pays différent...

A quick check

1 Complete the verbs in the following sentences, using the **conditional tense** of the verb given in brackets:

Vous (pouvoir) acheter une grande maison, si vous aviez beaucoup d'argent.

Elle croyait que son frère (se marier) avec une Écossaise.
Nous pensions que le voyage (coûter) moins cher.
Si Mark se mariait en France, nous y (revenir) avec grand plaisir.
J'(aimer) célébrer mes fiançailles à Noël.

2 Following the example given, write two sentences to say what you would do in each of the situations described – see **The main points 2**:

Exemple: Si nous avions un château en Espagne, nous y passerions les vacances d'été.

Si j'avais un oncle très riche,...
Si j'avais perdu les clés de la voiture,...
Si les Martiens envahissaient la terre,...

3 Make the following requests more polite (**The main points 3**) by using the verb in bold in the conditional:

Je **veux** que tu me prêtes ta voiture.
Nicolas, je **préfère** que tu ne sortes pas ce soir.
Chéri, tu sais, **j'aime mieux** que tu rentres sans aller au bar.

The next stage

1 The conditional to make suggestions

The conditional tense of **pouvoir** is used to suggest that something might happen, or that someone might do something:

Le mariage **pourrait** avoir lieu à Noël.	*The wedding could take place at Christmas.*
Nous **pourrions** réserver des chambres à l'hôtel pour les invités.	*We could book rooms at the hotel for the guests.*
Ne **pourriez**-vous pas attendre une année avant de vous marier?	*Couldn't you wait a year before you get married?*

Sometimes the impersonal expression **Il se peut/pourrait que** is used with the subjunctive:

Il se **pourrait** que le mariage **ait** lieu à Noël.	*It is possible that the wedding could take place at Christmas.*

2 The conditional in reported speech

In Unit 14 **The next stage 3**, you saw how the imperfect is used in indirect speech (reporting what other people said). When you are using indirect speech, a verb the speaker used in the future (**tuerai**) will be changed into the conditional (**tuerais**):

Je **tuerai** Nicolas s'il ne cesse pas de me taquiner.	*I'll kill Nicolas if he doesn't stop teasing me.*
Stéphanie a dit qu'elle **tuerait** Nicolas s'il ne cessait pas de la taquiner.	*Stéphanie said she would kill Nicolas if he didn't stop pestering her.*
Nicolas et moi, nous **irons** nous promener parce que nous ne voulons pas vous gêner.	*Nicolas and I will go for a walk because we don't want to get in the way.*
Georges a dit que lui et Nicolas **iraient** se promener parce qu'ils ne voulaient pas nous gêner.	*Georges said he and Nicolas would go for a walk because they didn't want to get in the way.*

3 The conditional perfect

The conditional tense of **avoir** or **être** + a past participle is used when speaking about conditions in the past – *would have* in English:

Je ne l'**aurais** jamais **cru**. On dirait que mes parents sont fous. C'est que ma soeur vient de se fiancer avec un Écossais. Tu te rends compte?	*I would never have believed it. You'd think my parents were mad. What's happened is that my sister has just got engaged to a Scot. Can you imagine?*
Ils **auraient accepté** un Italien, un Allemand **aurait posé** peut-être un petit problème, mais un Écossais!	*They would have accepted an Italian, a German would perhaps have caused a slight problem, but a Scot!*
Elle **aurait dû** choisir un Français. Si elle avait pensé à eux, elle se **serait mariée** avec un garçon de St Amand.	*She should have chosen a Frenchman. If she'd thought about them, she would have married a boy from St Amand.*

4 The conditional to give doubtful information

To suggest that something might not be true, or to cast doubt on a source of information, you can use the conditional in French.

In newspapers and other public accounts of events, it is sometimes necessary to show that one's sources are not absolutely certain to be accurate. In English expressions such as *alleged* or *suggested* are used. In French the conditional conveys this nuance:

Le marié **aurait** volé l'alliance.

The groom is supposed to have stolen the wedding ring.

Le mariage **aurait** coûté €16 000.

It is alleged that the wedding cost 16,000 euros.

Unit 8

Mark and Stéphanie plan to go horse-riding.

S   What do you want to do tomorrow, if it isn't raining? Do you want to go horse-riding or go for walks?

M   I don't know how to ride.

S   You can learn; it isn't difficult.

M   Are there riding schools in St Amand?

S   There are several, but I can ride at my friend Monique's; she has several horses. Can you see the pastures over there? They are hers. You can see the horses from here.

M   Do you have to wear special clothes?

S   Yes and no. You can wear jeans and trainers, but you have to wear a riding-hat. My father can lend you his. I'm going to phone Monique to see if we can ride tomorrow. By the way, when do your parents want to come?

M   They can come in July. They want to visit the north of France and perhaps go and spend a few days in Paris.

Unit 9

Mark asks Stéphanie if his parents can come in July.

M   Stéphanie, my mother has just asked me if she and dad can come to your house on July 7th. Is that all right with your parents?

S   I'm going to ask them the question straight away and you can phone her back later to give the answer.

Stéphanie calls her mum and gives her the news.

S   Mum, can Mark's parents come and see us on July 7th? They would like to spend three or four days with us, then visit the area and Paris as well.

I   Of course, with pleasure. Your dad can perhaps take a few days' holiday. How are they going to travel?

S   They're going to catch the plane from Glasgow to Paris and hire a car at the airport. Mark is going to give them a road map and a street-map of St Amand to help them.

Here are the instructions Mark is going to give his parents.

You arrive at the airport Roissy-Charles de Gaulle and you take the motorway to the north, the A1 up to Péronne.

Then go up the A2 right to the exit Cambrai/Valenciennes. Leave the A2 at Valenciennes and drive on to the Sentinelle. There you have to follow the A23 to the St Amand / Lille exit. Leave the A23 when entering St Amand and take the dual carriageway to the Raismes forest. At the second roundabout, turn left and you are at the chemin de l'Empire.

Unit 10

The Lemaires are planning how they will entertain the Dicksons.

I   What will happen? First they're going to hire a car at the airport. Then it takes two hours to get to our place. Then we'll have to have dinner,...

G   What do we usually do when we have guests? We show them the town and then we visit some of the local area. The Dicksons will surely be interested in the area around St Amand. So we could drive them to the forest and to Valenciennes. And we could also introduce them to our friends.

I   Yes, of course, but people go on holiday to have a rest! We'll have to give them time to relax and not try to do too many things. In any case, as this is their first time in France, we'll have to show them things that are typically French.

G   It's hard to decide what is interesting for Scottish people since we don't know Scotland.

I   It's better to ask them what they want to see – the countryside, the sea, towns,...

G   And then, it's important to introduce them to Stéphanie's friends because they will certainly want to get to know her better.

Unit 11

'What do you do?' Stéphanie, Mark, Alison and Georges speak about their work and their plans for the future.

S   The work I'm doing now doesn't interest me very much, but after my work placement I'll be able to find a job when I go back to France. It's my boss, Mr Williams, who is encouraging me to learn English and to improve my computing skills. "You'll always use English and computer skills" he tells me.

M   At the moment the job I have means I have to spend a lot of time off-shore. But I'll need this experience of drilling at sea. This is the practical experience which I'll need if I want to have a management post later on.

A   The work of a teacher is getting harder and harder. During the holidays, which always go too quickly for me, you don't rest. You have to prepare your classes because it's hard to find the time you need during the term. This evening, as usual, I'll be correcting homework and preparing the handouts I'll be using tomorrow.

G   A plumber never sleeps peacefully because at any moment the telephone might ring. You always have to help out people who have problems – problems that only happen at night or at the weekend. I hope my son will have a job that will allow him to sleep well and not work at impossible hours.

Unit 12

Nicolas, his mother and father are trying to work out how he can afford to go to Britain next year.

G   You ought to completely change your habits. You put money aside, you open a bank account, you deposit at least 150 euros each month and you don't spend anything!

N   It's easy for you! Do this! Do that! Don't do this! You give the orders and I obey. But for me it's not easy. Just think! I deprive myself of outings, clothes, books, the cinema. Think of the effect all that will have on me!

I   Yes, listen Georges! Help him! Don't give him orders. Better give him some advice.

G   That's what I'm trying to do. I want to help him. Don't criticize me for that! In any case I was going to suggest that we give him the money we have put aside for the new car. Let's give it to him! He really needs it.

I   Well really! No! Let's not do anything crazy! He's got a year to find the money. We'll have to think of other solutions because *I* want a new car!

N   Don't get mad! Let's stay calm. Please don't think I'm completely stupid. I'll find a little job, I'll do some baby-sitting and soon I'll have the money I need.

Unit 13

Isabelle tells a friend, Chloé, about the Dicksons' arrival at the airport.

I   We tried to learn a bit of English. Fortunately the Dicksons learnt French before they came.

C   Did they speak French straight away?

I   No. They started with a few words in English, but afterwards, they remembered their French lessons.

C   But what did you do? Didn't you feel a bit embarrassed?

I   Oh yes. I found the situation very difficult. People you've never met, and foreigners as well. And you must remember that Stéphanie made a great point of this visit! When they got off the plane, I was scared.

C   I really admire you! I've never been able to speak to people I don't know, and as I've never learned English ...

I   The beginning wasn't easy. But with good will we managed to communicate. They are perhaps our daughter's future in-laws, after all. And they were so nice to her. They welcomed her into their home and Alison especially helped her a lot. We got on well in the end.

Unit 14

Isabelle tells Alison about when Stéphanie was young.

I   She was very calm when she was small and she learned to talk and to walk earlier than Nicolas. She was three when she went to nursery school and she didn't like it much. Even when she was very small, she always sang in tune and I wasn't surprised when, later on, she decided to sing in the *Quatre Vents* choir. Before she went to Scotland, she sang with the choir twice a week.

All children draw at school, but for Stéphanie drawing was very important. She loved bright colours and for her birthday and at Christmas she always used to ask for colouring pencils or water colours. And she loved art galleries. We used to go fairly often to see exhibitions, at least two or three times a year. I remember an impressionist exhibition in Paris, when she was 12. She made such a fuss that I went to Paris with her and we saw the exhibition three times!

Unit 15

Alison writes to her French teacher in Scotland.

Dear Alan,

You asked me to write to you during our time in France. So I had started a letter the day we arrived, but we had too many things to do and everything was so interesting that I couldn't write sooner.

We had planned to spend a few days with the Lemaires and then to visit the area round St Amand. Several suggestions for things to see were given to us by Georges and Isabelle Lemaire and we are now going to leave St Amand and visit the battlegrounds from the First World War in the north of France. Then we'll go to Paris.

While Patrick was speaking to Georges, Isabelle and I chatted about our children, so now I understand Stéphanie better.

I hadn't thought about it, but my training as a History and Geography teacher is very useful for a trip abroad. I found out about the geographical situation of St Amand and because I've read several books about French history and the First World War, the north of France interests me very much.

We both thank you for your excellent French classes and we hope you're having a very enjoyable holiday. See you soon!

Best wishes from us both

Alison Dickson.

Unit 16

Here is a description of the area round the Louvre which Alison and Patrick visited in Paris.

What is remarkable in this area is the great number of monuments there are here. Tourists have to see not only the museum, but also the Cour carrée, the Colonnade, the Pyramide and the Arc de Triomphe du Carroussel.

The palace of the Louvre, whose architecture is very varied, was enlarged by Louis XIV. It is perhaps a pity that the Pyramide, the construction of which was completed in the 80s, should be so different from the rest of the palace.

It was President François Mitterrand who ordered a modern extension to be constructed at the **Louvre**. He insisted that the architect should have an international reputation.

Some French people find it regrettable that he should have chosen a foreign architect. They are afraid that the contrast between the historic buildings and the Pyramide will be too striking. However, people will have to get used to such developments if they want the historic buildings to continue to be used in the modern world.

Unit 17

Questionnaire of the month!

Your wishes? Your fears? Your plans?
Answer our questions to understand them all better!
Compare your replies with those of your family and friends!
Maybe you'll get a surprise?

The questions in our questionnaire have been prepared so that you can analyse for yourself the problems you are confronted with. Even though you may have a happy family life, it is possible that your plans and those of your nearest and dearest may not be compatible.

You don't believe such a conflict could arise? We hope you're right, however … Don't wait for the problems to overwhelm you!

• The first part of the questionnaire is about what you want. You'd like to travel? You want to change your job? You'd like to move house? What do the others think?

• In the second section, you will confront your nightmares.

Are you afraid that we'll all be killed by pollution? Are you scared to take a plane? And for your friends, your colleagues, your family? Do you think the future may have unpleasant surprises in store for them?

Finally, we give you the chance to think seriously about your future plans.
What can you do to overcome your fears and ensure a happy future?

Don't say it's too difficult! It's certain that, if you reply seriously, you will be able to think calmly about the unpleasant things life may have in store for you.

Unit 18

Extract from a letter from Stéphanie to her cousin Jeannette:

My dear little Jojo,

*You'd better sit down! What would surprise you the most?
Could you imagine your big cousin married — and to a foreigner? How would you feel about a spring wedding?*

*You'd be one of the bridesmaids and the other one would be
… a Scottish girl! because I'm getting married to Mark,
a Scots boy I met during my work placement.*

I know you thought I'd never get married, because I wanted to pursue my career. I'm starting to think that one could do both. You shouldn't agree to stay at home simply because you're married. I'm really determined to carry on working — what's the use of having done a work placement in Scotland if afterwards I can't take advantage of everything I've learnt?

*Have you ever thought about doing a work placement abroad?
I assure you that you'd benefit enormously from the experience — and maybe you'd meet someone as wonderful as Mark. I thought I'd be bored and that I'd find it hard to leave my family, but I quickly got used to life and work in a different country. …*

Unit 1

1

a Je vous **présente** Alison. Elle **a** 48 ans.

b Elle **est** professeur d'histoire-géographie.

c Voici Patrick. **Il a** 54 ans.

d Il **est directeur** (de supermarché).

e Ils **ont** trois enfants: Mark, Sandy, Andrew.

f Andrew **ne** travaille **pas**. Il **est/va** à l'école.

2

a Comment **s'appellent** les parents de Mark? Comment **vont** les parents de Mark?

b Quel âge **a** Sandy?

c **Est-ce que** Sandy travaille?

d Les Dickson **habitent**-ils (à) Aberdeen?

e Et Stéphanie? **Habite-t-elle** (à) Dundee?

3

a Ils s'appellent Alison et Patrick. Ils vont bien.

b Sandy a 20 ans.

c Elle ne travaille pas. Elle est étudiante.

d Ils n'habitent pas (à) Aberdeen. Ils habitent (à) Dundee.

e Elle n'habite pas (à) Dundee. Elle habite (à) Aberdeen.

Unit 2

1

a Qu'est-ce que **votre** maman fait comme passe-temps?

b Elle aime **les** randonnées en montagne, **la** photographie et faire **du** ski.

c Et **votre** père? **Quels** sports fait-il?

d Il joue **au** golf.

e **Où** est-ce qu'il joue au golf?

f **Qui** est sur **la** photo?

g C'est **mon** frère Andrew et ici c'est **ma** soeur Sandy.

h Qu'est-ce qu'elle fait dans **la** vie?

i Elle est étudiante. Elle fait **des** études de sciences humaines et de français.

2

Comment t'appelles-tu? / Comment tu t'appelles? / Tu t'appelles comment?

Où est-ce que tu habites? / Où tu habites? / Tu habites où?

Quand joues-tu au rugby? / Quand est-ce que tu joues au rugby?

3

Mon anniversaire est le *26 mai.*

Je suis né/e le *26 mai 1987.*

Aujourd'hui, la date est/c'est *le 25 février 20--*

Aujourd'hui, nous sommes *le 25 février 20--* C'est/nous sommes *le mercredi 25 février 20--).*

Unit 3

1 a

George est un homme **grand**. Il mesure **1.92m**.

Il est **blond**. Il **a** les cheveux **bouclés** et les yeux **bleus**.

Isabelle a les **cheveux bruns, mi-longs**. Elle est **mince** et **jolie**. Elle a les **yeux marron**.

Ils ont la **quarantaine**.

b

Stéphanie est **jolie**. Elle a les yeux **bleus**. Elle a les cheveux blonds, bouclés. Elle est blonde. Elle a les cheveux bouclés. Elle est mince. Nicolas est blond. Il a les cheveux blonds. Il est grand et mince. Il mesure 1.90m. Il a les yeux noisette.

2
231 456: deux cent trente et un mille quatre cent cinquante-six
245 985: deux cent quarante-cinq mille neuf cent quatre-vingt-cinq
3 500 765: trois million cinq cent mille sept cent soixante-cinq

12-hour system 6.15: Il est six heures et quart.
3.45: Il est quatre heures moins le quart.
3.05: Il est trois heures cinq.

24-hour system 13.55: Il est treize heures cinquante-cinq.
22.35: Il est vingt-deux heures trente-cinq.
23.45: Il est vingt-trois heures quarante-cinq.

Unit 4

1
a Je voudrais un kilo de belles pommes rouges.
b Quelle taille vous désirez acheter?/Vous désirez acheter quelle taille?
Quelle taille désirez-vous acheter?
c Je ne veux plus de viande, merci.
d Nous voudrions acheter du parfum pour ma mère.
e Laquelle de ces robes voudriez-vous?

2
a Isabelle voudrait **du** pâté, **du** beurre, **du** fromage, **des** pommes de terre, **de la** limonade, **des** croissants.
b Stéphanie a besoin de/d':
une bouteille de bordeaux.
un gros poulet.
un **kilo d'**oignons.
500 **grammes de** champignons.
une **livre / une plaquette de** beurre.
5 **kilos de** pommes de terre.

3
Je voudrais:
un pantalon	**Lequel** préfères-tu?
des bonbons	**Lesquels** préfères-tu
des cerises	**Lesquelles** préfères-tu?
du whisky	**Lequel** préfères-tu?

Unit 5

1
a Je **choisis** une fleur. Je prends **celle-ci.**

b Tu **choisis** un pot de confiture. Tu prends **celui-ci.**
c Il/Elle/On **choisit** un stylo-plume. Il/Elle/On prend **celui-ci.**
d Nous **choisissons** un livre. Nous prenons **celui-ci.**
e Vous **choisissez** des brochures. Vous prenez **celles-ci.**
f Ils/Elles **choisissent** des biscuits. Ils/Elles prennent **ceux-ci.**

2
a
A St Amand nous **entendons** les cloches de l'Abbaye sonner tous les jours
Ils **entendent** leurs voisins partir très tôt.
Quand Mark joue au rugby il **salit** son maillot.
Mark **réfléchit** et **choisit** l'assiette en porcelaine pour sa voisine.
b
A St Amand nous **les** entendons sonner tous les jours.
Ils **les** entendent partir très tôt.
Quand Mark joue au rugby il **le** salit.
Mark réfléchit et **la** choisit pour sa voisine.

3
Un hôtel quatre étoiles est **plus** luxueux **qu'**un hôtel deux étoiles.
Un hôtel deux étoiles est **moins** luxueux **qu'**un hôtel quatre étoiles.

La Tour Eiffel est **plus** haute **que** la Tour de Blackpool.
La Tour de Blackpool est **moins** haute **que** la Tour Eiffel.

Mark est **plus** âgé **que** Stéphanie.
Stéphanie est **moins** âgée **que** Mark.
Elle est **plus** jeune **que** Mark.

Unit 6

1
a Je vais visiter l'Abbaye de St Amand.
b Est-ce que tu vas acheter des cartes postales?
c J'aimerais aller voir les sangliers dans le bois de St Amand.

2
a Mark **écrit** des cartes postales **de** St Amand et **les** envoie à sa famille à Dundee et à ses amis.
b Les parents de Mark **vivent dans** un quartier résidentiel **de/à** Dundee.
c Mr Dickson **prend** le bus **pour / afin de** se rendre au travail le matin.
d Il est directeur **d'**un supermarché à quelques kilomètres **du** centre

ville **près de** / **au bord de** la rivière Tay.

e   Il **part** à 8 heures le matin et **revient** à 18 heures, **sauf** le jeudi soir car il travaille **jusqu'à** 21 heures.

3

Dundee occupe une position **très/vraiment** privilégiée sur la côte est de l'Écosse. Les deux collines, Balgay et Law, offrent une vue **vraiment** superbe de la Tay et de la campagne. Dundee est une ville **très/principalement/**bien connue pour le bateau Discovery et l'observatoire de Balgay avec ses vues féériques. Dundee est une ville **toujours/très/vraiment** accueillante pas très loin de St Andrews, **mondialement/très** célèbre pour le golf.

Unit 7

1

Où se trouve votre maison?   Où se trouve **la vôtre?**
Andrew ne trouve pas ses disques compacts. Andrew ne trouve pas **les siens.**
Il prend mes disques. Il prend **les miens.**
J'oublie souvent de rendre tes disques. J'oublie souvent de rendre **les tiens.**

2

C'est le dictionnaire **de** Sandy.
Ce magazine appartient **à** Sandy.
Ce livre n'est pas à **toi.** C'est **le mien.**
Leurs voisins sont plus aimables que **les nôtres.**
Ce catalogue *La Redoute* **appartient** à Sandy.
«Est-ce qu'il y a des photos de **toi** dans ce catalogue?», demande Andrew.
La voiture garée en face de la maison des Dickson est à **eux.**
La nouvelle Peugeot 405 n'est pas **la leur.** C'est celle de **leurs** voisins.

Unit 8

1

S   Je vais demander à mes parents s'ils **veulent** rester chez nous à ce moment-là. Je crois que Papa ne **doit** pas travailler le 14 juillet car c'est férié.
Est-ce que tu **sais** combien de temps ils **peuvent/veulent** rester?

M   Je ne **sais** pas exactement. Une quinzaine de jours. Ils **veulent /
ont envie d'**inviter tes parents à venir en Écosse l'année prochaine. Est-ce que tu crois que tes parents

ont **envie de/veulent** venir à Dundee?

S   Oui, j'en suis sûre. Cette année ils ne **peuvent** pas partir en vacances.

2

Est-ce que vous **savez** parler français?
Est-ce que tu **veux** aller au cinéma?
Est-ce qu'il **peut** rentrer tard?
Est-ce que nous **devons** ranger nos affaires?

Unit 9

1

Tu arrives à l'aéroport Roissy-Charles de Gaulle et **tu prends** l'autoroute du nord, la A1, jusqu'à Péronne.
Ensuite **tu prends** la A2 jusqu'à la sortie Cambrai/Valenciennes.
Quitte la A2 à Valenciennes et **continue** jusqu'à la Sentinelle. Là, **tu dois** prendre la A23 jusqu'à la sortie St. Amand/Lille.
Quitte la A23 à l'entrée de St Amand et **prends** la voie rapide jusqu'à la forêt de Raismes. Au deuxième rond-point, **tourne** à gauche et **tu es** au chemin de l'Empire.

2

Prenez la première à droite / à gauche.
Continuez tout droit jusqu'au coin.
Descendez la rue de Lille.
Tournez à gauche / à droite.

3

a   Tu **leur** dis que c'est d'accord.
b   Tu **lui** téléphones pour dire quand tu vas revenir.
c   Tu **leur** donnes les directions.
d   Patrick **lui** demande les directions exactes.

Unit 10

1   (model answer): Pendant les vacances, nous voulons nous reposer, mais nos parents préfèrent être très actifs.
C'est pour cette raison que nous essayons de nous lever le plus tard possible.
D'abord nous mangeons un petit déjeuner copieux.
Puis nous prenons une douche et nous nous habillons très lentement.
Alors nous discutons interminablement le programme du jour.

Il est donc midi et nous n'avons
pas pris une décision.
Après avoir mangé, il faut
accepter de sortir car nos parents
commencent à se fâcher.
Finalement, tout le monde est
prêt, et nous pouvons enfin partir.

Unit 11

Stéphanie   Aujourd'hui je
travaillerai au bureau.
Je **taperai** des lettres
pour mon chef et
j'assisterai à une
réunion des membres du
département de
ressources humaines.
Est-ce que tu **viendras**
me chercher à 17 heures
30? On **achètera** de quoi
manger à **Marks et
Spencer.**

Mark   Ce soir je **mangerai** avec
Stéphanie. Mardi je ne
serai pas ici car je **prendrai**
l'hélicoptère et je
recommencerai à travailler
sur une plate-forme BP. Je
règlerai l'appareil de
forage et je le **contrôlerai**
par ordinateur. Nous
serons sur plate-forme
pour trois semaines. Je ne
verrai pas Stéphanie et elle
me **manquera** beaucoup.

Alison   Aujourd'hui à 4 heures
nous **aurons** une réunion
de tous les enseignants.
Elle **durera** au moins 2
heures et demie et je ne
rentrerai pas avant 7
heures 30. Vous **préparerez**
vous-mêmes le dîner – et il
ne **faudra** pas oublier de
faire la vaisselle!

Georges   Est-ce que nous **pourrons**
manger à 9 heures ce soir?
La réparation de la
tuyauterie chez Madame
Vincent ne **sera** pas
terminée et je **devrai** aussi
remplacer les robinets
dans sa salle de bains.

Unit 12

1   (model answer)
Utilise ta carte Cirrus à la banque.
Achète tes repas dans les
restaurants avec ta carte Visa.
Utilise tes travellers dans les
magasins.
Utilise ta carte Visa dans les
grands magasins.

Change tes devises à la banque.
Achète une ceinture porte-
monnaie.

2   (model answer)
N'ouvrez pas votre porte-monnaie
dans le métro!
Ne changez pas vos travellers à
l'hôtel!
Ne laissez pas votre carte de crédit
et votre passeport dans votre
chambre!
Ne laissez pas votre porte-
monnaie dans le métro!

3   (model answer)
Tu nous donnes ton numéro de
téléphone.
Il apporte la rose à Stéphanie.
Nous offrons les cadeaux à toi,
Maman!

4
Oui, je **le lui** donne. Non, je ne **le
lui** donne pas.
Oui, je **les leur** apporte. Non, je
ne **les leur** apporte pas.
Oui, nous **le leur** recommandons.
Non. nous ne **le leur**
recommandons pas.

Unit 13

1   Par exemple:
Nous **avons laissé** la voiture dans
le parking. Ma femme **a** tout de
suite **reconnu** les Dickson. Ils **ont
appris** à parler français, et ma
femme leur **a parlé** lentement.

2   Quel voyage! D'abord le taxi n'**est
pas arrivé** à l'heure. Nous **avons
téléphoné** à la compagnie et ils
ont envoyé un autre taxi, mais
nous **sommes arrivés** à la gare
deux minutes avant le départ du
train. Nous **avons couru** et nous
avons attrapé le train de justesse.
Avec des valises très lourdes et
tous les paquets des enfants, nous
avons eu du mal à trouver des
places. Finalement, nous **nous
sommes assis** dans un wagon
fumeurs. Naturellement ça m'**a
donné** la migraine!

3   (model answer)
Oui, nous **sommes parti(e)s** en
vacances en été.
Nous **sommes allé(e)s** à St Omer.
Nous **avons vu** la mer et
beaucoup de gens sur la plage.
Non, je **n'ai pas acheté** de
souvenirs parce que je n'ai pas
d'argent.

Bien sûr que oui! Elle **a acheté** des choses stupides – des animaux en peluche et une assiette horrible.

Unit 14

1 (model answer)
Nous habitions San Francisco aux États-Unis.
J'aimais le pont qui s'appelle le *Pont d'or*.
Je n'aimais pas la brume.
Mon père était ingénieur et il travaillait souvent dans d'autres villes.
Nous n'avions pas de famille à San Francisco, car mes parents sont français.
Mes frères et mes soeurs étaient très contents de se trouver aux États-Unis.
Ce qui nous amusait, c'était de cacher le chat dans la corbeille à linge.

2
imparfait – **tu te souviens; pendant mon enfance**
passé composé – **un jour; ce jour-là**

Tu te souviens, Stéphanie? Moi, j'**étais** toujours plus petit que toi et pendant mon enfance, j'**avais** honte, parce que ma soeur **était** plus grande que moi. Et puis, un jour, j'**ai remarqué** que je **mesurais** quelques centimètres de plus que toi. Ce jour-là, j'**ai fait** la fête!

Unit 15

1 Avant la première guerre mondiale, les Allemands **avaient** bien **préparé** leurs armées, de sorte que les armées des alliés **ont perdu** des millions d'hommes dans des batailles dans le nord de la France. A Verdun, des millions de soldats **sont morts** et les Allemands **ont traversé** facilement la Ligne Maginot.

2
a Dans le nord de la France la terre est très plate, **donc** le paysage est quelquefois monotone, **mais** les villages sont agréables à voir.

b On célèbre le jour de l'Armistice le 11 novembre **parce que / car** la guerre a cessé le 11 novembre **et** on achète des coquelicots ce jour-là en Grande-Bretagne, **car / parce que** les coquelicots poussent dans les champs de la Flandre.

Unit 16

1 *'Signals'*   *Verbs*
il faut que   soient
a peur que   (ne manquent
a insisté que   se calme
veut que   soit

2 (model answers)
Comme je veux apprendre le français, il faut que je travaille beaucoup.
Pour bien parler français, il est important que tu assistes à toutes les classes.
Je voudrais aller au cinéma ce soir, mais mon père insiste que nous restions à la maison.
Ma mère va au supermarché demain. Qu'est-ce que tu veux qu'elle achète?

3
• Tout ce que ma femme veut faire c'est visiter les musées de Paris.
• Ce qui est intéressant c'est la différence entre le Palais du Louvre et la Pyramide.
• Ce qu'il faut voir, c'est le Musée du Louvre.

Unit 17

1 (model answer)
J'espère que mes parents aimeront les Lemaire.
J'ai peur qu'ils aient du mal à comprendre le français.

J'espère que mon père m'achètera un nouvel ordinateur.
Je crains qu'il n'ait pas suffisamment d'argent.

2 (model answer)
J'espère aimer les Lemaire.
J'ai peur d'avoir du mal à parler français.

J'espère acheter un nouvel ordinateur.
Je crains de ne pas avoir suffisamment d'argent.

3
Bien que j'aime bien mes collègues, je vais changer d'emploi.
Bien que mes enfants veuillent rester ici, je vais changer d'emploi.
Bien que ma femme soit contente ici, je vais changer d'emploi.

4 (model answer)
J'ai décidé d'inviter tous mes cousins britanniques à la réunion

afin que nous puissions les rencontrer.

J'ai décidé de louer plusieurs chambres à l'hôtel pour que tout le monde soit ensemble.

J'ai décidé de faire une grande réunion familiale en été de sorte que tous nos parents soient libres au même moment.

Unit 18

1 Vous pourriez acheter une grande maison, si vous aviez beaucoup d'argent.
Elle croyait que son frère se marierait avec une Écossaise.
Nous pensions que le voyage coûterait moins cher.
Si Mark se mariait en France, nous y reviendrions avec grand plaisir.
J'aimerais célébrer mes fiançailles à Noël.

2 (model answers)
Si j'avais un oncle très riche, je lui demanderais de m'acheter une voiture.
Si j'avais un oncle très riche, il me donnerait des cadeaux merveilleux.

Si j'avais perdu les clés de la voiture, j'irais à la police.
Si j'avais perdu les clés de la voiture, je serais affolé(e).
Si les Martiens envahissaient la terre, nous verrions qu'ils ne sont pas verts.
Si les Martiens envahissaient la terre, tout le monde aurait peur.

3 Je voudrais que tu me prêtes ta voiture.
Nicolas, je préférerais que tu ne sortes pas ce soir.
Chéri, tu sais, j'aimerais mieux que tu rentres sans aller au bar.

Key irregular verbs in different tenses

.. = past participle repeated

– = part in bold repeated

avoir *to have* Present participle: **ayant** Past participle: **eu/e/s**

Present (Imperative)	Future	Conditional	Imperfect	Perfect (Past Historic)	Pluperfect	Present Subjunctive (Perfect Subjunctive)
j'ai	aurai	aurais	avais	ai eu	avais eu	aie
tu as	auras	aurais	avais	as eu	avais eu	aies
il/elle/on a	aura	aurait	avait	a eu	avait eu	ait
nous avons	aurons	aurions	avions	avons eu	avions eu	ayons
vous avez	aurez	auriez	aviez	avez eu	aviez eu	ayez
ils/elles ont	auront	auraient	avaient	ont eu	avaient eu	aient
(aie, ayons, ayez)				(eus, eus, eut, eûmes, eûtes, eurent)		(aie eu, aies eu, etc.)

être *to be* Present participle: **étant** Past participle: **été**

Present (Imperative)	Future	Conditional	Imperfect	Perfect (Past Historic)	Pluperfect	Present Subjunctive (Perfect Subjunctive)
je suis	serai	serais	étais	ai été	avais été	sois
tu es	seras	serais	étais	as été	avais été	sois
il/elle/on est	sera	serait	était	a été	avait été	soit
nous sommes	serons	serions	étions	avons été	avions été	soyons
vous êtes	serez	seriez	étiez	avez été	aviez été	soyez
ils/elles sont	seront	seraient	étaient	ont été	avaient été	soient
(sois, soyons, soyez)				(fus, fus, fut, fûmes, fûtes, furent)		(aie été, aies été etc.)

s'asseoir *to sit down* Present participle: s'asseyant Past participle: assis/e/s

Present (Imperative)	Future	Conditional	Imperfect	Perfect (Past Historic)	Pluperfect	Present Subjunctive (Perfect Subjunctive)
je m'assieds	– assiérai	– assiérais	– asseyais	– suis assis(e)	– étais assis(e)	– asseye
tu t'assieds	– assiéras	– assiérais	– asseyais	– es assis(e)	– étais ..	– asseyes
il s'assied	– assiéra	– assiérait	– asseyait	– est assis(e)	– était ..	– asseye
nous nous asseyons	– assiérons	– assiérions	– asseyions	– sommes assis(e)s	– étions ..	– asseyions
vous vous asseyez,	– assiérez	– assiériez	– asseyiez	– êtes assis(e)s	– étiez ..	– asseyiez
ils s'asseyent	– assiéront	– assiéraient	– asseyaient	– sont assis(e)s	– étaient ..	– asseyent
(assieds-toi, asseyons-nous, asseyez-vous)				(– assis, – assis, – assit, – assîmes, – assîtes, – assirent)		(– sois assis(e), – sois assis(e) etc.)

aller *to go* Present participle: allant Past participle: allé/e/s

Present (Imperative)	Future	Conditional	Imperfect	Perfect (Past Historic)	Pluperfect	Present Subjunctive (Perfect Subjunctive)
je vais	irai	irais	allais	suis allé(e)	étais allé(e)	aille
tu vas	iras	irais	allais	es allé(e)	étais ..	ailles
il va	ira	irait	allait	est allé(e)	était ..	aille
nous allons	irons	irions	allions	sommes allé(e)s	étions ..	allions
vous allez	irez	iriez	alliez	êtes allé(e)(s)	étiez ..	alliez
ils vont	iront	iraient	allaient	sont allé(e)s	étaient ..	aillent
(va, allons, allez)				(allai, allas, alla, allâmes, allâtes, allèrent)		(sois allé(e), sois allé(e) etc.)

boire *to drink* Present participle: buvant Past participle: bu/e/s

Present (Imperative)	Future	Conditional	Imperfect	Perfect (Past Historic)	Pluperfect	Present Subjunctive (Perfect Subjunctive)
je bois	boirai	boirais	buvais	ai bu	avais bu	boive
tu bois	boiras	boirais	buvais	as bu	avais ..	boives
il boit	boira	boirait	buvait	a bu	avait ..	boive
nous buvons	boirons	boirions	buvions	avons bu	avions ..	buvions
vous buvez	boirez	boiriez	buviez	avez bu	avaient ..	buviez
ils boivent	boiront	boiraient	buvaient	ont bu		boivent
(bois, buvons, buvez)				(bus, bus, but, bûmes, bûtes, burent)		(aie bu, aies bu etc.)

croire *to believe* Present participle: croyant Past participle: cru/e/s

Present (Imperative)	Future	Conditional	Imperfect	Perfect (Past Historic)	Pluperfect	Present Subjunctive (Perfect Subjunctive)
je crois	croirai	croirais	croyais	ai cru	avais cru	croie
tu crois	croiras	croirais	croyais	as cru	avais ..	croies
il croit	croira	croirait	croyait	a cru	avait ..	croie
nous croyons	croirons	croirions	croyions	avons cru	avions ..	croyions
vous croyez	croirez	croiriez	croyiez	avez cru	aviez ..	croyiez
ils croient	croiront	croiraient	croyaient	ont cru	avaient ..	croient
(crois, croyons, croyez)				(crus, crus, crut, crûmes, crûtes, crurent)		(aie cru, aies cru etc.)

devoir *to have to / to owe* Present participle: devant Past participle: dû *(for owed only: dû/s/due/s)*

Present (Imperative)	Future	Conditional	Imperfect	Perfect (Past Historic)	Pluperfect	Present Subjunctive (Perfect Subjunctive)
je dois	devrai	devrais	devais	ai dû	avais dû	doive
tu dois	devras	devrais	devais	as dû	avais ..	doives
il doit	devra	devrait	devait	a dû	avait ..	doive
nous devons	devrons	devrions	devions	avons dû	avions ..	devions
vous devez	devrez	devriez	deviez	avez dû	aviez ..	deviez
ils doivent	devront	devraient	devaient	ont dû	avaient ..	doivent
				(dus, dus, dut, dûmes, dûtes, durent)		(aie dû, aies dû etc.)

dire *to say* Present participle: disant Past participle: dit/e/s

Present (Imperative)	Future	Conditional	Imperfect	Perfect (Past Historic)	Pluperfect	Present Subjunctive (Perfect Subjunctive)
je dis	dirai	dirais	disais	ai dit	avais dit	dise
tu dis	diras	dirais	disais	as dit	avais ..	dises
il dit	dira	dirait	disait	a dit	avait ..	dise
nous disons	dirons	dirions	disions	avons dit	avions ..	disions
vous dites	direz	diriez	disiez	avez dit	aviez ..	disiez
ils disent	diront	diraient	disaient	ont dit	avaient ..	disent
(dis, disons, dites)				(dis, dis, dit, dîmes, dîtes, dirent)		(aie dit, aies dit etc.)

dormir *to sleep*   Present participle: **dormant**   Past participle: **dormi**

Present (Imperative)	Future	Conditional	Imperfect	Perfect (Past Historic)	Pluperfect	Present Subjunctive (Perfect Subjunctive)
je dors	dormirai	dormirais	dormais	ai dormi	avais dormi	dorme
tu dors	dormiras	dormirais	dormais	as dormi	avais ..	dormes
il dort	dormira	dormirait	dormait	a dormi	avait ..	dorme
nous dormons	dormirons	dormirions	dormions	avons dormi	avions ..	dormions
vous dormez	dormirez	dormiriez	dormiez	avez dormi	aviez ..	dormiez
ils dorment	dormiront	dormiraient	dormaient	ont dormi	avaient ..	dorment
(dors, dormons, dormez)				(**dormis**, –is, –it, –îmes, –îtes, –irent)		(aie dormi, aies dormi etc.)

envoyer *to send*   Present participle: **envoyant**   Past participle: **envoyé/e/s**

Present (Imperative)	Future	Conditional	Imperfect	Perfect (Past Historic)	Pluperfect	Present Subjunctive (Perfect Subjunctive)
j'envoie	enverrai	enverrais	envoyais	ai envoyé	avais envoyé	envoie
tu envoies	enverras	enverrais	envoyais	as envoyé	avais ..	envoies
il envoie	enverra	enverrait	envoyait	a envoyé	avait ..	envoie
nous envoyons	enverrons	enverrions	envoyions	avons envoyé	avions ..	envoyions
vous envoyez	enverrez	enverriez	envoyiez	avez envoyé	aviez ..	envoyiez
ils envoient	enverront	enverraient	envoyaient	ont envoyé	avaient ..	envoient
(envoie, envoyons, envoyez)				(**envoyai**, –as, –a, –âmes, –âtes, –èrent)		(aie envoyé, aies envoyé etc.)

faire *to do*   Present participle: **faisant**   Past participle: **fait/e/s**

Present (Imperative)	Future	Conditional	Imperfect	Perfect (Past Historic)	Pluperfect	Present Subjunctive (Perfect Subjunctive)
je fais	ferai	ferais	faisais	ai fait	avais fait	fasse
tu fais	feras	ferais	faisais	as fait	avais ..	fasses
il fait	fera	ferait	faisait	a fait	avait ..	fasse
nous faisons	ferons	ferions	faisions	avons fait	avions ..	fassions
vous faites	ferez	feriez	faisiez	avez fait	aviez ..	fassiez
ils font	feront	feraient	faisaient	ont fait	avaient ..	fassent
(fais, faisons, faites)				(fis, fis, fit, fîmes, fîtes, firent)		(aie fait, aies fait etc.)

Present (Imperative)	Future	Conditional	Imperfect	Perfect (Past Historic)	Pluperfect	Present Subjunctive (Perfect Subjunctive)

falloir *to be necessary* Present participle: **fallant** Past participle: **fallu/e/s**

Present (Imperative)	Future	Conditional	Imperfect	Perfect (Past Historic)	Pluperfect	Present Subjunctive (Perfect Subjunctive)
il faut	il faudra	il faudrait	il fallait	il a fallu (il fallut)	il avait fallu	il faille (il ait fallu)

offrir *to offer* Present participle: **offrant** Past participle: **offert/e/s**

Present (Imperative)	Future	Conditional	Imperfect	Perfect (Past Historic)	Pluperfect	Present Subjunctive (Perfect Subjunctive)
j'offre	offrirai	offrirais	offrais	ai offert	avais offert	offre
tu offres	offriras	offrirais	offrais	as offert	avais ..	offres
il offre	offrira	offrirait	offrait	a offert	avait ..	offre
nous offrons	offrirons	offririons	offrions	avons offert	avions ..	offrions
vous offrez	offrirez	offririez	offriez	avez offert	aviez ..	offriez
ils offrent	offriront	offriraient	offraient	ont offert	avaient ..	offrent
(offre, offrons, offrez)				(**offris**, –is, –it, –îmes, –îtes, –irent)		(aie offert, aies offert etc.)

ouvrir *to open* Present participle: **ouvrant** Past participle: **ouvert/e/s**

Present (Imperative)	Future	Conditional	Imperfect	Perfect (Past Historic)	Pluperfect	Present Subjunctive (Perfect Subjunctive)
j'ouvre	ouvrirai	ouvrirais	ouvrais	ai ouvert	avais ouvert	ouvre
tu ouvres	ouvriras	ouvrirais	ouvrais	as ouvert	avais ..	ouvres
il ouvre	ouvrira	ouvrirait	ouvrait	a ouvert	avait ..	ouvre
nous ouvrons	ouvrirons	ouvririons	ouvrions	avons ouvert	avions ..	ouvrions
vous ouvrez	ouvrirez	ouvririez	ouvriez	avez ouvert	aviez ..	ouvriez
ils ouvrent	ouvriront	ouvriraient	ouvraient	ont ouvert	avaient ..	ouvrent
(ouvre, ouvrons, ouvrez)				(**ouvris**, –is, –it, –îmes, –îtes, –irent)		(aie ouvert, aies ouvert etc.)

Present (Imperative)	Future	Conditional	Imperfect	Perfect (Past Historic)	Pluperfect	Present Subjunctive (Perfect Subjunctive)

partir *to leave* Present participle: **partant** Past participle: **parti/e/s**

Present (Imperative)	Future	Conditional	Imperfect	Perfect (Past Historic)	Pluperfect	Present Subjunctive (Perfect Subjunctive)
je pars	partirai	partirais	partais	suis parti(e)	étais parti(e)	parte
tu pars	partiras	partirais	partais	es parti(e)	étais ..	partes
il part	partira	partirait	partait	est parti(e)	était ..	parte
nous partons	partirons	partirions	partions	sommes parti(e)s	étions ..	partions
vous partez	partirez	partiriez	partiez	êtes parti(e)(s)	étiez ..	partiez
ils partent	partiront	partiraient	partaient	sont parti(e)s	étaient ..	partent
(pars, partons, partez)				(partis, –is, –it, –îmes, –îtes, –irent)		(sois parti(e), sois parti(e) etc.)

pouvoir *to be able to* Present participle: **pouvant** Past participle: **pu**

Present (Imperative)	Future	Conditional	Imperfect	Perfect (Past Historic)	Pluperfect	Present Subjunctive (Perfect Subjunctive)
je peux	pourrai	pourrais	pouvais	ai pu	avais pu	puisse
tu peux	pourras	pourrais	pouvais	as pu	avais pu	puisses
il peut	pourra	pourrait	pouvait	a pu	avait pu	puisse
nous pouvons	pourrons	pourrions	pouvions	avons pu	avions pu	puissions
vous pouvez	pourrez	pourriez	pouviez	avez pu	aviez pu	puissiez
ils peuvent	pourront	pourraient	pouvaient	ont pu	avaient pu	puissent
				(pus, pus, put, pûmes, pûtes, purent)		(aie pu, aies pu etc.)

prendre *to take* Present participle: **prenant** Past participle: **pris/e/s**

Present (Imperative)	Future	Conditional	Imperfect	Perfect (Past Historic)	Pluperfect	Present Subjunctive (Perfect Subjunctive)
je prends	prendrai	prendrais	prenais	ai pris	avais pris	prenne
tu prends	prendras	prendrais	prenais	as pris	avais ..	prennes
il prend	prendra	prendrait	prenait	a pris	avait ..	prenne
nous prenons	prendrons	prendrions	prenions	avons pris	avions ..	prenions
vous prenez	prendrez	prendriez	preniez	avez pris	aviez ..	preniez
ils prennent	prendront	prendraient	prenaient	ont pris	avaient ..	prennent
(prends prenons, prenez)				(pris, pris, prit, prîmes, prîtes, prirent)		(aie pris, aies pris etc.)

recevoir *to receive* Present participle: recevant Past participle: reçu/e/s

Present (Imperative)	Future	Conditional	Imperfect	Perfect (Past Historic)	Pluperfect	Present Subjunctive (Perfect Subjunctive)
je reçois	recevrai	recevrais	recevais	ai reçu	avais reçu	reçoive
tu reçois	recevras	recevrais	recevais	as reçu	avais ..	reçoives
il reçoit	recevra	recevrait	recevait	a reçu	avait ..	reçoive
nous recevons	recevrons	recevrions	recevions	avons reçu	avions ..	recevions
vous recevez	recevrez	recevriez	receviez	avez reçu	aviez ..	receviez
ils reçoivent	recevront	recevraient	recevaient	ont reçu	avaient ..	reçoivent
(reçois, recevons, (recevez)				(reçus, –us, –ut, –ûmes, –ûtes, –urent)		(aie reçu, aies reçu etc.)

savoir *to know* Present participle: sachant Past participle: su/e/s

Present (Imperative)	Future	Conditional	Imperfect	Perfect (Past Historic)	Pluperfect	Present Subjunctive (Perfect Subjunctive)
je sais	saurai	saurais	savais	ai su	avais su	sache
tu sais	sauras	saurais	savais	as su	avais ..	saches
il sait	saura	saurait	savait	a su	avait ..	sache
nous savons	saurons	saurions	savions	avons su	avions ..	sachions
vous savez	saurez	sauriez	saviez	avez su	aviez ..	sachiez
ils savent	sauront	sauraient	savaient	ont su	avaient ..	sachent
(sache, sachons, sachez)				(sus, sus, sut, sûmes, sûtes, surent)		(aie su, aies su etc.)

sortir *to go out* Present participle: sortant Past participle: sorti/e/s

Present (Imperative)	Future	Conditional	Imperfect	Perfect (Past Historic)	Pluperfect	Present Subjunctive (Perfect Subjunctive)
je sors	sortirai	sortirais	sortais	suis sorti(e)	étais sorti(e)	sorte
tu sors	sortiras	sortirais	sortais	es sorti(e)	étais ..	sortes
il sort	sortira	sortirait	sortait	est sorti(e)	était ..	sorte
nous sortons	sortirons	sortirions	sortions	sommes sorti(e)s	étions ..	sortions
vous sortez	sortirez	sortiriez	sortiez	êtes sorti(e)(s)	étiez ..	sortiez
ils sortent	sortiront	sortiraient	sortaient	sont sorti(e)s	étaient ..	sortent
(sors, sortons, sortez)				(sortis, –is, –is, –îmes, –îtes, –irent)		(sois sorti(e), sois sorti(e) etc.)

Present (Imperative)	Future	Conditional	Imperfect	Perfect (Past Historic)	Pluperfect	Present Subjunctive (Perfect Subjunctive)

tenir to hold   Present participle: **tenant**   Past participle: **tenu/e/s**

Present (Imperative)	Future	Conditional	Imperfect	Perfect (Past Historic)	Pluperfect	Present Subjunctive (Perfect Subjunctive)
je tiens	tiendrai	tiendrais	tenais	ai tenu	avais tenu	tienne
tu tiens	tiendras	tiendrais	tenais	as tenu	avais ..	tiennes
il tient	tiendra	tiendrait	tenait	a tenu	avait ..	tienne
nous tenons	tiendrons	tiendrions	tenions	avons tenu	avions ..	tenions
vous tenez	tiendrez	tiendriez	teniez	avez tenu	aviez ..	teniez
ils tiennent	tiendront	tiendraient	tenaient	ont tenu	avaient ..	tiennent
(tiens, tenons, tenez)				(tins, tins, tint, tînmes, tîntes, tinrent)		(aie tenu, aies tenu etc.)

voir to see   Present participle: **voyant**   Past participle: **vu/e/s**

Present (Imperative)	Future	Conditional	Imperfect	Perfect (Past Historic)	Pluperfect	Present Subjunctive (Perfect Subjunctive)
je vois	verrai	verrais	voyais	ai vu	avais vu	voie
tu vois	verras	verrais	voyais	as vu	avais ..	voies
il voit	verra	verrait	voyait	a vu	avait ..	voie
nous voyons	verrons	verrions	voyions	avons vu	avions ..	voyions
vous voyez	verrez	verriez	voyiez	avez vu	aviez ..	voyez
ils voient	verront	verraient	voyaient	ont vu	avaient ..	voient
(vois, voyons, voyez)				(vis, vis, vit, vîmes, vîtes, virent)		(aie vu, aies vu etc.)

vouloir to want   Present participle: **voulant**   Past participle: **voulu/e/s**

Present (Imperative)	Future	Conditional	Imperfect	Perfect (Past Historic)	Pluperfect	Present Subjunctive (Perfect Subjunctive)
je veux	voudrai	voudrais	voulais	ai voulu	avais voulu	veuille
tu veux	voudras	voudrais	voulais	as voulu	avais ..	veuilles
il veut	voudra	voudrait	voulait	a voulu	avait ..	veuille
nous voulons	voudrons	voudrions	voulions	avons voulu	avions ..	voulions
vous voulez	voudrez	voudriez	vouliez	avez voulu	aviez ..	vouliez
ils veulent	voudront	voudraient	voulaient	ont voulu	avaient ..	veuillent
(veuille, veuillons, veuillez)				(**voulu**s, –us, –ut, –ûmes, –ûtes, –urent)		(aie voulu, aies voulu etc.)

Other irregular verbs

The forms given here are for the first person singular (**je**) and plural (**nous**).

Verb *meaning* present participle past participle	*Present	Future/ Conditional	Imperfect
CONDUIRE *to drive* conduisant conduit/e/s	conduis conduisons	**conduir**ai/-ais **conduir**ons/-ions	conduisais conduisions
CONNAÎTRE *to know* connaissant connu/e/s	connais connaissons	**connaîtr**ai/ais **connaîtr**ons/-ions	connaissais connaissions
COURIR *to run* courant couru/e/s	cours courons	**courr**ai/ais **courr**ons/-ions	courais courions
CRAINDRE *to fear* craignant craint/e/s	crains craignons	**craindr**ai/-ais **craindr**ons/-ions	craignais craignions
CUEILLIR *to pick* cueillant cueilli/e/s	cueille cueillons	**cueiller**ai/-ais **cueiller**ons/-ions	cueillais cueillions
ÉCRIRE *to write* écrivant écrit/e/s	écris écrivons	**écrir**ai/-ais **écrir**ons/-ions	écrivais écrivions
LIRE *to read* lisant lu/e/s	lis lisons	**lir**ai/-ais **lir**ons/-ions	lisais lisions
METTRE *to put* mettant mis/e/s	mets mettons	**mettr**ai/-ais **mettr**ons/-ions	mettais mettions

*These forms are also the **tu** and **nous** forms of the imperative.
For the **vous** form just add -**ez** to the stem: e.g. **conduis**ez.

Perfect/ Pluperfect	Past Historic	Present Subjunctive	Perfect Subjunctive
ai/avais conduit	conduisis	conduise	aie conduit
avons/avions conduit	conduisîmes	conduisions	ayons conduit
ai/avais connu	connus	connaisse	aie connu
avons/avions connu	connûmes	connaissions	ayons connu
ai/avais couru	courus	coure	aie couru
avons/avions couru	courûmes	courions	ayons couru
ai/avais craint	craignis	craigne	aie craint
avons/avions craint	craignîmes	craignions	ayons craint
ai/avais cueilli	cueillis	cueille	aie cueilli
avons/avions cueilli	cueillîmes	cueillions	ayons cueilli
ai/avais écrit	écrivis	écrive	aie écrit
avons/avions écrit	écrivîmes	écrivions	ayons écrit
ai/avais lu	lus	lise	aie lu
avons/avions lu	lûmes	lisions	ayons lu
ai/avais mis	mis	mette	aie mis
avons/avions mis	mîmes	mettions	ayons mis

Verb	Present	Future/ Conditional	Imperfect
MOURIR *to die* mourant mort/e/s	meurs mourons	**mourr**ai/-ais **mourr**ons/-ions	mourais mourions
PARTIR *to leave* partant parti/e/s	pars partons	**partir**ai/-ais **partir**ons/-ions	partais partions
PLAIRE *to please* plaisant plu	plais plaisons	**plair**ai/-ais **plair**ons/-ions	plaisais plaisions
PLEUVOIR *to rain* pleuvant plu/e/s	il pleut	il pleuvra / il pleuvrait	il pleuvait
RIRE *to laugh* riant ri	ris rions	**rir**ai/-ais **rir**ons/-ions	riais riions
SOUFFRIR *to suffer* souffrant souffert/e/s	souffre souffrons	**souffrir**ai/-ais **souffrir**ons/-ions	souffrais souffrions
SUIVRE *to follow* suivant suivi/e/s	suis suivons	**suivr**ai/-ais **suivr**ons/-ions	suivais suivions
VALOIR *to be worth* valant valu/e/s	il vaut	il vaudra il vaudrait	il valait
VENIR *to know* venant venu/e/s	viens venons	**viendr**ai/-ais **viendr**ons/-ions	venais venions
VIVRE *to live* vivant vécu/e/s	vis vivons	**vivr**ai/-ais **vivr**ons/-ions	vivais vivions

Perfect/ Pluperfect	Past Historic	Present Subjunctive	Perfect Subjunctive
suis/étais mort(e)	mourus	meure	sois mort(e)
sommes/étions mort(e)s	mourûmes	mourions	soyons mort(e)s
suis/étais parti(e)	partis	parte	sois parti(e)
sommes/étions parti(e)s	partîmes	partions	soyons parti(e)s
ai/avais plu	plus	plaise	aie plu
avons/avions plu	plûmes	plaisions	ayons plu
il a plu/avait plu	il plut	il pleuve	il ait plu
ai/avais ri	ris	rie	aie ri
avons/avions ri	rîmes	riions	ayons ri
ai/avais souffert	souffris	souffre	aie souffert
avons/avions souffert	souffrîmes	souffrions	ayons souffert
ai/avais suivi	suivis	suive	aie suivi
avons/avions suivi	suivîmes	suivions	ayons suivi
il a/avait valu	il valut	il vaille	il ait valu
suis/étais venu(e)	vins	vienne	sois venu(e)
sommes/étions venu(e)s	vînmes	venions	soyons venu(e)s
ai/avais vécu	vécus	vive	aie vécu
avons/avions vécu	vécûmes	vivions	ayons vécu

Some -er verbs which have spelling changes in the present and future tenses:

Present tense

acheter *to buy* j'achète, tu achètes, il achète, nous achetons, vous achetez, ils achètent

appeler *to call* j'appelle, tu appelles, il appelle, nous appelons, vous appelez, ils appellent

commencer *to begin* je commence, tu commences, il commence, nous commençons, vous commencez, ils commencent

enlever *to take off/out* j'enlève, tu enlèves, il enlève, nous enlevons, vous enlevez, ils enlèvent

envoyer *to send* j'envoie, tu envoies, il envoie, nous envoyons, vous envoyez, ils envoient

jeter *to throw* je jette, tu jettes, il jette, nous jetons, vous jetez, ils jettent

placer *to place* je place, tu places, il place, nous plaçons, vous placez, ils placent

préférer *to prefer* je préfère, tu préfères, nous préférons, vous préférez, ils/elles préfèrent

promener *to take for a walk* je promène, tu promènes, il promène, nous promenons, vous promenez, ils/elles promènent

Future tense

acheter j'achèterai, tu achèteras, il achètera, nous achèterons, vous achèterez, ils achèteront

appeler j'appellerai, tu appelleras, il appellera, nous appellerons, vous appellerez, ils appelleront
Verbs following the same pattern: **épeler, rappeler.**

enlever j'enlèverai, tu enlèveras, il enlèvera, nous enlèverons, vous enlèverez, ils enlèveront
Verb following the same pattern: **relever.**

jeter je jetterai, tu jetteras, il jettera, nous jetterons, vous jetterez, ils jetteront

promener je promènerai, tu promèneras, il promènera, nous promènerons, vous promènerez, ils promèneront

This glossary is here to help you with some of the technical grammatical terms in *Teach Yourself French Grammar*. Words which have their own entry in the glossary are in bold (**noun**) so that you can check them easily. The unit where you will find fuller explanations and examples is shown in square brackets [Unit 1]. You will get the best results if you use the glossary in conjunction with the index (page 270).

active voice *(la voix active)* See **voice**.

adjective *(adjectif)* A word which qualifies a **noun**. In French adjectives agree (see **agreement**) in **gender** and number with the noun they qualify, i.e. their **ending** changes according to whether the noun is masculine or feminine, singular or plural. French adjectives usually come after **nouns,** although there are a few important short ones *(petit, grand* etc.) that can come before [Unit 3].

> **demonstrative adjective** *(un adjectif démonstratif)* ce, cet, cette, ces *(this, that, these, those)* + **noun** [Unit 2].

> **interrogative adjective** *(un adjectif interrogatif) quel, quelle, quels, quelles (which, what)* + **noun** [Unit 4].

> **possessive adjective** *(un adjectif possessif) mon, ton, son, mes, tes, ses* etc. *(my, your, his, her)* + **noun** [Unit 2]. See **possessives**.

adverb *(un adverbe)* A word (or group of words) which modifies the meaning of a **verb,** an **adjective** or another adverb. Adverbs never change their form. They describe *how, when* or *where* something happens. In English they usually end in *-ly,* in French usually in *-ment*. Their **stem** is normally an adjective *(**principalement** mainly;* **heureuse**ment *happily)*. Their usual position is after the **verb** or before the **adjective** or adverb they modify [Unit 6].

agreement (*un accord*) The matching of a **verb** with its **subject** [Unit 1] or an **adjective** with a **noun** [Unit 3]. In French, words agree in number (singular / plural) and in **gender**.

article (*un article*) A short word which goes with a **noun**.

> **definite article** (*un article défini*) *le, la, l', les* the [Unit 1].
>
> **indefinite article** (*un article indéfini*) *un, une* a/an, *des* some [Unit 1].
>
> **partitive article** (*un article partitif*) *du, de la, d', des* some/any [Unit 4].

auxiliary verb (*le verbe auxiliaire*) A **verb** used with other verbs to construct different **tenses**: *être* to be; *avoir to have* [Unit 13].

clause (*la proposition*) A group of words including a **verb** and its subject (**main clause, relative clause, subordinate clause**)

comparative (*le comparatif*) Used to compare or contrast two ideas: *plus / moins ... que more/less ... than; aussi ... que as ... as* [Unit 6].

compound sentence (*la phrase complexe*) A **sentence** which has more than one **clause**, a **main** or principal clause and a **surbordinate clause** or clauses [Units 10, 15].

compound tense (*le temps composé*) A **tense** made up of more than one word: an **auxiliary verb** + the **past participle**, e.g. the **perfect, pluperfect** or **future perfect**.

conditional tense (*le conditionnel*) The **tense** that tells you what _could / would / should happen_: a single word in French, **infinitive stem + imperfect** endings [Unit 18].

> **conditional perfect tense** (*le passé du conditionnel*) A **compound** tense made from the **conditional** tense of the **auxiliary** *être* or *avoir* + **past participle**. It tells you what _could / would have_ happened [Unit 18].

conjunction (*la conjonction*) Words which join two **clauses**, either **coordinating** conjunctions *et, mais and, but* or **subordinating** conjunctions *parce que, bien que, quand because, although, when* [Unit 10].

direct object (*un objet direct*) The person or thing acted on directly by the **verb** [Unit 6]. See also **indirect object**.

ending (*la terminaison*) Added to a verb **stem** to form **tenses** (*dis – ais*), **adjectives** (*intéress – ante*) or **adverbs** (*vrai – ment*).

future tense (*le futur*) This tense tells you what _will happen_ (a single word in French). The **endings** -ai,-as,-a, -ons, -ez, -ont are added to the **infinitive** of -er, -ir regular verbs (minus -e for -re verbs) [Unit 11].

future perfect tense (*le futur antérieur*) The future of the auxiliary verb + the **past participle** [Unit 11].

immediate future (*le futur immédiat*) To speak about something that *is going to happen* soon: the present tense of *aller to go* + the **infintive** [Unit 6].

gender *(le genre)* All French **nouns** have a **gender** (masculine or feminine). This is indicated by the **article**: *le voyage*; *la rencontre* [Unit 1].

imperative (*un impératif*) Used to give an **order**, an **instruction** or to make a **suggestion**. The imperative has no **subject pronoun** [Unit 9].

imperfect (*un imparfait*) A one-word **tense** describing on-going past situations and actions or events which happened often in the past. The **endings** -ais, -ais, -ait, -ions, -iez, -aient are added to the **stem** of the first person plural (*nous*) form of the present **tense** of the **verb**: *allais, parlions* (equivalent of *was doing, used to do, would do*) Unit 14].

impersonal verb (*le verbe impersonnel*) A **verb** without a personal **subject**: *il faut, il s'agit de, il y a*: *It is necessary, It concerns, There is* ...These expressions cannot be used with another subject [Units 8, 10, 16].

indicative mood (*le mode indicatif*) All French **verbs** except those in the **subjuctive** and **imperative** belong to the indicative [Unit 12].

indirect object (*un objet indirect*) A **noun**, a group of words or a **pronoun** which goes with a **verb**. It is usually introduced by the **preposition** *to* in English [Units 9, 12]. See also **direct object**.

infinitive (*un infinitif*) The main form of the **verb**. It is a single word in French: *habiter, appeler, faire to live, to call, to do*. Infinitives have these **endings** in French: *-er, -ir, -re, -oir, -oire*.

interrogative (*un interrogatif*) Used for asking **questions** [Units 1, 6].

interrogative adjective See **adjective**.

interrogative pronoun See **pronoun**.

inversion (*une inversion*) The **verb** and the **subject** change position, usually to ask a **question** [Units 1, 13].

main clause (*la proposition principale*) The main part of a **sentence**. It has a **subject** and a **verb** and may have **objects**. It may be extended by a **subordinate** or a **relative clause**.

modal verbs (*le verbe modal*) **Verbs** which are used to express possibilities: *vouloir, pouvoir, devoir should, might, would, could* [Unit 9].

mood of a **verb** (*le mode*): See **indicative, subjunctive, imperative**.

negative (*la négation*) This is often expressed by two words in French: *ne ... pas; ne ... jamais; ne ... plus not, never, no longer* etc. [Units 1, 4, 11, 12, 13].

noun (*le nom*) Nouns can be **concrete** (things, people, animals, anything tangible), abstract (concepts, ideas or feelings) or proper (names). All French nouns have a **gender,** i.e. they are either masculine or feminine [Unit 2].

passive voice (*la voix passive*) A form of the **verb** which tells us that the **subject** has something done to it by someone / something else. It is formed from the verb *être* in the appropriate **tense** + **past participle** [Unit 10]. In French, only the **direct object** of an **active voice verb** can become the **subject** of a passive verb. For English forms such as *He has been given ...* use *on*.

past historic tense (*le passé simple*) A past **tense** only used in writing, never orally, to replace the **perfect** [Unit 17].

past participle (*le participe passé*) Used with **auxiliary verbs** to form **compound tenses**. The commonest **ending** for an English past participle is *-ed*. In French the past participles of regular *-er* verbs end in *é, -ir* verbs in *i, -re, -oir* verbs in *u*. The past participle of verbs which take *être* usually **agrees** in number and **gender** with the **subject** [Unit 10; Unit 13]. Past participles can also be used as **adjectives**.

perfect tense (*le passé composé*) The usual past **tense** in French. It is a **compound tense,** made up of the **auxiliary verb** *avoir* or *être* + the **past participle**. It is used both for the English *have done* and *did* (*j'ai fait*). It describes actions that are already completed or finished or which happened at a specific time in the past [Unit 13].

phrase (*la locution*) A group of words which does not contain a **verb**. Phrases often begin with a **preposition:** *près de la source; au centre*.

pluperfect tense (*le plus-que-parfait*) A **compound tense** formed from the **imperfect** of *avoir* or *être* + **past participle** [Unit 15].

possessives (*les possessifs*)

possessive adjective (*un adjectif possessif*) Agrees in **gender** and number with the thing possessed, **not with the possessor:** *mon, ma, mes, ton, son, notre, vos, leur my, your, his/her* etc. [Unit 2].

possessive pronouns (*le pronom possessif*) A **pronoun** which replaces the thing possessed: *le mien, le tien, la nôtre, les leurs* etc. *mine, yours, his/hers* etc. [Unit 7].

preposition (*la préposition*) A word (or group of words) closely connected to a **noun**, **pronoun** or **verb**. Like **adverbs**, they often indicate *where, when, how* or *why*: *dans, à, sur, avant, après, avec, pour, de, par in, at, on, before, after, with, for, from, of, by* [Unit 6].

present participle (*le participe présent*) This part of a **verb** ends in *-ing* in English and *-ant* in French. The present participle can also be used as an **adjective** [Units 3, 6].

present tense (*le présent*) French only has one **present** tense but English has two: *does* and is *doing*. For regular *-er* **verbs** the **endings** are *-e, -es, -e, -ons, -ez, -ent* (according to the **subject**: je, *tu, il/elle/on, nous, vous, ils/elles*) [Unit 1]. For regular *-ir* **verbs** the endings are *-is, -is, -it, -issons, -issez, -issent* [Unit 5]. For regular *-re* **verbs** the **endings** are *-s, -s, -, -ons, -ez, -ent* [Unit 5]. The present tense in French is sometimes also used when talking about **future** actions [Unit 11].

pronoun (*le pronom*) A word that stands in place of a **noun**. It agrees in **gender** and number with the **noun** it replaces.

demonstrative pronouns (*le pronom démonstratif*) *celui(-ci), ceux(-là), celle(-là), celles(-ci) this, that, these, those; this one, that one etc.* [Unit 6].

emphatic / stressed pronouns (*le pronom fort*) are used after **prepositions** and for emphasis [Units 1, 7].

interrogative pronouns (*le pronom interrogatif*) such as *qui? who?* are used to ask a question [Unit 4].

object pronouns (*pronoms compléments d'objet direct*) Object pronouns can be **direct** and **indirect**. They come before the verb in French. If there is more than one object pronoun, there are strict rules in French about order [Unit 12].

direct the person(s)/thing(s) acted on by a **verb** [Unit 5].

indirect the person(s)/thing(s) to/for whom/which the action is done [Unit 9].

possessive pronouns (*le pronom possessif*) See **possessives**.

reflexive pronouns (*le pronom réfléchi/réciproque*) are used with **reflexive verbs** showing that people do something to themselves or to one another. The same words are used as for **direct object pronouns**: *me, te, se, nous, vous, se* and they have the same position before the verb [Units 3, 6, 13].

relative pronouns (*le pronom relatif*) link the **main clause** to a **clause** related to a noun in the main clause: *qui, que, dont, lequel* etc. [Units 11, 16].

compound relative pronouns (*le pronom relatif composé*) are formed when the **relative pronoun** *lequel, laquelle* etc. comes after the **prepositions** *à* or *de* [Units 11, 16].

subject pronouns (*le pronom sujet*) are the subjects of **verbs** and the verbs agree with them in number and sometimes in **gender**: *je, tu, il, elle, on, nous, vous, ils, elles* [Unit 1].

question (*la question*) There are several ways of asking a question in French [Units 1, 2]. Some of the words which are used to ask questions are **interrogative adjectives** and **interrogative pronouns**. Other question words are *Quand? Où? Comment? Pourquoi?* [Unit 2].

reflexive pronouns See under **pronouns**.

reflexive verbs (*le verbe pronominal/réciproque*) **Verbs** where the **subject** and the **object** are the same person, showing that the subject does something to him/herself (*pronominal*) or that the subject and another person do something to one another (*réciproque*) [Units 3, 6]. See **pronouns**.

relative clause (*la proposition relative*) A group of words including a **verb** and its **subject**, related to the **main clause** by a relative **pronoun**.

sentence (*la phrase*) A group of words containing at least one **clause**, the **main clause**. It usually also has a **subject** and often an **object**.

stem (*la racine*) Part of the **verb** to which the **endings** are added to indicate the **subject**, the **tense** and the **mood**.

subject (*le sujet*) The person or thing that performs the action expressed by the **verb**. See also **subject pronouns**, under **pronouns**.

subjunctive mood (*le mode subjonctif*) A **mood** of the **verb** which only survives in English in a few set expressions, e.g. '*If I <u>were</u> you*', '*Peace <u>be</u> with you*'. In French, the subjunctive **must** be used after the structure *il faut que* and after verbs of necessity, possibility, will, strong desire, emotion, doubt [Unit 17].

subordinate clause (*la proposition subordonnée*) A part of a **compound sentence** which has its own **verb**. It is joined to the **main clause** by a **conjunction** or a **relative pronoun**.

superlative (*le superlatif*) Used to say that something or someone is *the most ...*: *le plus intelligent; la plus intéressante; les plus délicieuses*. Often shown in English by **adjectives ending** in *-est* [Unit 6].

tense (*le temps*) The form of the **verb** that shows when an action was done: **present** [Unit 1], past (**perfect** [Unit 13], **imperfect** [Unit 14], **pluperfect** [Unit 15]), **future** [Unit 11], **conditional** [Unit 18].

transitive verb (*le verbe transitif*) A **verb** which takes a **direct object** is transitive. **Verbs** which cannot take a **direct object** are intransitive. **Verbs** which are transitive in English may be intransitive in French [Units 9, 12].

verb (*le verbe*) A verb is the main word in a sentence. It expresses an action, a state or an event. Verbs change their form according to who or what did the action (**subject**), when the action was done (**tense**) and the purpose of the action (**voice**).

voice (*la voix*) A form of the **verb**. A verb can be in the active or **passive voice**.

   active The usual form of the verb showing that the **subject** does something.

   passive See **passive voice**.

index